"The authors of *[Lights, Camera...Faith!]* know the power of film and they have tapped it to illustrate and illuminate the meaning of God's Word in the liturgy. With this volume, teachers and preachers can help believers see more deeply into God's message and also help them to incorporate that message into their lives."

REV. ROBERT E. LAUDER,
Department of Philosophy, St. John's University, Jamaica, NY

"...Challenging and insightful. With our culture's deep interest in motion picture entertainment, *Lights, Camera...Faith!* is not just a practical guide, but a strategic cultural tool that rightly assigns the purpose of stories to the inculturation of moral values."

STAN WILLIAMS,
Motion Picture Producer, Director

"This splendid movie lectionary brings together the imaginative power of the Scriptures and the revelatory possibilities of the Screen. Peter Malone and Rose Pacatte have supplied us with visual and printed liturgical agents capable of transforming our lives and...transfiguring our world."

SCOTT YOUNG,
Cofounder,
City of Angels Film Festival

"Who would have thought that the movies we see on Saturday night could enlighten our reading of the Gospel on Sunday morning? ...By introducing serious and respectful conversation between the life of faith and 21st century media culture, *Lights, Camera...Faith!* provides both a model and a method for a deep and rich media literacy movement among all Christian denominations."

ELIZABETH THOMAN,
Founder,
Center for Media Literacy

"...A clever approach, long overdue. Connecting faith and culture is the challenge all ministers face today. Film, which is now woven into the fabric of our storytelling and conversations in everyday life, can be applied to the Gospel in unique and creative ways. This is one approach that is worth our consideration and investment of time and energy.

"How can faith and culture meet in the liturgical year celebrations? How can we influence Christians to approach film with a critical, reflective mind and to discern how Gospel values can challenge or affirm what we see and hear in a film? How can someone be challenged, the next time he or she sees a movie, to apply Gospel sensitivity and values to the experience? Malone and Pacatte's book guides us in this direction."

ANGELA ANN ZUKOWSKI, MHSH, D.MIN.,
Member of the Pontifical Council for Social Communications

"To me, *Lights, Camera...Faith!* is the most imaginative and engaging contemporary contribution to the art of preaching: 72 well-known films integrated with the liturgical year, in dialogue with the Gospel. It makes Hollywood a splendid resource for the pulpit instead of simply a threat to morality. Informative and stimulating, provocative and practical, appreciative and critical, it should send preachers to the movies with fresh eyes, and bring revived enthusiasm into discussion groups. The homilies are still to be written by us, and many of the films are still to be seen, but the method is now ours for the taking."

WALTER J. BURGHARDT, SJ,
Senior Fellow, Woodstock Theological Center,
Georgetown University

A Movie Lectionary—Cycle C

LIGHTS CAMERA... FAITH!

A Movie Lover's Guide to Scripture

By Peter Malone, MSC with Rose Pacatte, FSP

Pauline
BOOKS & MEDIA
Boston

Library of Congress Cataloging-in-Publication Data

Malone, Peter.
  Lights, camera...faith! : a movie lectionary. Cycle C / by Peter
Malone, MSC with Rose Pacatte, FSP.
      p. cm.
Includes bibliographical references and index.
  ISBN 0-8198-4501-9 (pbk.)
  1. Bible. N.T. Gospels — Criticism, interpretation, etc. 2. Motion
pictures — Religious aspects — Christianity. I. Title.
  BS2565 .M27 2001
  261.5'7— dc21
                              2001001422
                              Rev.

Scripture quotes are taken from the New American Bible, copyright © 1970, 1997, 1998 Confraternity of Christian Doctrine, Inc., Washington, D.C. All rights reserved.

Cover design by Helen Rita Lane, FSP

Printed and published in the U.S.A. by Pauline Books & Media, 50 Saint Pauls Avenue, Boston, MA 02130-3491.

www.pauline.org

Pauline Books & Media is the publishing house of the Daughters of St. Paul, an international congregation of women religious serving the Church with the communications media.

1 2 3 4 5 6 7 8 9   11 10 09 08 07 06 05 04 03

Contents

ADDITIONAL CELEBRATIONS

Foreword

Bedtime was seven or so. A patent injustice—it was light outside; even the birds were still flying about. But the little boy was sent off to his room. And there in the bottom bunk, he'd miserably toss about listening to the sounds of a summer evening in which he had no share. But one night the sounds were different! From the living room came gunfire, the whinny of a horse, tap dancing feet, and canned laughter: a din too wonderful for words and utterly irresistible.

Even pushed firmly against the wall, the bowed back of the old family couch left a small amount of space, a kind of tunnel between the sofa's worn floral back and the white wall behind. The space was not quite large enough for the family's Irish setter and even the suction end of the vacuum cleaner had never banged its way into this nether world; and yet the tunnel was whistle clean, for it was scoured nightly by that same little boy who secretly wriggled its length. This was his favorite hideaway, unknown to all outsiders. Even his parents never learned the truth of that tunnel. I know all this because I was that boy, and the zippered pajamas covered in dust balls were mine.

I must have been three or four when I first stumbled on that magical rabbit hole and found…well, not Wonderland exactly, but Hollywood! Yes, Hollywood! By snaking along that forbidden passage to the sofa's far end (oh, watch out for that lamp cord in the wall socket!) I discovered a spectacle finer than an Albert Bierstadt (1830–1902, German-American landscape artist) panorama. There, along the back wall of the living room, was a newly uncrated cabinet-style 21" black-and-white television with a magical name! I'd only known of two words that began with a Z—zoo and zebra—

both magical concepts to a child. But on that box the splendid word Zenith was added to my universe.

Those first broadcast images play out in my recollection as fitfully as the old films themselves, but one memory persists: my first movie was *Frankenstein*. There was the monster, flailing about in a burning windmill, hurling his victims down onto the wooden sails. The lick of those flames and the terrible canine growling of Karloff remain with me still. The little boy in his living-room tunnel was transfixed, horrified, and yes, hopelessly hooked.

Slowly came the dawn: acting! That's it! I would be an actor! I soon began to pull faces out of thin air, practice dialects, imitate teachers, then the principal (and then I began to visit the principal's office!). But the laughter of friends had more impact than the paddle's sting. Throughout childhood I juggled many passions—dinosaurs and telescopes, the FBI, the Forestry Service—but by high school I'd parted with all of my hobbies but acting. The movies just would not let go of me. And they still have me in their hold.

Films have not only delighted me, transported me, enchanted, terrified, and informed me; they have, in the best instances, shaped me. No priest or homily so calibrated my moral compass as did movies. No classroom lecture so humanized me as did Hollywood. *How Green was My Valley, Lassie Come Home, The Yearling, My Friend Flicka, David Copperfield* had boys my approximate age right at their center. They were marvelous stories, but they were also voices for the strength of family and the power of decency—stories that subtly instilled in me a vision of life as a journey, with laughter and sadness intermixed, and joy and adversity waiting inevitably around each episodic bend.

The Boy with Green Hair, Imitation of Life, and the magisterial *To Kill a Mockingbird* were stirring lectures against prejudice. The annual holiday broadcasts of *It's a Wonderful*

Life, Ben-Hur, The Song of Bernadette, even the breezy film sermons of *Going My Way* and *The Bells of St. Mary's,* were far more responsible for my Christianization than anything I learned at Sunday school. These movies were "conversion experiences" in my life, and each viewing left me the better for it.

Somewhere in this book you now hold, there may well be such a movie for you—a story with the power to alter your worldview, enlarge your humanity, sweep aside smallness, sourness, self-contentedness. Movies can do just that!

—PETER MACNICOL, ACTOR

# Introduction

Storytelling

Whether we are scientists, mathematicians, philosophers, parents, or laborers, all of us are storytellers. We like to hear and tell stories.

One of the most frequently used story-telling device is that of metaphor. A metaphor is a word, phrase, or entire story that compares a person, place, or thing to another. A metaphor is a figure of speech and is not meant to be taken literally. An allegory is another literary form that is used in cinematic storytelling and that audiences use when they think about what a story might mean. An allegory is an extended metaphor that parallels the original story and sometimes evokes even deeper meaning. Allegories are similar to fables and parables. An analogy parallels or compares one thing to another. For example, Jesus used analogies and metaphors in the parables he told. He did this to teach people about divine realities. He often said, "The kingdom of heaven is like…." A parable is a fable or moral tale that uses metaphor, allegory, and analogy to teach truth, though not always "facts." It is helpful to keep in mind the distinction between "truth" and "fact." When people tell stories and tales, they often communicate "truth," but this does not mean the stories are, or have to be, "factual."

When the Word was made flesh, Jesus appeared on earth, one might say, in a narrative dramatic story form. He was born. He lived quietly in Nazareth before embarking on a mission to preach the Good News of repentance, forgiveness of sin, and the coming of God on earth. He suffered, died, and, as an extra dimension to the human story, he rose from the dead. By dying he said the ultimate "yes" to his Father's will and the Father, receiving it, could only love him back into risen life.

That is our Christian story.

Sunday by Sunday, feast day by feast day, we listen to chapters of that story. Some of the story is familiar; some of it seems a little strange at times. Through the liturgy, we are invited to open up the scriptures to fuller understanding to deepen our faith and to grow in our relationship with God.

The *Lights, Camera...Faith! A Movie Lectionary* series is designed to help us appreciate the gospel stories as well as the other Scripture readings that have been selected to accompany them. The method is to take a popular movie story and to create a dialogue between the movie and the Gospel. The movie/movie story is chosen not because it has a "good moral" per se, but because its themes can illuminate the Gospel. Sometimes the film's theme will parallel the Scripture readings, while at other times, the film provides a contrast. Conversely, the gospel story can help us find deeper levels of meaning in the movies and in the stories they tell.

During the Cycle A liturgical year, the gospel readings are principally from St. Matthew's Gospel. The movies often illustrate Jesus' teaching rather than events in his life.

With Cycle B, it is rather different. The readings come mainly from St. Mark's Gospel, although during the course of the year, there is a five-week series of readings from John 6 on the Bread of Life. Mark's Gospel is the most direct of the four in its storytelling. It is vivid and detailed in its portrait of Jesus. It is also what one might call "tough," because it includes episodes where Jesus confronts devils, tells stories of demonic possession, commands us to take up the cross as a disciple. It also recounts hostile interchanges between Jesus and the religious leaders of his time.

This means that some of the movies chosen here correspond to this "toughness." In faith terms, we could say that these gospel stories and these movies challenge us to a stronger and more resilient faith. For some congregations or groups, watching the whole movie might be too difficult. In this case, leaders can select sequences that contain the essentials of the movie and could be watched by all.

In Cycle C, we read principally from St. Luke's Gospel. Traditionally, Luke's Gospel is considered to be the Gospel of compassion. The portrait of Jesus we see in this Gospel has a warm humanity. He is not as didactic as the Jesus of Matthew's Gospel, or as simple and plainspoken as the Jesus of Mark's Gospel.

The infancy narrative in Luke is longer and far more detailed than the narrative in Matthew's Gospel. The parallel between John the Baptist and Jesus is highlighted with the stories of the annunciation to Zechariah and to Mary, and of the two births. There are stories of Jesus' childhood, the naming, the presentation, the finding in the temple, and of Jesus going back to Nazareth, obedient to Mary and Joseph.

Many characters with whom we are familiar appear only in Luke's Gospel: the widow of Nain, the ten lepers, Zacchaeus, the good thief. It is a gospel where Jesus encounters many women: Martha and Mary, the woman caught in adultery, the group of women who ministered to Jesus, the women of Jerusalem on the way to Calvary, Mary Magdalene and the women who came to the tomb. The well-known story of the disciples on the road to Emmaus is the principal resurrection story in Luke.

Several of Jesus' best-known parables are found only in Luke: the Good Samaritan, the Prodigal Son, the Pharisee and the Publican, the Unjust Judge.

We have tried to choose movies that will appeal to the widest audience in selecting the movies for *Lights, Camera... Faith! A Movie Lectionary*. Some films have achieved classic status, like *Chariots of Fire* and *Schindler's List*; others are popular films like *As Good As It Gets* and *The Deep End of the Ocean*.

Some may not be the best movies ever made, but their themes are particularly relevant to a certain Sunday or feast-day celebration and its readings, such as *Bless the Child* and *What Dreams May Come.*

In preparing these volumes, Sister Rose Pacatte has collaborated as primary editor and has made invaluable suggestions about movies to include as well as amplifying the synopsis and dialogue sections and clarifying the commentary. Her special and particular contribution is the section "For Reflection and Conversation." We have shared an ongoing journey through the Movie Lectionary series.

The Format

The format of *Lights, Camera…Faith!* is simple and accessible.

Synopsis: Not all readers may have seen every movie included in this book, although it is strongly recommended you see a movie before using it in a homily or with a group. The synopsis offers details that may be helpful in recalling movie characters, plot, and sequence.

SYNOPSIS

Commentary: Each movie commentary provides information about the movie itself: actors, directors, producers, related films, etc.

COMMENTARY

Dialogue with the Gospel: This is the core of each chapter: how the movie and its themes relate to the liturgical readings. Some movies and gospel passages harmonize quite well. Other pairs do not correspond as clearly—for the most part, moviemakers probably did not intend a scriptural message! Therefore, each dialogue begins with a short "Focus" to point the reader in the right direction.

DIALOGUE WITH THE GOSPEL

Key Scenes and Themes: To enrich the dialogue, I highlight several sections of the movie that would be worth dis-

KEY SCENES AND THEMES

cussing thematically or showing as a clip during group discussions, liturgy preparation, or course presentation if the scenes are sequential.

FOR REFLECTION AND CONVERSATION

For Reflection and Conversation: These practical, thought-provoking comments and questions provide a focus for living the gospel message in daily life.

Prayer

Prayer: My editor had the rather beautiful idea of adding a short prayer to bring the reflections to a conclusion.

The subtitle *A Movie Lectionary*, rather than *The Movie Lectionary*, is intentional. It would be possible to match the same readings with seventy-five other movies. In that sense, this lectionary is a set of samples; you might like to start constructing your own version as well!

Most of the movies used here have been released during the last fifteen years and are available on video or DVD. However, some earlier movies have been chosen because of their relevance to the Gospel. They, too, should be available, at least on video.

How to Use Lights, Camera...Faith!

Individuals who appreciate deeper meanings in movies may want to watch the film, read the scriptures, and use both for personal reflection and prayer.

Homilists will find suggestions for sermon preparation.

Young adult groups will discover new ways to bring the gospel message to bear on contemporary culture.

Parish study and discussion groups might find that watching a movie or sections of it will lead to discussion, further reading and viewing, and a deeper entry into the Liturgy of the Word.

Professors and students of film and media criticism will find a useful text for discussing the phenomenon of faith in film.

Again, it is recommended that you see a movie before using it. The nature of some movies may suggest working with a film clip, since not every movie is suitable for wide audiences. Some themes demand greater maturity than that of adolescents; there may be certain movie sequences that are too strong or explicit regarding language, sexuality, or violence for some audiences. *Lights, Camera...Faith!* is not meant to be a "viewing guide." Checking with a publication that provides this type of information will be useful, although such guidelines often differ in their opinions.*

Each of the movies represented in *Lights, Camera...Faith!* has been chosen because in some way the movie portrays the real-life struggles of people—human struggles that beg a human response—and connects these struggles to the Christian story found in the Sunday liturgy's Scripture readings. While not every movie may work for you, I do hope that the majority of them will.

— PETER MALONE, MSC

---

*From an international point of view, such publications might seem arbitrary in their comments. While acknowledging objective norms of truth and morality, sometimes what is objectionable to one culture is not to another; "infrequent coarse language" in one culture seems "far too frequent" in another. Modesty and nudity norms differ from one country to another. One culture deplores violence; another has a greater tolerance for visual violence. (See the "Movie Ratings Chart" at the end of this book.) These are the hazards when movies are shown internationally.

Deep Impact

U.S.A., 1998, 120 minutes
Cast: Tea Leoni, Robert Duvall, Morgan Freeman, Elijah Wood,
Vanessa Redgrave, Maximilian Schell, James Cromwell,
Ron Eldard, Blair Underwood, Leelee Sobieski
Writers: Michael Tolkin, Bruce Joel Rubin
Director: Mimi Leder

Deep Impact

Signs in the Heavens

An ambitious journalist, Jenny Lerner, thinks she has uncovered a Washington political sex scandal. What she has stumbled on, instead, is a sensational story about the U.S. government's efforts to respond to an oncoming disaster. An asteroid is hurtling toward the earth and scientists predict that a tidal wave will destroy the eastern seaboard of the United States and beyond when it hits. The administration, in conjunction with other world powers, has formed a contingency plan for a select number of talented people to survive. They are to be chosen by lottery; anyone over fifty will be automatically excluded.

Jenny is close to her mother, Robin, who is depressed because of her divorce and her husband's remarriage. Amidst everything, Jenny tries to reconcile with her father.

Meanwhile Leo Bierdeman, the young student who discovered the asteroid and notified the authorities, wants to save his girlfriend, Sarah, and her family. However, their names are not chosen in the lottery. Leo and Sarah decide to marry.

SYNOPSIS

The president reveals his plans to the American public. He appeals to the people to remain calm, but they panic. Looters and rioters cause mayhem.

Jenny's mother commits suicide. Leo and Sarah escape to a mountain to avoid the massive tsunami. Jenny gives up her seat in the rescue helicopter and joins her father at their beach house, where the wave engulfs them. The damage is not as severe as expected because the team of experts, who had gone into space to try and deflect the asteroid, are partially successful. They give their lives in the attempt. People begin to emerge from the caverns where they have sought safety and start to rebuild their lives.

COMMENTARY

There is a lot more going on in *Deep Impact* than its special effects, which are very impressive at times. With a veteran cast of lead and character actors, the movie looks at personal crises as a way to comprehend impending disaster. Mimi Leder (*ER, The Peacemaker, Pay it Forward*) is an experienced director who deftly incorporates human dimensions into what would otherwise be just another action flick.

Tea Leoni plays the investigating journalist. Veteran actors Vanessa Redgrave and Maximilian Schell play her parents and give the movie a sense of dignity amidst chaos. Elijah Wood, now famous for his role in the *Lord of the Rings* Trilogy, and Leelee Sobieski of *Joan of Arc* fame, represent the younger generation. Morgan Freeman is stately and impressive as the president. This is a movie about people facing the end of the world.

DIALOGUE WITH THE GOSPEL

Focus: Advent begins with warnings about taking stock of our lives so that we may be "blameless in holiness," both now and when our lives end. Those who are faithful will be able to face any catastrophe and welcome Christ's coming. Deep Impact *imagines the end of the world and the different ways people cope or respond to that moment.*

The first reading refers to the time when God will fulfill his promise and raise up a "just shoot," a "faithful remnant" that will do what is right for the land. Jeremiah utters these hopeful words when he is in prison and Jerusalem is under attack. The day of justice is coming for his chosen people who will be saved because of their fidelity, humility, and integrity. The reading alerts us to the fact that throughout history there have always been disasters, yet hope endures because of God's promise.

The Gospel is part of an eschatological discourse from Jesus, a meditation on the end of time. It is a warning about the judgment of God and uses apocalyptic images from Old Testament books like Ezekiel and Daniel. These images were further developed in the New Testament book of Revelation. The symbols are expressed in imaginative, colorful, hyperbolic stories and dramatic warnings.

Deep Impact is a contemporary dramatization of this kind of apocalyptic disaster. It shows signs in the "heavens" and nations are in terror as the asteroid hurtles toward earth. There are disturbances in the seas and, ultimately, destruction from a gigantic tidal wave.

Jesus warns his listeners to take stock of their lives and prepare for whatever is to come. He says that the disaster will confront everyone on the earth and that our response is to "stand erect and raise your heads because your redemption is near at hand." This apocalyptic threat and how people respond to it is what *Deep Impact* suggests so well. Some people flee; some are bewildered; others loot and destroy. The challenge for everyone is to review their lives and take stock. While some opt out, others calmly face the inevitable. Many discover a kind of generosity, forgiveness, and heroism.

KEY SCENES AND THEMES

- The discovery of the asteroid and the reaction of the scientists; the American government's plan for saving some millions; the caves, the provisions, the lottery, and the exclusion of those over fifty.

• Jenny's ambitions, her love for her mother, her anger with her father, her mother's suicide, Jenny's giving up her seat in the helicopter, dying with her father; Leo and his status as discoverer of the asteroid, his girlfriend and their not being chosen to be saved, her parents and the bus, fleeing to the mountain.

• The president and government plans, his speeches to the people, his urging of trust in God; the people's reactions, their calm and panic, fears and looting, roads clogged; the saved going into the caves; the impact of the wave and the cosmic disaster and destruction; the survivors beginning to rebuild the world.

FOR REFLECTION AND CONVERSATION

1. *Deep Impact* and *Armageddon* formed part of Hollywood's millennium apocalyptic response to the ending of the twentieth century and the birth of the twenty-first. Other films such as *End of Days* and *Bless the Child* are also part of this genre. At first glance, these movies seem to play off the fears that people had that the end of the world would indeed occur at the turn of the millennium. (Some of this kind of thinking emerged in the mid-1800s in a theology that interpreted apocalyptic literature literally, giving us the popular, though misinformed, notions of "the Rapture" and "the Remnant" even today.) Philosophy says that time does not exist, but is, rather, a mental construct with roots in reality. What do you think "time" really means for humanity, now and at the end of the world?

2. St. Paul tells us to "abound in love for one another and for all" at the coming of Jesus. How did the char-

acters in the film prepare for the end of their world and for what they believed to be coming? Which character impressed you the most? Why? How do you think you would have acted in his or her place? As winter approaches in the northern hemisphere the earth seems to be dying. Advent begins at this time and the readings provide a way for us to reflect communally on the Word of God that speaks to us of the end times. How have I prepared for the end of my world, whenever God may call me? What are some ways we can prepare to greet the Lord peacefully with a good conscience?

3. What does the title of the film mean? Talk about the various ways the central event of the film affected the lives of the characters, society, and the world. Discuss the role the media played in the story. Did the news coverage "impact" or "influence" people? What is the difference between the two? Did the people respond or react to the news of impending disaster? Again, what is the difference?

Prayer

Lord of heaven and earth, the disasters we experience in our world remind us of how fragile our lives are. Help us to face the tragedies of life with authentic courage and humility. Amen.

SECOND SUNDAY OF ADVENT

Baruch 5:1–9;
Philippians 1:4–6, 8–11;
Luke 3:1–6

Beyond Rangoon

U.S.A., 1995, 99 minutes
Cast: Patricia Arquette, U Aung Ko, Frances McDormand,
Spalding Gray, Victor Slezak
Writers: Alex Lasker, Bill Rubenstein
Director: John Boorman

Beyond Rangoon

Journey in Hope

SYNOPSIS

Laura Bowman goes on a trip to Rangoon, Burma, with her sister Andy to get over the tragedy of her husband and son's murders. Laura, a doctor, feels trapped in her grief and depression. She no longer wants to practice medicine. One night she goes walking and comes across a protest march led by Aung Sang Suu Kyi. When the soldiers bar the leader's way and threaten to shoot her, she calmly walks through their midst.

Laura's passport is stolen so she remains in the capital while Andy and the tourists return home. She meets a guide, a former professor named U Aung Ko, who had been imprisoned for helping dissident students. They travel into the country to visit a Buddhist monastery and Laura talks freely to him about her worries. The professor takes her to a railway station but Laura sees him being beaten by the military and gets out of the train. She helps him to a riverboat, goes to get medicine in a village where she is confronted by a colonel, and manages to shoot him before he rapes her.

Martial law has been declared. When Laura and U Aung Ko return to the city, they witness a massacre of peaceful protesters. Once again, she escapes with the professor and joins another group of students. They make their way to the Thai border, pursued by soldiers and heavy gunfire. Many are killed but the professor is reunited with his family and Laura decides to stay and help the refugees as a doctor.

Director John Boorman (*Point Blank, Deliverance, Excalibur, Hope and Glory*) uses the familiar structure and conventions of the action chase but pauses dramatically before he recreates a walk by Burma's (Myanmar) opposition leader, Aung San Suu Kyi, through the streets of Rangoon (Yangon). She walks majestically and memorably through the night lights to the cheers of the crowds. When troops bar the way, rifles poised, she looks the soldiers in the eye and calmly moves through their ranks. And the audience begins to understand the plight of Burma and the democratic hopes of the people.

Beyond Rangoon is an entertainment film, not a documentary. It was made for a Western audience, using Western cinema styles and techniques. A film made from the Burmese perspective would be entirely different in focus and would probably not have been well received by non-Asian audiences (and therefore, not financially viable). So Boorman tells the story from Laura's point of view and wagers that his audience will identify with her efforts to use her wits to decide what must be done to resolve the dramatic conflicts that arise.

COMMENTARY

Focus: Laura Bowman's stay in Rangoon is an Advent time for her. She is a woman in need of comfort who shares the longings of the people. Her journey beyond Rangoon, inspired by Aung Sung Suu Kyi, is a journey of hope toward salvation toward which today's scriptures point.

DIALOGUE WITH THE GOSPEL

Today's Gospel begins with a description of the political situation in Palestine at the beginning of Jesus' ministry. It was a time of occupation by the Romans, with Herod and his brother as the day-to-day administrators. It was a time of oppression and hardship. Yet, this was the context for hope as well as a call for repentance as the people anticipated the coming of God's kingdom to free them from tyranny. This promise of hope is a constant theme in the Jewish scriptures.

The words of Baruch proclaim the end of mourning and the donning of the splendor of God's glory to the people during the time of the Babylonian captivity (587–537 B.C.). To get his message of hope across, he sings a song of how a new road will be constructed, leading the exiles home. Today's Gospel includes a quotation from Second Isaiah that announces the triumphant arrival of the Lord again using the analogy of pathways and roads. The spirituality of Advent is one that contemplates in hope the fulfillment of God's promises.

Beyond Rangoon presents audiences with a desperate political situation marked by military rule. The Burmese people are hopeful, strengthened by the Buddhist spirituality of purification through suffering and endurance. As we watch the dignified progress of the leader during the protest march, we see a woman of great presence, dignity, and power whom the soldiers do not resist. Like Jesus, who also had persecutors, Aung Sung Suu Kyi passes through their midst. It is a sign that the obstacles to freedom and democracy will be laid low and paths will be made straight for the liberation of the people. The protest depicted in the film actually occurred in 1988. Following it, Aung Sung Suu Kyi was placed under house arrest twice, finally winning unconditional release in 2002. The subtext of the film portrays what turned out to be a protracted experience of Advent longing and waiting for an entire nation.

Laura Bowman, like all of us, has experienced her own tragedies. Baruch's words seem to address her directly because now she can take off the robe of mourning and misery. Inspired by Aung Sung Suu Kyi and encouraged by the kindness of the professor, she ventures beyond Rangoon and the confines of her depression. The movie shows her Advent journey as well as that of the professor and the students.

Beyond Rangoon takes place in a Buddhist culture, which can contribute much to a dialogue with Christianity about its hopes and its spirituality. Aung Sung Suu Kyi is a Buddhist heroine whose life can be seen to parallel that of Jesus. For Laura Bowman, her Advent journey culminates in a realization that she has come out of herself and her loneliness to save lives. Her suffering can bear fruit in a spirituality of joy that Paul describes for the Philippians.

KEY SCENES AND THEMES

- Laura, depressed in Rangoon, with memories and dreams of her dead husband and son, walking the streets and witnessing the protest march, watching the progress of Aung Sung Suu Kyi and her peaceful walking through the barricade of armed soldiers; Laura's sense of liberation.

- The professor as a teacher and guide, his self-sacrifice for the students, his poverty and dependence on tourists; his listening enables Laura to "confess" her life and worries; the visit to the monastery; seeing the professor beaten and coming to his aid.

- Laura's physical, emotional, and spiritual journeys; obtaining the medicine, resisting the colonel, meeting the students, witnessing the massacre, the exodus through the jungle, the escape to freedom across the river; the fulfilment of her hopes.

FOR REFLECTION AND CONVERSATION

1. Compare *Beyond Rangoon* with other films that focus on Asian culture and recent history, such as *Kundun, Seven Years in Tibet, Paradise Road, The Year of Living Dangerously, The Killing Fields*. All these films are based on true stories. Research the people whose stories

these films tell (e.g., Aung Sung Suu Kyi, the Dalai Lama, Sydney Shanberg, and Heinrich Harrer) and discuss the current personal, religious, and political situations as they exist today in the light of today's readings. As a believer, how do these stories resonate with your own desire for justice in the world?

2. A good story-telling technique is to focus on the personal life of a character, fictional or real, in order to help the audience grasp a broader religious, sociological, political, or human reality. What are Laura's personal challenges? What are the issues and challenges facing the people of Burma as depicted in the film? Is it fair to compare the life of a privileged American woman with the plight of the oppressed people of Burma? Why or why not? What do you see through Laura's eyes? What response can you offer in your own environment to similar situations in the world today?

3. Last week's Scripture readings presented us with visions of hope amid descriptions of the world coming to an end. This week, we are once again encouraged by the readings to hope, because God is leading his people in joy, mercy, and justice toward freedom and salvation. How does Laura, who grieves for her dead husband and son, begin to hope and once again find joy? What role do her sister Andy, the professor, and the refugees play in Laura's healing process? How do you and your family and faith community minister to those who grieve, especially during this time of Advent? Laura's grief turned to hope and became practical; identify some ways you can help those with whom you share faith to grow in hope.

Prayer

In our Advent time, Lord, we find it very difficult to see past the obstacles in our lives. Make our paths straight that they may lead us in hope to your glory. Amen.

The Year of Living Dangerously
Australia, 1982, 115 minutes
Cast: Mel Gibson, Sigourney Weaver, Linda Hunt,
Michael Murphy, Bill Kerr
Writers: David Williamson, Peter Weir
Director: Peter Weir

The Year of Living Dangerously

What Should We Do?

SYNOPSIS

During 1965, Indonesia is in a state of unrest. This will ultimately lead to revolution and the end of the regime of President Sukarno. The press corps in Jakarta is on the lookout for news scoops while living the easy life in the clubs and bars of the city. They also work embassy contacts for story leads.

Guy Hamilton, an Australian journalist, teams up with a Chinese-Australian photographer, Billy Kwan. Billy is a dwarf and is gifted with a mystical sense of identification with the country and its people. He idolizes Sukarno until he sees how the president fails to help his people when a child whom Billy has befriended dies of poverty and lack of medical attention. Billy is disillusioned and dies violently, a witness against Sukarno's oppression.

Guy falls in love with Jilly, an assistant on the staff of the British embassy. She is scheduled to return to London soon. Against her better judgment, she tells Guy about a secret communiqué the embassy received about a shipload of arms China is sending to the PKI (Communist Party) in Jakarta. Although he knows it jeopardizes Jilly, Guy works the story with his local staff, seeking independent confirmation to keep his source safe. The arms arrive and the PKI stages a coup. Guy does not want to break the story until he is sure Jilly is safe but he, too, must escape when the coup fails. They leave amid the terror and chaos of the political unrest.

The most striking character in Peter Weir's movie, which is based on the award-winning 1978 novel by Christopher Koch, is the Chinese-Australian cameraman Billy Kwan. American actress Linda Hunt (television's *The Practice, Eleni, Ready to Wear, Kindergarten Cop, Dragonfly*) plays Billy, and she won an Oscar for Best Actress in a Supporting Role for her performance. In fact, Linda Hunt was the first woman to ever receive an Oscar for playing a man.

COMMENTARY

The movie was filmed on location in the Philippines and Australia and, according to the press, accurately recreates the filth and poverty of Jakarta in the 1960s. Peter Weir (*Gallipoli, Witness, Dead Poets Society, Fearless, The Truman Show*) is Australia's most celebrated filmmaker. He has the marked ability to challenge social, political, and military power structures in history and current events in ways that evoke a thoughtful response from audiences.

A very young Mel Gibson gives a credible performance in the role of the foreign journalist Guy Hamilton. Sigourney Weaver's role is functional but necessary as she provides the information that causes the sequence of events in the latter part of the film. Bembol Roco is excellent as Kumar, Guy's assistant, who is a communist seeking help for his people.

Focus: Just as 1965 was a year that anticipated great change and hope for the betterment of the Indonesian people, so Advent is a time for challenge and change in the hope that Jesus' coming will bring justice and peace.

DIALOGUE WITH THE GOSPEL

Both the novel and the screenplay for *The Year of Living Dangerously* make explicit reference to Luke's Gospel by asking the same question as does John the Baptist at the Jordan,

"What should we do?" This is an Advent question, a question that suggests repentance, change, and a new way of living. It is a question of great import for those who want to be ready for the coming of Jesus.

The movie offers a parallel between the year of living dangerously and the year of Jesus' coming into the world. There is a feeling of expectancy, of change in the air. Some will choose violence to achieve revolution and redress; others will choose political agitation to overthrow a harsh government. Still others seek the way of love.

Like Jesus, Billy Kwan sees the people confused and harassed, in need of food, water and the ordinary amenities of life. But who will provide them? This is the challenge he offers to Guy and begs him to look at the masses of Asian people suffering from poverty.

Billy Kwan possesses a mythical aura. He is the conscience-counselor who understands local lore and the significance of the *wayang*, the shadow-puppet tales of Indonesia. When he confronts the journalist hero, Guy, with the overwhelming experience of Asian poverty, he quotes Luke 3:10, "What should we do?" These words are the people's response to the preaching of John the Baptist and his challenge to repent. Fellow journalists taunt Billy for his fervor. They mock him and accuse him of wanting to be crucified.

When his trust in authority and his hope in Guy are dashed, Billy can see no other way than to follow the lead of the person whom John the Baptist is announcing, Jesus. Billy must die in protest, trying (ineffectually, it would seem) to alert others to the plight of Indonesia's suffering. Billy Kwan is presented as a Christ-figure through explicit references to the Gospel. In laying down his life for others and witnessing to the abuses in Indonesia, Billy is a "redeemer-figure."

KEY SCENES AND THEMES

- Billy and Guy as partners at work; Billy inviting Guy into the streets of Jakarta to see the poverty of Asia;

Billy confronting the journalists in the bar; their talk about him as being like Jesus and wanting to be crucified.

- The *wayang*, the Indonesian puppets that are used to tell mythical tales; Billy's explanation of their function that shows Billy himself as a mythical character; Billy's banner of protest against Sukarno and the president's not seeing it; Billy falling to his death.

- Guy's experiences with the PKI secretary who risks his position by taking Guy to the outer areas to experience the reality of Indonesia; Jilly supplying the information, her dismay at Billy's death, and her worries about the news story; Guy's injury, escape to the airport, and departure with Jilly.

FOR REFLECTION AND CONVERSATION

1. Guy Hamilton is a reporter and Billy Kwan is a photographer who promises to help Guy obtain pictures of what is really happening in Indonesia. Billy is a dwarf and can go anywhere because it's as if no one notices him. How does Billy become Guy's eyes? Why does he keep files on people "he cares about"? What is Billy looking for? How is *The Year of Living Dangerously* a movie about "seeing" the injustices of the world? When Guy's eye is seriously injured at the end of the film, is he really in danger of going blind or does he finally "see"? What are some of the ways the film directs our attention to really seeing and understanding what is going on right in front of us as well as beyond our borders? What, indeed, are we to do in this time of Advent?

2. *The Year of Living Dangerously* is a film about the media, specifically journalism and journalists. What kind of stories does Billy want the foreign journalists to

write? Why do they refuse? What are their criteria for reporting their stories? What are Billy's criteria? If you were a journalist in a culture different from your own, how would you report the realities of the situation to your audience? What criteria would you use? Would people want to read, see, or hear the stories you would report? Why or why not? What makes for responsible journalism in situations such as those that existed in Jakarta in the 1960s and continue to exist in our world today?

3. There is much dialogue in the film that asks the audience to reflect on deeper realities than the here and now. When Billy suggests that Guy give money to the poor, Guy refuses because it won't do any good in the larger scheme of things. Billy tells Guy not to think about the major issues. He says, "Just think about the misery in front of you. Add your light to the light in front of you." Who do you agree with, Billy or Guy? Why?

Prayer

Jesus, we look forward to your coming into our world at Christmas. As we prepare for this feast, we ask what we must do. Please answer our heartfelt cry for justice in the world. Amen.

About Schmidt

U.S., 2002, 126 minutes
Cast: Jack Nicholson, Hope Davis, Kathy Bates,
Dermot Mulroney, Len Cariou, Howard Hesseman
Writers: Alexander Payne, Jim Taylor
Director: Alexander Payne

About Schmidt

Blessed By a Child

SYNOPSIS

At a farewell banquet for his retirement as an assistant vice president at an insurance company, Warren Schmidt is dismayed to realize his life has not amounted to much. As he adjusts to retirement, he sees an infomercial asking people to sponsor a child in Tanzania for $22.00 a month and he decides to sponsor an orphan. When his wife of forty-two years suddenly dies, his accustomed routines go with her. However, he begins writing to the six-year-old orphan, Ndugu. The letters become a means to examine the purpose and meaning of his life as well as a way to confess his shortcomings, concerns, and joys.

He is surprised and upset when he finds some letters among his wife's things that show she had an affair with his best friend, Ray, twenty-five years before. He angrily confronts Ray but soon realizes that it was long ago and that he may have contributed to his wife's behavior.

Schmidt sets out for Denver, aiming to arrive ahead of time for his daughter Jeannie's wedding to a free-spirited waterbed salesman, Randall. He wants to persuade her not to marry him. When Schmidt is almost there, he calls and she tells him not to come yet. He calls Ray and apologizes

17

and then sets off on a road-trip detour. He revisits the places of his early life and education. He upsets a hospitable woman at a trailer park by his inappropriate advances. As he travels, he continues to examine his life. He finally arrives in Denver and is taken aback by Randall's even more free-spirited parents. Schmidt's daughter, whom he has largely ignored until now, resents his interference. At the wedding, rather than voice his disappointment, he makes a noncommittal speech and realizes that he has to let his daughter live her own life.

When he returns home, he receives a letter from a missionary sister in Tanzania writing on Ndugu's behalf. She thanks him for his letters and his help. Since Ndugu is too young to read and write, he sends Warren a picture he has drawn instead. Warren is so moved by the image of a little boy holding the hand of a man that he realizes his life does have meaning, especially to a little child in a faraway land.

COMMENTARY

In *Election*, his satirical high school comedy, director Alexander Payne showed talent for examining the foibles of human nature in incisive yet inspired ways. Now, he moves to the senior citizen age bracket with an even stronger sensitivity.

Jack Nicholson gives one of his best and most restrained—even understated—performances. For an actor who does "crazy" so well, Schmidt is a much-deserved compliment to Nicholson, who never crosses the line. With a wealth of intimate detail, Payne and Nicholson give us a portrait of an ordinary "everyman" who is forced to revisit his life, reassess his judgments on people, and learn forgiveness and tolerance as he asks himself if his life has made any difference to anyone. The movie is based on the novel by Louis Begley.

Jack Nicholson received another Oscar nomination for his role as Schmidt. Hope Davis as his daughter brings an edge of melancholic realism to her role, as she did in *Hearts of Atlantis*. An almost unrecognizable Dermot Mulroney plays

Randall. Kathy Bates was also nominated for an Academy Award as she again shows her versatility as Randall's free-spirited and surprisingly uninhibited mother.

Focus: Mary goes on a purposeful Advent journey to Elizabeth. Warren Schmidt goes on an Advent journey late in life, to look for meaning. He is transformed when he reaches out to a savior child who, in turn, reaches out to him.

DIALOGUE WITH THE GOSPEL

Today's readings suggest two Advent themes: the journey and salvation through a child. *About Schmidt* echoes these themes.

Warren Schmidt is at a new crossroads and he feels the need to examine his life and change because there is nowhere else to go. This is a journey he must make.

In the words of the reading from Hebrews, Schmidt had obeyed the law throughout his life and become the person he thought he was supposed to become. Yet, his life was merely the equivalent of sacrifices and sin offerings, of which he had made so many. Still, a richer understanding of his call in life was possible for Schmidt. Now he needs to find it, face it, and embrace it.

Mary's personal Advent journey was arduous and motivated by love. She traveled south from Nazareth, when she herself was pregnant, to visit her dear and unexpectedly pregnant cousin. Elizabeth's Advent prayer for Mary is a blessing that Mary's hopes would be fulfilled. Schmidt first goes on a journey into his past, a journey of self-discovery. His journey to do the right thing for his daughter brings him to people that he does not understand or like. If he is to discover his true self, he has to respect these people and let them live their lives their way, not his.

In Micah, the child is the symbol of the fulfillment of Advent hopes. In the Gospel, we see that Jesus, about to be born, is this savior. The other child, John, will have a key role in pointing out the path to salvation for people then and now. For Warren Schmidt, the child Ndugu points out the way to salvation. He is the poor, orphaned child who "listens" to Schmidt and becomes his "confessor." Ndugu is the catalyst for Schmidt's new "conversion" because the little boy gives meaning and purpose to his life. Schmidt realizes that he has made a difference during his lifetime. The final letter from the missionary sister enclosing Ndugu's gift is a wonderfully gentle affirmation of the ministry of the Church in Africa for its children.

KEY SCENES AND THEMES

- Warren Schmidt's last day in his office, the farewell dinner and speeches, his dissatisfaction; the routines at home with Helen, not being wanted at the office, the suddenness of Helen's death; the discovery of the letters, the confrontation with Ray; Jeannie and her resentments; Schmidt's being at a crossroads.

- His decision to leave early for Denver, Jeannie telling him not to come now, his journey to his old home and the college; the incident in the trailer park; his arrival in Denver, the clashes with Jeannie, his negativity to Randall, his surprise at Roberta's attitudes and behavior; his waterbed injury and the consequences; his neutral speech at the wedding reception.

- The infomercial about ChildReach, his decision to send money, and being given Ndugu as his foster child; beginning to write letters about his life to Ndugu; the letter from the sister and the gift of art from Ndugu and their effect on Schmidt.

FOR REFLECTION AND CONVERSATION

1. In literature and film, a motif is a theme or recurring idea that helps move the story along to its conclusion. *About Schmidt* is full of visual motifs. Identify some of them (e.g., Helen's collections of Hummels, the rain,

stars, Native Americans, meat and beef cattle from the restaurant back to the trucks that haul them to market, the endless roads and side roads, clocks and keeping time, desolate and barren cityscapes, religion, alcohol, the music and sounds) and talk about how these motifs support and add meaning to the story. The film is billed as a comedy, and indeed, humor is a motif in the film as well. But is it truly a comedy? How did all of these elements or motifs help create meaning for you? What do you think of the film?

2. The poet John Donne wrote in Meditation XVII: "All mankind is of one author, and is one volume; when one man dies, one chapter is not torn out of the book, but translated into a better language; and every chapter must be so translated.... As therefore the bell that rings to a sermon, calls not upon the preacher only, but upon the congregation to come: so this bell calls us all: but how much more me, who am brought so near the door by this sickness.... No man is an island, entire of itself...any man's death diminishes me, because I am involved in mankind; and therefore never send to know for whom the bell tolls; it tolls for thee." How do the themes of interconnectedness (the island) and mortality (the bell) parallel Schmidt's journey? How does Ndugu's picture capture these themes?

3. The Gospel focuses primarily on the story of two women. One of the major themes in *About Schmidt* is also women. Talk about the different women in Schmidt's life, who they are, and the role they play in the story: Helen, Jeannie, Roberta, Saundra, the woman at the RV park, and Sister Nadine. They are all presented to us through Schmidt's eyes and experiences. What are the stages he goes through in the

way he perceives the women in his life? Does he ever really come to care about any of them? What do you think about the women in the film? Could their characters have been drawn differently? Should they have been?

Prayer

Lord, guide us as we stand at crossroads in our Advent journeys. May we find the right person who will help us along the path from despair to hope in the fulfillment of your promises. Amen.

Mel Gibson and cast in *Braveheart*.

CHRISTMAS MIDNIGHT

Isaiah 9:1–6;
Titus 2:11–14;
Luke 2:1–14

Braveheart

U.S.A., 1995, 180 minutes
Cast: Mel Gibson, Patrick McGoohan, Sophie Marceau,
Catherine McCormack, Angus MacFadyen, Brian Cox
Writer: Randall Wallace
Director: Mel Gibson

Braveheart

A Savior of His People unto Death

There is political turmoil in Scotland in the year 1280. Young William Wallace flees the Highlands after seeing many of his family killed during the incursions and oppression by Edward Longshanks, King of England. The adult William returns home, a natural leader, and secretly marries his childhood sweetheart, Murron. A local lord's soldier assaults Murron; after Wallace tries to protect her, Wallace and Murron flee. Murron is captured and killed as a lesson to the village. Wallace, ready for vengeance, pretends to surrender, but instead leads a devastating attack on the lord and his forces. Wallace, although somewhat reluctant, becomes a leader of the rebellion against the English and begins to attack English towns.

There are many claimants to the throne of Scotland, including Robert the Bruce. William Wallace wants to support him, but ultimately the Bruce sides with England. Edward, who is retired, urges his effete son to fight for Scotland. Disappointed in his ineffectual behavior, Edward sends his French daughter-in-law, Isabelle, to negotiate with Wallace. She fails, but they are attracted to one another and have a

SYNOPSIS

liaison. After the battle of Falkirk, where Bruce sides with the English, Isabelle returns to be with Wallace. However, Wallace is betrayed and taken to London where he is tortured and brutally killed. His final cry on the block is "Freedom!" At the same time, Edward is dying and his son is powerless. Isabelle mourns Wallace and she discovers she is carrying his child. The Bruce contemplates the confusion and brutality of the wars. Later, Robert the Bruce unites Scotland under the English.

COMMENTARY

Braveheart was the unexpected winner of the 1995 Oscar for Best Film as well as Best Director for Mel Gibson. His previous directing project was the sensitive movie, *Man Without a Face.* Another epic of seventeenth century Scots history was released in 1995, *Rob Roy,* starring Liam Neeson.

The English film critics in particular argued about the historical accuracy of the movie, which is clearly partisan Scots mythmaking. Patrick McGoohan portrays Edward Longshanks as a calculatingly powerful tyrant. Angus McFadyen is a heroic but ultimately compromising Robert Bruce.

The movie is long, a blend of more intimate sequences and extraordinary battles with enhanced computer-generated troops, a technique that was used in another more recent film starring Mel Gibson, Roland Emmerich's *The Patriot.* The drama in *Braveheart* culminates with the death of William Wallace. He is shown throughout the movie as a kind of messianic hero who rose from among his people, leads them to victory and is then killed as a martyr. There are many visual and thematic references to the passion and death of Jesus in these sequences. Though fact-based, *Braveheart* is in many ways a grim, mythic parable about the fight for freedom and about liberation emerging from oppression and defeat.

DIALOGUE WITH THE GOSPEL

Focus: Jesus is born as savior of the world. He has come to bring us peace and freedom. Among the many historical and mythi-

*cal heroes who fight for peace and freedom, William Wallace,
the "braveheart," is a powerful example.*

Braveheart may seem, at first glance, a strange choice for
a movie dialogue for Midnight Mass. The Christmas atmosphere is gentle as we focus on the traditional crib and the
visit of the shepherds. However, the Nativity is the beginning
of a life that ends in Jesus' execution on Calvary, a laying
down of life for all of us who have sinned and are in need of
redemption.

The responsorial psalm refrain reminds us that Jesus is
our savior. The psalm itself has a cosmic tone, because we get
a sense of the vastness of God's interaction with the world:
"God comes to rule the earth...he shall rule the world with
justice and the peoples with constancy."

The reading from Isaiah evokes and almost foreshadows
the *Braveheart* story. The people are in darkness and deep
shadow and they long for light. The son who will be born is
going to take away the yoke from people's shoulders, the rod
of the oppressor and all the apparel of battle and war will be
consumed by fire. Jesus' life will become the pattern of hope
for all who are bowed down and in need of liberation because he too was born into a world of oppression.

Paul's Letter to Titus is about waiting in hope for the
appearance of Christ Jesus so that we might be delivered from
all lawlessness. The Scots waited in hope, and, though their
champion was martyred, his cry for freedom and therefore,
for human dignity resounds throughout all of history.

- The Scots village, its poverty, oppression; the young
  children, victims of the massacres and those who survive; Wallace as local hero, his love for Murron, his
  defense of the people against despotic rule; Murron's
  death.

**KEY SCENES
AND THEMES**

- The king's arrogance, lust for power; the squabbles and betrayals of the Scots nobility; the battles; the king's disappointment with Robert the Bruce; Isabelle.

- Wallace betrayed, his imprisonment, interrogations and torture, the wagon carrying him to the place of execution, and his outstretched arms evoke constant parallels in image and symbol with Jesus' passion; Wallace's death and his cry for freedom; the aftermath of his death for king, prince, princess, and Robert the Bruce.

FOR REFLECTION AND CONVERSATION

1. What are some of the images in the film that suggest William Wallace as a Christ-figure, that is, a man or woman whose life parallels, in some redemptive way, the life of Christ? Do you agree that he is one? Why or why not?

2. One of the most poignant scenes in the film is when William realizes that Robert the Bruce has sided with the English. It had seemed that the men were not only compatriots, but that they admired and respected one another as well—that they were friends. How does this betrayal foreshadow the life of Jesus? Have you ever experienced the darkness of the death of a friendship? In what ways could the feast of Christmas help restore joy and gladness even amid the sadness of broken friendships and relationships in your life?

3. The distance between Nazareth and Bethlehem is about seventy miles as the crow flies. Tonight's Gospel describes Mary's ordeal of traveling while almost ready to give birth, and we can empathize with her discomfort. Perhaps she worried that something might happen along the way; she may have been hungry and

thirsty as well. And all this because a despot in far-away Rome made a decision to count people for his own benefit and without regard for human needs. How does this experience of oppression mirror situations in the world today? In what ways, however small, can we contribute to human freedom and the promotion of human dignity in the world so that the light of Jesus may shine in the lives of the spiritually and/or physically poor?

Prayer

Jesus, in the darkness of night you came to redeem a people in darkness. Be a light of salvation and peace for our world. Amen

Powder

U.S.A., 1995, 107 minutes
Cast: Mary Steenburgen, Sean Patrick Flanery, Jeff Goldblum,
Lance Henricksen, Susan Tyrell, Ray Wise
Writer: Victor Salva
Director: Victor Salva

Powder

When Humanity Surpasses Technology

SYNOPSIS

A Texas mother who has been struck by lightning dies in childbirth while her albino son, Jeremy, survives. Rejected by his father, Jeremy Reed is raised by his grandparents and known by his nickname, "Powder," because he is so white and has no hair. When his grandfather dies, local authorities place Jeremy in an institution for boys. A sympathetic social worker, Jessica, discovers that he is physically fit and highly intelligent. In fact, he has read and memorized every book in his grandfather's study. During a demonstration in his physics class, he draws electricity into himself to the amazement of the teacher, Donald, who tries to help him develop his abilities. Tests indicate that Jeremy is a genius.

The boys at the institution mock and bully him. Things come to a head when the deputy sheriff, Duncan, takes some boys hunting and shoots a deer with great relish. Powder holds the dying animal and grips Duncan, transmitting the painful experience of the deer's death to the man. The sheriff, Doug, has tried to help Powder but remains wary of him. After listening to his deputy's story, he takes Jeremy home, hoping that he can heal his dying wife. Instead, Powder communicates what the wife is thinking to Doug. This enables her to die peacefully and Doug and his estranged son to reconcile.

The boys take Jeremy out into a storm, strip and humiliate him. An electrical shock kills John, his main tormentor. Powder had told John that he knew his secrets about his stepfather's abuse. Powder brings John back to life. He then rebels against Jessica and runs away to his grandparents' home, now all boarded up. Jessica and Donald realize where he has gone, and they follow. So do the sheriff and deputy. During a powerful storm, Powder runs into a bolt of lightning and absorbs it into himself. He is drawn from the earth into a bright sky.

COMMENTARY

Powder works well on several levels and less well on others. This 1995 film is a parable that teaches us that people who are different can contribute to our lives and that fearing them harms us more than the person who is gifted or different. It is a fantasy about realizing that our salvation is right here, among us. The film works less well because it is largely predictable and it isn't as subtle as the intriguing introduction would lead us to believe. Writer/director Salva's criminal conviction on child molestation charges has caused some audiences to interpret some of the scenes in disturbing ways. But if the viewer doesn't know this background, the film can stand on its own.

Two years later, Jon Turteltaub's *Phenomenon* dealt with similar themes as *Powder*. The character, played by John Travolta, is transformed for a short time into a genius and a savior by what seems like a lightning strike.

Powder is played with dignity by Sean Patrick Flanery, who later appeared in many films, including *Simply Irresistible* and *The Suicide Kings,* as well as in television series such as *Adventures of the Young Indiana Jones.* Director/writer Victor Salva has had a checkered career, going from *Powder* in 1995 to dramatic thrillers and horror films, notably the *Jeepers Creepers* franchise in 2001 and 2003.

**DIALOGUE WITH
THE GOSPEL**

Focus: The savior's birth is a mysterious sign of contradiction that brings blessing to those who believe in him. Meanwhile, he will suffer rejection by others, beginning in his infancy. Powder *is a story that parallels that of the savior, Jesus.*

With the popular image of the Christmas crib in our minds, with the baby lying in the manger, surrounded by Mary and Joseph, the first reading takes us back to the anticipated Old Testament hope at the prospect of the coming of the messiah: "your savior comes!" Both the Gospel that speaks of angels and the responsorial psalm that refers to the heavens add a cosmic dimension to our joy on this day when "light dawns for the just; and gladness, for the upright of heart."

Powder opens with a difficult birth amidst a raging storm. The mother loses her life in giving her son to the world. He is special—so much so, that his father cannot accept him. The child is raised by his grandparents. When the authorities find Powder/Jeremy after their deaths, he is hidden away in darkness, because as an albino he is sensitive to light. Yet he himself *is* light, both physically white as well as intellectually bright and full of electric energy. This child is a blessing for those who can appreciate him. Like Jesus, Powder is a sign of contradiction for those who cannot accept him. He draws out the goodness and kindness present in Jessica, Donald, and the sheriff. Like Jesus, Powder can read minds and hearts. Like Jesus, he can soothe those who suffer, bring about reconciliation between father and son, and teach compassion and empathy to those who exult in cruelty. He can raise the dead. Powder's goodness illustrates the blessings we find in the reading from Titus: "When the kindness and generous love of God our savior appeared…."

The Gospel takes us back to the crib, to the wonderful child who is sought out by the shepherds who hear the message of peace from the angels. Powder draws people to him, transforms them, and gives them his gift of peace. The first scene was a hard birth. The final scene is an "ascension" in which Powder leaves behind his "disciples," those who will remember him and tell his story. The movie offers an almost complete parallel to the gospel story of Jesus.

The reference to Einstein, the genius who was so instrumental in the development of the good and, at the same time, destructive powers of twentieth-century technology, is important for our Christmas reflection. Technology is not an end, but a means. The crib reminds us that in Jesus, humanity has already surpassed technology.

KEY SCENES AND THEMES

- The pregnant mother and her suffering, her being struck by lightning, her death in childbirth; the father's rejection of his son, the boy's albino condition, the brain scans; the boy who was born "light" but in darkness, who hid in the darkness of the family cellar but emerged into the light.

- Jeremy's experience in the institution, the mockery of John and the boys, the demonstration of energy with the spoons; the physics class and Jeremy's drawing the energy into himself; the contrast between his transmitting the energy of the dying deer into the deputy sheriff and his communicating the wife's thoughts and wishes to the sheriff.

- John's cruelty and humiliation of Jeremy and Jeremy's bringing him to life; Jeremy's desire to go home, realizing that it would never be possible to live a free life, going open-armed into the storm to absorb the energy to go home to the heavens.

FOR REFLECTION AND CONVERSATION

1. The teacher, Donald Ripley, discusses a quotation from Einstein with Jeremy: "It has become appallingly clear that our technology has surpassed our humanity." He continues: "When I look at you, I have hope that maybe one day our humanity will surpass our technology." Take some time to walk through the rooms of your home very slowly, as if seeing everything that is there for the first time. How much "technology" is present, from appliances to information (computers) and entertainment media (televisions, VCRs, DVD players, CD players, etc.)? How much time do you spend each day with "technology"? Do you think these things enhance your humanity and your ability to live as a Christian with your family, friends, colleagues, and those with whom you share faith? What about the bigger picture of technology: war machines, genetic engineering of food, equitable access to the means of production and living? How does the birth of Jesus remind us of our humanity? How do Jesus' birth, life, death, and resurrection make us more human? What does it mean to be a human being?

2. *Powder* is the story of a boy who is physically different from others, who is mocked by his peers and forced to live in an institution from which he finally escapes. It is the story of a prodigy who is capable of reading the inner thoughts of people and can heal them and bring them back to life. *Powder* is a parable that teaches us that some individuals have powers beyond that which we are able to imagine, but that if we will get to know them, we will learn new things and receive blessings from them. Just because a person is different, why does this make him or her a target for our fears? Why do people strike out at what they do not know?

Both love and hate are four-letter words: how can Jesus' birth help us to speak a language of love rather than hate?

3. The movie suggests that there is a physical explanation to Powder's abilities. It focuses on electricity, energy, and the commands of the brain to describe why he is the way he is. The film also leaves the way open for more mysterious, cosmic, mystical, perhaps more supernatural explanations for Powder. Audiences that are familiar with the gospel stories will have no difficulty in seeing the parallels that the screenplay draws between Powder's life and that of Jesus. How does the film take us from his strange birth through his hidden life, his acceptance and rejection, a passion, and his literal ascension into the heavens? Contrast this story with other films that have similar themes: *Edward Scissorhands* and *Phenomenon* in particular. What are the elements of parable (a short fictitious story to teach a moral) and fantasy (fiction that has elements of imaginary persons, places, and events) in each of these stories? What is the lasting impression you are left with after viewing these films? Why?

Prayer

Jesus, you provide an abundance of kindness and blessing for those who rejoice in your coming. May this be your Christmas gift to us today. Amen.

CHRISTMAS DAY
Isaiah 52:7–10;
Hebrews 1:1–6;
John 1:1–18

Catch Me If You Can
U.S.A., 2002, 144 minutes
Cast: Leonardo DiCaprio, Tom Hanks, Christopher Walken,
Jennifer Garner, Nathalie Baye, Martin Sheen,
Amy Adams, James Brolin
Writer: Jeff Nathanson
Director: Steven Spielberg

 *Catch Me If You Can*

A Father's Day

SYNOPSIS

In 1963, Frank Abignale Jr. turns sixteen. He attends a prep school and is devoted to his upper-middle class New York family. He admires his would-be entrepreneur father, Frank Sr., who loves his French-born wife but is continually in trouble with the IRS. One day, his father asks the innocent Frank to pose as his chauffeur and he is introduced to the world of role-playing and fraud. Things go badly for Frank Sr., the family has to move to an apartment, and Frank has to go to public school. There, he pretends to be a French teacher and gets away with it. Frank is shocked when he hears that his parents are divorcing and he runs away from home.

Frank wants to find a way for the family to be together again. He needs money and one day realizes that airline pilots are trusted and can have their checks cashed in hotels instead of at banks. He poses as a high-school journalist and discovers how PanAm works. He disguises himself and pretends to be a co-pilot, "dead-heading" from city to city but never flying a plane. He also develops a talent for doctoring checks and a system for eluding detection. It isn't long before the FBI uncovers his schemes. Carl Hanratty, a serious,

36

completely dedicated agent, is deceived at first by Frank but then devotes his career to chasing him.

Frank decides to impersonate a doctor and gets his training from soap operas. He falls in love with a hospital desk assistant, Brenda. She has been estranged from her family and Frank proposes to her as a way to bring them together again. They go to visit her family in New Orleans, and now Frank claims also to be a lawyer, like Brenda's father. He tells her parents that all he has to do is pass the bar exam, which he does. At their engagement party, Hanratty catches up with Frank, but Frank escapes to Europe.

Frank meets his father several times and tries to give him gifts to make up for all that his father has lost. His mother has remarried. Frank calls Hanratty on Christmas Eve every year to make contact because he is lonely. After traveling the world, he is arrested in France while printing fake checks. Hanratty has him extradited to the U.S. and he is found guilty and imprisoned. Hanratty then offers Frank the opportunity to advise the FBI on check fraud, a career that he has pursued for twenty-five years.

COMMENTARY

Frank W. Abignale Jr. told journalists during the promotion junkets for *Catch Me If You Can* that the events portrayed in the film were basically accurate. He also assured audiences who might think the movie promotes the notion that "crime pays" that he has paid his debt to society by serving a prison sentence (though he has earned and continues to earn a substantial income from consultancies to counter the kinds of fraud that he indulged in).

Leonardo DiCaprio still looks boyish enough to convince us that he is a teenage imposter. While Tom Hanks has a role that is the opposite of the flamboyant Frank, he is completely convincing as humorless, conscientious, and dedicated FBI officer Carl Hanratty. Christopher Walken is by turns endearing and sinister as Frank Sr. and was nominated for an Oscar for his performance.

After several very serious movies *(Amistad, Saving Private Ryan, A.I.: Artificial Intelligence, Minority Report),* director Steven Spielberg seems to have enjoyed making this over-long, poignant though colorful, and often comic movie which takes up his recurring theme of abandoned children. The film is based on the book of the same title by Frank Abignale Jr. and Stan Redding.

DIALOGUE WITH THE GOSPEL

Focus: Christmas images invite us to celebrate the relationship between a mother and son, but today's liturgy urges us to reflect on Jesus as the Son of the Father. When Frank Abignale's father fails his son in Catch Me If You Can, *the FBI agent acts as a surrogate father, especially on Christmas Eve. The film reminds us of the bonds between fathers and sons.*

Several key sequences of *Catch Me If You Can* take place on Christmas Eve. The first year that Frank is on the run, he calls Carl Hanratty to make some kind of contact with someone he knows and learns that Carl is working late and alone in his office. As the movie progresses, it is clear that they are bonding like father and son. Christmas makes us think of Mary and her son, Jesus, but the readings for Christmas Day are much more focused on the image of God as "Father." The prologue of St. John's Gospel makes for serious reading on this day, but perhaps thinking of Frank's escapades that end with a father-figure showing care and love for him in *Catch Me If You Can* adds a human touch to John's Christology.

St. John tells us at first that the Word was with God and was made flesh, and dwelt among us. By the end of the prologue, he is referring to the father-son relationship: the Son is always at God's side and reveals the Father. In the more poetic translation from the Jerusalem Bible, John says, "It is the Son who is nearest to the Father's heart who has made him known." This is reinforced in the Letter to the Hebrews that quotes God as saying of Jesus, "I will be a father to him and he shall be a son to me."

Part of the charm as well as the poignancy of Frank Abignale's story is his deep love for his father. Frank admires Frank Sr. and thinks he can do no wrong. He shares his father's sense of prankish fun by tweaking his nose at authority. He successfully pretends to be a teacher, pilot, doctor, and lawyer, while in reality he is driven to make up for all that his father lost. His parents' divorce is traumatic and drives him away from home. Frank's final visits with his father sadden him and the news of his death is a shock. In the meantime, he has found another father in Carl Hanratty. Just as Frank "manifested" or "revealed" his own father's traits in his daring and fraudulent escapades, he "reveals" the qualities of Carl Hanratty for the rest of his life by working for the FBI in tracking down con artists like himself.

Although Frank Abignale was no angel, he tried to be a good son and he repaid his debt to society. He found the redemption that Isaiah speaks of in the first reading. Frank is a kind of Matthew-figure or a Zacchaeus-figure because of their connection to money and unfair taxes, and yet both became special friends of Jesus. When Jesus was born in the stable, he committed himself to associating with every Matthew and every Zacchaeus the world would ever know in order to offer them peace and salvation. Perhaps this is the peace Frank Abignale sought on those lonely Christmas Eves when he telephoned Carl and wanted to make contact with a father who cared.

- Frank Abignale's love for his father, his admiration when he receives the award, remembering the mouse story, his delight in being with his father; watching his father dance with his mother, the conversations

KEY SCENES AND THEMES

in the restaurants and bars after Frank runs away; Frank wanting to make up for all his father's financial losses; the final conversation with his dad and his sense of separation.

- Frank's escapades; his impersonations as teacher, pilot, doctor, lawyer; his relationship with Brenda and telling the truth to her father; calling Carl every Christmas Eve.

- Carl's tracking Frank down in his mother's hometown; Frank's being found guilty, going to jail, Carl visiting him; assisting the fraud squad; Carl having failed as a father to his daughter but succeeding with Frank.

FOR REFLECTION AND CONVERSATION

1. Like almost every Spielberg movie (as we shall see later on this year in the movies *Schindler's List* and *Signs*), *Catch Me If You Can* is about a lonely child (although Frank is more like the Peter Pan of *Hook* than the children in Spielberg's other films, because Peter Pan was a lost boy who never wanted to grow up and had to just the same). Most audiences went to the theater expecting to see a comedy, but it soon becomes evident that, despite its comedic moments, *Catch Me If You Can* is an affecting tale of a lost boy. Did you like the film? Why or why not? What was the most emotional moment for you? Talk about how Hanratty was a "savior" to Frank, and how Frank offered Hanratty the chance to be a father once again.

2. *Catch Me If You Can* is about a father and son, but it is also about the family. Although it does not seem appropriate to dwell on divorce and its effects on Christmas, it is actually a wonderful opportunity to

contemplate what parents and families can do to stay together. What undermined Frank Sr.'s seemingly stable marriage? What were the effects of his parents' divorce on Frank? Have you known divorce and its effects? How would you encourage divorced people or children of divorce at Christmas, when we long more than ever for signs of God's love?

3. *Catch Me If You Can* is full of visual motifs and even Catholic imagery. How many times do images of Mary appear in the film? How does the repetition of the color blue and the PanAm logo create a visual theme that moves the story along? How does Christmas itself function as the framework for telling the story? How many Christmases go by during the film? Do you think *Catch Me If You Can* works as a Christmas movie when the world celebrates the moment in time when the Father, who so loved the world, sent his only Son into the world? Talk about your response.

Prayer

On this Christmas Day, Lord, bless all fathers so that they deepen their love for their children. Amen.

Jodie Foster and Adam Hann-Byrd in *Little Man Tate*.

Little Man Tate

U.S.A., 1991, 99 minutes
Cast: Jodie Foster, Diane Weist, Adam Hann-Byrd,
Harry Connick Jr., Debi Mazar, David Hyde Pierce
Writer: Scott Frank
Director: Jodie Foster

Little Man Tate

Little Man Jesus

SYNOPSIS

DeDe, a single mother, is devoted to her only son, Fred Tate, who is a gifted child. Fred narrates the story about how he is usually bored at school but at home he writes poetry, plays the piano, and is a whiz at math and physics. It's not so much what he knows, but what he understands that makes him different.

Fred comes to the attention of Jane, an expert in dealing with gifted children. She offers him a place in her three-week travel program called "Odyssey of the Mind" in view of attending her special school in the fall. With some reluctance, DeDe agrees. Fred has no friends until he slowly makes friends with the other children on the trip, especially the "magician." Jane decides to write a book about Fred that she will call *Little Man Tate*. She wants to keep him with her so she can observe and test him. She asks DeDe if Fred can take a course in quantum physics at a college during the summer instead of going to Florida with his mother. Fred is the youngest student at the school and some of the students tease him, but he begins to enjoy the experience and performs well.

Fred gradually gets lonely for his mother and craves affection. He experiences disappointment when adults make promises and don't fulfill them. He finds that Jane cannot express affection. He deliberately fails to perform tasks meant to show his genius during a special television program designed to display the talents of gifted children. He says his mother is dead and runs away to return home. DeDe watches the program in Florida and comes home to Fred.

On his eighth birthday, Fred has a party with his mother and his friends. Jane arrives and joins in the celebration.

COMMENTARY

Little Man Tate marks the directing debut of Jodie Foster (who won acting Oscars for *The Accused* and *Silence of the Lambs*). She also plays DeDe in the film, a single mother who discovers she has an extraordinary child and is reluctant to let him go. She gives her character a warmth and down-to-earth quality that is especially vulnerable when she cannot keep pace with her son's intelligence. Diane Weist is the quietly ambitious expert who discovers her emotional limitations. These two actresses complement each other's roles with intelligence and sensitivity. Adam Hann-Byrd plays Fred Tate beautifully.

Scott Frank's screenplay contains closely observed details of the behavior of gifted children and convincingly portrays the inner world of such children and the difficulty they have fitting in.

DIALOGUE WITH THE GOSPEL

Focus: Fred Tate is a child who steps out from the security of his family to develop the extraordinary gifts he has received. Jesus did the same thing at twelve years old in the Temple.

Today's Gospel shows Jesus as a gifted child. The story of "the finding in the Temple" portrays a child who amazes his teachers but who dismays his parents. They seem at a loss to understand why the child they have raised is now acting in a way they have not seen before. This gospel story should be read in the light of the bar mitzvah ceremony and its place in the life of a Jewish boy as he moves toward adulthood and takes his place as a reader in the synagogue.

Little Man Tate is the story of another gifted child. At seven, Fred is much younger than Jesus is during this gospel account, but his story helps us imagine Jesus as he left his parents to be with the learned men at the Temple. The movie shows that the child has a rich inner life of learning, intelligence, and skills that he does not necessarily express in his outer world. At school Fred is considered quiet and perhaps somewhat slow, until one day he lets his teacher see how intelligent he really is.

When the opportunity arises, gifted children can feel at home with peers and display their abilities with some comfort. Instead, Jesus is at home with the religious leaders and teachers, asking them questions, discussing issues.

DeDe is a loving single mother. The father of the child is absent and she has experienced the critical curiosity of strangers regarding her pregnancy and the paternity of her child. The movie shows the mother's appreciation of her son but her inability to fully understand him. When he goes to live with the expert, she feels she is losing him.

DeDe and Fred Tate's story is perhaps even more reminiscent of the story of Hannah as recounted in the reading from First Samuel. Hannah presented her son at the "temple" of Shiloh, to learn the ways of the Lord. DeDe gave her son into the care of Jane at the "temple" of learning, hoping that this was the best for her son.

In the Gospel, Mary asks Jesus after he has been in the Temple for three days, "Son, why have you done this to us? Your father and I have been looking for you with great anxiety." On television, Fred, the lonely little boy, tells the interviewer that his mother is dead. When his mother hears this, it is as if her heart has been wounded. DeDe's experience as a mother parallels that of Mary and Hannah on an emotional level. As the audience and as participants in this liturgy, we can empathize with all of these mothers.

Finally, Jesus went back to Nazareth with Mary and Joseph, in loving obedience to them. Fred returns to his mother and settles into a life of love while still remaining the gifted boy that he is.

KEY SCENES AND THEMES

- Fred's voice-over about his birth, his mother, and his life; his mother's love for him, the discovery that he could read; DeDe proud of his abilities but reluctant to let him go on the trip to Jane's estate; Fred's age, being considered slow in school; his poetry, piano playing, his knowledge and appreciation of art, science, music; his extraordinary understanding.

- Fred's response to Jane, the other children, the appreciation of his abilities; his remarkable responses to the quizzes; beginning college, his disappointment in the promises of adults, Eddie and learning to play pool, Jane's suggestion that he get a drink of water as a way to deal with his nightmare.

- Fred's saying on television that his mother was dead, DeDe watching and wounded but also giving the kiss of life to the boy who was floating in the pool; Fred returning home and breaking the telephones that he liked to play with; DeDe's return, her love for him; the joy and wholeness of the birthday party.

FOR REFLECTION AND CONVERSATION

1. Stories about mothers and their children are the fabric of life. As Mary loved Jesus, so DeDe loved Fred. We know that Mary did not fully understand her son's mission or what he was doing at the Temple for three days, or she would not have asked, "Son, why have

you done this? Your father and I have been looking for you with great anxiety." DeDe was aware of how much she did not know about her son, and was perhaps shamed by the fact that he was so much more intelligent than she. How did this awareness affect her love for him? Which events in the film proved that though Fred was more intelligent, as a person, DeDe had her own particular gifts and value? What was the "defining" moment of her awareness of her love for Fred? Why?

2. Today's Gospel passage often evokes questions about the nature of Jesus' knowledge. Was Jesus, as a human person, endowed with a true human knowledge (cf. *Catechism of the Catholic Church*, nn. 472–474)? What does the Church teach about what Jesus really knew about his Father? If we can account for Jesus' knowledge, how do we account for the gift of genius that some people have? Compare the gifts of DeDe with those of Jane. In the final analysis, what do you think is most important about the gifts that God gives each person? How important is the gift of knowledge?

3. Consider the characters of DeDe, Fred, Jane, the other gifted children, and Eddie as individuals. How did they respond to life around them? How did the adults relate to one another, the adults to the children and the children to each other? How mature are the adults? How did you feel about the characters as the story unfolded and we came to know each of them? What was Eddie's role in the film? Is there a moral to the story of *Little Man Tate*? What do you think it is and why? Can the film be seen, perhaps, to mirror Jodie Foster's own life as an acting prodigy?

Prayer

Jesus, you had your first experience of being adult in the Temple. You knew it was a time when you had to achieve some distance from Joseph and Mary. Give your courage to young adults as they move toward their independence and grant your wisdom to their parents. Amen.

The Elephant Man

U.K., 1980, 118 minutes
Cast: Anthony Hopkins, John Hurt, Anne Bancroft,
John Gielgud, Wendy Hiller, Freddie Jones, Kenny Baker
Writers: Christopher DeVore, Eric Bergren, David Lynch
Director: David Lynch

The Elephant Man

I Am a Human Being

Frederick Treves, a celebrated surgeon at the London Hospital, goes to a carnival to see one of the "freak" exhibits, "The Elephant Man." Treves convinces Bytes, the cruel proprietor, to let the tragically deformed man, John Merrick, be the subject of a medical examination and presentation to the London medical society. Bytes agrees, but mistreats Merrick. Treves goes to their dank lodgings and takes Merrick to the hospital. Treves wants to arrange for Merrick, though ultimately incurable and probably unintelligent, to live at the hospital. When Treves and Mr. Carr Gomm hear Merrick recite the twenty-third psalm, they realize that he is a man of learning and culture who has suffered great humiliation and physical pain.

Queen Victoria intervenes with the hospital board to allow Merrick to stay there permanently. John goes to Treves's home for tea and is treated kindly by Mrs. Treves. Mrs. Kendal, a famed London actress, presents him with her photo and a volume of Shakespeare's plays. Together they recite lines from *Romeo and Juliet* and she kisses him. London society begins to visit Merrick. Mrs. Mothershead, the head nurse, warns Treves

SYNOPSIS

49

that he is no better than Bytes who exposed Merrick to the public.

The night watchman sees a way to make money by getting his pub friends to pay him to see the "Elephant Man." When they invade his room, Bytes joins them, abducts Merrick, and takes him to France. When Merrick collapses, Bytes puts him in a cage with monkeys. The other carnival "freaks" free Merrick and pay his way to London where a crowd pursues him. He confronts them, telling them he is not an animal but a human being.

When he is at home again at the hospital, Mrs. Kendal invites him to the theater. The audience gives him a standing ovation. On his return he removes the pillows that prop him up in bed so that he can breathe properly. He wants to sleep like other people do. He thinks of his mother, whom he has always loved but never known, and dies.

COMMENTARY

In the 1970s, David Lynch made a striking if esoteric small-budget psychological drama, *Eraserhead*, which quickly became a cult classic. Lynch went to England for his second feature, *The Elephant Man*. He skillfully blends his re-creation of Victorian London in black and white with the surrealistic images, dreams, and nightmares of *Eraserhead*. John Morris's evocative score, a blend of dramatic themes with circus melodies, adds to the atmosphere.

The Elephant Man was nominated for eight Academy Awards, losing out on all counts. After all, it was the year of *Raging Bull, Ordinary People, Star Wars: The Empire Strikes Back, Fame,* and *Tess.*

The film was based on *The Elephant Man, a Study in Human Dignity* by Ashley Montagu (1971), and on *The Elephant Man and Other Reminiscences* by Sir Frederick Treves, published in 1923. The film carries a disclaimer that it is not based on the play or on any other accounts of the story of Joseph Carey Merrick, the true name of the "Elephant Man."

Anthony Hopkins is perfectly cast as Treves. John Hurt is one of nature's gentlemen as John Merrick. Dame Wendy Hiller (*A Man for All Seasons*), Sir John Gielgud, and Anne Bancroft add to the impressive casting of this moving drama.

Focus: The Incarnation means that the Word was made flesh. Like John Merrick, Jesus would be rejected and made to suffer. John Merrick's goodness is an image of the human and compassionate Jesus.

DIALOGUE WITH THE GOSPEL

At Christmas we celebrate the wonder of the Incarnation. We try to appreciate how Jesus lived in the world as we do. Toward the end of *The Elephant Man*, John Merrick cries out to the pursuing crowd, "I am not an animal. I am a human being. I am a man." Jesus came to earth to live our lives with us, especially with those as afflicted as John Merrick.

The reading from Sirach declares that divine wisdom has been sent by God to dwell on earth. All of us are meant to be images of God and divine wisdom. We see God's compassion in Dr. Treves. John Merrick is patient, a man of great sensitivity and courtesy, thankful for his experience of life. The Governor, Mr. Carr Gomm, the matron, Mrs. Mothershead, and the actress, Mrs. Kendall all portray glimpses of humane care.

St. Paul's hymn in the Letter to the Ephesians sings of God's loving plan for all of us, to be holy and without blemish before him. John Merrick is considered by some to be nature's blemish, but is instead the epitome of holiness.

Parallels can be drawn between John the Baptist and Dr. Treves and between Jesus and John Merrick in light of the prologue to St. John's Gospel. Treves found Merrick and announced him to the world. He then had to examine his conscience about his motives for displaying Merrick to society. Like the Baptist, Treves had to become less important, to step back from the limelight.

John Merrick came into the world as a light in society's darkness. "His own received him not." Bytes was brutal and the porter exploited him cruelly, "just for a laugh." For those who recognized John's deep humanity, he empowered them to become children of God in their love and compassion. John Merrick was full of grace and truth.

<table>
<tr><td>

KEY SCENES AND THEMES

</td><td>

- The prologue with Merrick's mother experiencing the trauma of the elephants; Merrick's dreams; his mother's photo and his wish that he could find her and that she would be proud of him; his dying and her receiving him.

- Treves, the surgeon, the anatomist; his visit to the carnival; his examination and display of Merrick; the deal with Bytes; persuading Mr. Carr Gomm to let John stay; their hearing him recite more of Psalm 23 than Treves had taught him; Mrs. Kendal's visit, *Romeo and Juliet,* and the kiss; the intervention of the queen with the hospital board; Merrick at home in the hospital.

- The carnival, exposed to the crowds, Bytes beating him; the treatment of Merrick by the porter and his drunk mates; kidnapped by Bytes, back in the carnival, his collapse, in the cage with the monkeys, his friends freeing him; the journey and the pursuit in the station; the declaration of his humanity; his death.

</td></tr>
<tr><td>

FOR REFLECTION AND CONVERSATION

</td><td>

1. For years, it was thought that John Merrick suffered from neurofibromatosis, the most common nervous system genetic defect caused by a single gene, leading to symptoms such as those he exhibited. Now, however, it is commonly believed that Merrick suffered from Proteus Syndrome (www.proteus-syndrome.org),

</td></tr>
</table>

an unrelated condition, only identified in 1979. To-day, there are only 120 people known to have this condition worldwide. Why do you think that John Merrick was so badly mistreated? How do people deal with those they perceive as "different" from themselves or as "other" in our own day and age? As Christians, what are some things we can do to help us focus on our common humanity rather than on distinctions between peoples?

2. What caused Mr. Treves to reflect on his motivations for seeking out John Merrick in the first place? Was he wrong to encourage John to entertain celebrities? How and why did Mr. Treves, Mr. Carr Gomm, the head nurse, Nora, and others change in their attitude toward John? When did they become his true friends? How did the movie make you feel about people you may have avoided because of their external looks or limitations? How can a movie like *The Elephant Man* change our way of seeing people? What function do the mirror and photographs play in the film?

3. One of the most emotional moments in the film is after Mr. Treves coaches John to repeat certain things to impress Mr. Carr Gomm. At first it seems John can only repeat what he was told, but then they overhear him actually praying the twenty-third psalm. What religious images are in the film? What function do they play, especially the cathedral? At the end, when John is being pursued by the mob, he yells out, "I am not an animal! I am a human being! I am a man!" What are your thoughts at the conclusion of this bi-ography of a man who wanted so much to be like ev-

ery other member of the human race? Who else besides John Merrick is an image of the human and compassionate Jesus in the film?

Prayer

*Jesus, you came to live among us, you took on our limitations and
you shared our sufferings. Help us to see your face in every man and
woman we meet. Amen.*

Martin Sheen (left) in *The Fourth Wise Man.*

The Fourth Wise Man
U.S.A., 1985, 72 minutes
Cast: Martin Sheen, Alan Arkin, Eileen Brennan,
Ralph Bellamy, Richard Libertini, Harold Gould,
Lance Kerwin, Sidney Penny, Adam Arkin
Writer: Tom Fontana
Director: Michael Ray Rhodes

The Fourth Wise Man

The One Who Never Arrived

SYNOPSIS

In Persia, three magi prepare to set out for Israel to seek the Messiah. Another "wise man," Artaban, a physician who has recently lost his family in a fire, realizes that his astrological charts were correct when he sees a star appear that will lead him to the king of Israel. Artaban's father allows him to go, asking the slave, Orontes, to accompany him and keep him safe. Artaban sells all his possessions to buy three precious jewels to take as gifts for the newborn king. The men set out to join the magi, but because they stop to help someone, they arrive after the other three magi have started out. Artaban tells Orontes to sell one of the gems to buy camels and provisions for a caravan because he believes they can catch up. Later, they give a ruby to one of Herod's soldiers to save a baby in Bethlehem, and once again miss finding Jesus.

The men continue their search and are ambushed and robbed by people from a colony of outcasts and lepers. Artaban and Orontes stay with the group for thirty years, helping the colony. Eventually, another member of the magi from Artaban's homeland who is now a successful trader visits them with his daughter.

When Artaban hears that Jesus is in Jerusalem, he and Orontes follow, reaching the Upper Room just as Jesus leaves for Gethsemane. The men follow Jesus' movements that night and when Artaban hears Jesus being scourged, he himself collapses. When Jesus is about to be executed, Artaban tries to follow him along the road to Calvary but becomes ill and cannot continue immediately. Just as he reaches his goal, Artaban and Orontes see the young daughter of their countryman being taken away by soldiers. Artaban gives his precious pearl, his last jewel, to pay her ransom.

Artaban dies after he has a vision of Jesus who tells him that all he did for others, he did for him. Orontes stays on to work in the colony.

COMMENTARY

The Fourth Wise Man is based on a story, "The Story of the Other Wise Man," originally written by Henry Van Dyke in 1895 and published as "The Other Wise Man" by Harper in 1927. Fr. Ellwood Kieser, the Paulist priest who produced the *Insight* programs as well as the films *Romero* and *Entertaining Angels*, produced *The Fourth Wise Man*. The story was adapted for television by Tom Fontana, who also wrote the script for the 2001 Paulist production, *Judas*. Michael Ray Rhodes, who produced *Romero* and *Entertaining Angels*, directed *The Fourth Wise Man*.

The movie was written as a blend of "homily and entertainment," according to writer Tom Fontana. The basis for *The Fourth Wise Man* is the narrative in Matthew's Gospel about the visit of the Magi to Bethlehem.

Martin Sheen gives a heartfelt performance as Artaban, and Alan Arkin plays the film's comic relief, the slave Orontes. Members of the Sheen and Arkin families (including Charlie Sheen as a Roman) also appear in the movie.

DIALOGUE WITH THE GOSPEL

Focus: Today's Gospel tells us about the three magi who followed the star and reached Bethlehem to honor Jesus. The Chris-

tian imagination has invented many stories surrounding the life of Christ; this film tells a fictitious tale about a fourth wise man who searched for the Child but never arrived because he stopped on the journey to help the poor.

The first reading, written about five hundred years before the coming of Jesus, sets a tone for the story of the magi coming from the East, riding camels and bearing gifts of gold, frankincense, and myrrh. Themes of light and glory in darkness permeate the reading. The responsorial psalm celebrates the gathering of the kings of "the nations" to pay tribute and serve the Child. We now call the magi "kings."

The Fourth Wise Man offers us images to fill in some of the detail of the rather spare descriptions in today's Gospel. According to the tale, the magi are not only wise men; they are wealthy and well-educated physicians and astronomers. Their studies of sacred writings tell them that a star will rise because the king of the world is to be born in Israel.

The film asks us to suspend our literal understanding of today's Gospel and imagine another wise man who is completely selfless in his search for Jesus. Artaban gives his gifts to those who are in immediate need, forgives those who steal from him, and remains in the leper colony to heal the sick. Artaban continually postpones his departure until thirty years have passed. He lives Jesus' teaching in his daily life, something Jesus confirms at the end of the film when he appears to Artaban and tells him, "Whatever you did for the least of my brothers and sisters, you did for me."

The Epiphany is a feast of the manifestation of Jesus to the world. This movie is an inspiring reminder that Jesus reveals himself not in palaces and the circles of the great and mighty but to the poor and the marginalized. When he is dying, Artaban has a vision of Jesus. It is an epiphany that reveals to this generous seeker that all that he has done for others, he has done for Jesus. This is the gift he brings to Christ today.

KEY SCENES AND THEMES

- Artaban and his enthusiasm to find the Messiah, seeking Jesus in Israel, saving one of the "holy innocents," continuing the search; the contrast between Artaban and Orontes, who only wants to return home.

- The lepers and outcasts robbing Artaban; his compassion for the lepers; his years serving in the colony; teaching the colonists how to sow and reap their crops.

- The final search for Jesus, the Upper Room, in Gethsemane, at Pilate's palace, on the road to Calvary; Artaban giving his pearl to the young girl; his death and Jesus' final revelation to him.

FOR REFLECTION AND CONVERSATION

1. Taking up a quest is to make one or a series of long journeys and adventures, to wander far and wide in search of something. Stories of odysseys and quests abound in world literature. In cinema, this genre is sometimes called "road movies," and is often more about people finding their way in life through crime and mishap rather than about serving others. How is the journey of Artaban and ultimately that of Orontes a quest? What is the goal of their journeys and adventures? Artaban seeks both a person and meaning. Do these mean the same thing? How do the events in Artaban's life lead him "to find him and serve him, the only one who can lead me to life's real meaning"?

2. In *The Fourth Wise Man,* we have the story of a man whose sorrow leads him to seek truth through service in a community. What other films tell similar stories, even if they are not specifically religious; for example, *Beyond Rangoon, Restoration, The Searchers,* and *Men With Guns*? What impressed you about these stories? How do different people "travel" together toward their

goals and the "truth" they are seeking? Does today's film work as an example of people from different faith traditions, as well as political, economic, and cultural situations, walking side by side toward justice, charity, and truth? Why or why not? Is the film more "sermon" or "entertainment," or does it satisfy on both levels? Why?

3. Epiphany means "manifestation." Today's feast is not about differences but about God's self-revelation to all people, about being partners on our path to God. What are some ways that you practice the manifestation of God in your own life? Through ecumenical, interreligious or interfaith efforts? Talk about some practical ways you can "incarnate" today's feast in your prayer, personal life, and community.

Prayer

Jesus, on this day we celebrate your revelation to the world by the Father. Help us to see your face in the faces of all those who are in need of compassion. Amen.

The Saint of Fort Washington
U.S.A., 1994, 98 minutes
Cast: Danny Glover, Matt Dillon, Rick Aviles,
Ving Rhames, Joe Seneca, Nina Siemaszko
Writer: Lyle Kessler
Director: Tim Hunter

The Saint of Fort Washington

Anointing a Secular Saint

SYNOPSIS

The decrepit Hotel Jefferson in Manhattan is being demolished. Many street people who found it a refuge, including a young photographer named Matthew, now must spend their nights in the Fort Washington armory, a vast dormitory where the men run the risk of being harassed and robbed. Matthew has been diagnosed as schizophrenic and has spent time in an institution.

Matthew takes a photo of Vietnam veteran Jerry with his camera that has no film. Although Jerry is upset and they clash, he protects Matthew when Leroy and his gang go on the prowl for trouble at the armory. A father-son relationship develops between Jerry and Matthew. Jerry notices Matthew being kind to strangers and, making a parallel with Joan of Arc and her voices, he proclaims Matthew a saint. Later, he pours water over him, thus "anointing" him the Saint of Fort Washington. Matthew and Jerry clean car windshields near the George Washington Bridge. At first Matthew is awkward, but soon he learns the rhythms of the work. He even begins to tell jokes like Jerry and earns some money.

Jerry's friend, Spits, offers the hospitality of his van to the two men, who plan to eventually rent an apartment together.

When Jerry's injured knee causes him agony and he has no more painkillers, Matthew massages him and "cures" him, at least temporarily. Matthew also massages and heals Spits's arthritic fingers.

The van is towed away by the city. The weather is freezing and the authorities force the street people to go into the shelters. While Jerry gets away, Matthew is taken to the armory where a vengeful Leroy stabs him to death. Jerry goes to Matthew's unmarked grave in Potters Field. He continues to clean car windows, recalling his friendship with Matthew and inspired by his spirit.

COMMENTARY

The Saint of Fort Washington is a blend of the tough and the gentle, contrasting the hardships, language, and violence of the streets on the one hand with the goodness of spirit of so many who are dismissed as "drifters" on the other. It did not receive a wide theatrical release and found its audience with groups who like to discuss movies and their messages.

While the message of *The Saint of Fort Washington* inspires, the film itself runs the danger of seeming a little too predictable for some audiences. However, it has excellent credentials. Danny Glover, who is convincing as Jerry, has made a career of portraying characters who are serious (*Places in the Heart, Grand Canyon, To Sleep with Anger*) or who are tough (and comedic: the *Lethal Weapon* series). Matt Dillon as Matthew underplays his schizophrenic role rather than using the histrionic style many actors adopt when playing people with mental impairment. Ving Rhames is almost too credible as the sleazy Leroy. The film was directed by Tim Hunter (who previously directed Dillon in *Tex*).

DIALOGUE WITH THE GOSPEL

Focus: Just as John baptized Jesus at the beginning of his ministry, Jerry's "anointing" Matthew as the Saint of Fort Washington singled him out to be an instrument of God's grace.

The reason for choosing *The Saint of Fort Washington* for the feast of the baptism of Jesus is obvious. In the middle of the movie, Jerry, who already declared Matthew a saint, takes some water, pours it on Matthew, and uses it to symbolize his being anointed as a saint.

The world cries out for role models, for men and women who can make the meaning of saintliness more credible in our time. There is a long literary tradition of novel characters that have a mental illness being filled with the spirit of God and doing good for others, even when they are ridiculed and rejected. Dostoyevsky's *The Idiot* is a classic example, as is Steinbeck's *Of Mice and Men.* In the movie world, there have been a number of idiot savants, autistics like Raymond in *Rain Man* and, of course, *Forrest Gump.*

The first reading takes up the theme of the revelation of God's glory that is a principal feature of the celebration of the Lord's baptism. The people yearn for comfort and, while God is powerful, the savior holds lambs tenderly and leads them with care. This is the kind of saint Matthew is.

Matthew can in fact be considered a Christ-figure. When he is kind to people, when he goes out of his way to help them with little things, when he cures the sick—all this resembles the Jesus of the gospels. When Jerry suddenly "baptizes" him, it seems entirely fitting. There is no spectacular "epiphany," as occurred with Jesus and John at the Jordan, but God could nevertheless identify Matthew as one of his beloved sons in whom he was well pleased. Jerry reminds us of many gospel figures. When he claims Matthew as his son, he is a Joseph-figure; when he anoints Matthew, he is a Baptist-figure; when he visits Matthew's grave, he reminds us of Nicodemus.

The water theme is ever present in *The Saint of Fort Washington*, especially in the cleaning of the cars, which Jerry refers to as making things beautiful. The waters of baptism have always been seen as a symbol for cleansing, therefore an image of dying and being born again.

It is worthwhile reading the selections from Isaiah and Titus in the light of what Matthew achieved in his short and limited life. He was a means of comfort to God's people and a sign of God's grace.

- Matthew and his "photographs"; the initial clash with Jerry but Jerry's protecting him, calling him his son, proclaiming him the saint, baptizing him, being healed by him, failing to save him from death, burying him, and "proclaiming" him after his death.

- Matthew's acts of kindness and generosity, his healing powers, his awkwardness washing car windows but learning how to do the work, finding the humor and the right greeting and affirmation for the drivers; the effect he had on Jerry, Rosario, Tamsin, and Spits.

- Leroy's aggression, his sleazy violence; Jerry protecting Matthew from Leroy; Matthew helping the young man in the armory; Leroy turning on Matthew and killing him; Matthew buried in a pauper's grave.

KEY SCENES AND THEMES

1. "Maybe you ain't schizophrenic. Maybe you're just a saint," Jerry tells Matthew. In some ways Matthew is like St. Benedict Joseph Labre, who was born in France in 1748. Labre was the oldest of fifteen children and tried eleven times to enter a monastery, but it was obvious he did not have a religious vocation. He then became a homeless pilgrim, walking all over Europe to visit many religious shrines until he settled in Rome in 1774. He begged in the streets, slept in the colosseum, prayed in the various churches during the day, and cured the sick. He was a mystic and even wrote a prayer for protection against lightning, thunder, and storm. He collapsed in the street and died at the age of thirty-five. He is the primary patron saint of the

FOR REFLECTION AND CONVERSATION

mentally ill. What is mental illness? What is holiness and what are the conditions for it to flourish? Who is a saint? Who can be a saint?

2. At any given time, 1 percent of the U.S. population, that is, 2.3 million adults and children, are homeless. According to some sources, 50 percent of homeless women and children are fleeing domestic violence. In Canada, homelessness is calculated by how many people use homeless shelters; today in Toronto, the homeless number about 5,000, an increase of 20% in ten years. Australia and the United Kingdom also maintain statistics on those who sleep in the rough. Do some research on the causes of homelessness. What are they? Who are the homeless in your area? When a homeless person washes your car window, what is your response?

3. What does *The Saint of Fort Washington* reveal about human nature? How do the locations in which the film is shot, as well as the symbols in the film, help create its meaning? How do issues of Christian social justice emerge from the story of Matthew, Jerry, and the people with whom they interacted? What did the story mean to you in the light of your baptismal commitment?

Prayer

Lord, you call us all to be ordinary saints in our daily lives. We are to be kind and patient and to work for justice and charity as you did. At this celebration of the beginning of your public life, be with us as we renew our baptismal promises and strengthen us to live your holiness. Amen.

ASH WEDNESDAY

Joel 2:12–18;
2 Corinthians 5:20—6:2;
Matthew 6:1–6, 16–18

On the Waterfront

U.S.A., 1954, 103 minutes
Cast: Marlon Brando, Eva Marie Saint, Karl Malden,
Lee J. Cobb, Rod Steiger, Leif Ericsson, Martin Balsam
Writer: Budd Schulberg
Director: Elia Kazan

On the Waterfront

The Waterfront: This Is My Church

SYNOPSIS

Johnny Friendly, along with his bookkeeper, Charlie Molloy, runs the longshoremen's union on the New York waterfront. When Joey Doyle speaks to the crime investigators about waterfront corruption, Friendly uses ex-boxer Terry Molloy as an unknowing decoy so that Doyle can be murdered. Edie Doyle wants to know the truth about her brother's death. Terry is attracted to her, and when he realizes his role in the murder, eventually confesses to her what he has done. Parish priest Fr. Barry becomes involved in the waterfront troubles, holding meetings in his church and encouraging men to speak to the authorities. He tells them that any murder on the docks is another crucifixion.

When a second worker is killed, Fr. Barry confronts Terry about his duty to speak out. Friendly urges Charlie to control Terry, but Terry reminds Charlie that he could have been someone, a professional boxer, except for Charlie's forcing him to take falls for betting set-ups. Charlie backs off and is murdered by Friendly's men.

After Terry testifies at a hearing, the men shun him. Then Friendly challenges him, and they fight. Friendly's thugs converge on Terry and beat him. The men gang up against

67

Friendly and refuse to work unless Terry leads them in. Urged on by Fr. Barry, Terry walks and the men follow.

COMMENTARY

On the Waterfront is a classic Hollywood movie with a social conscience. It is also a powerful look at how a priest and the church can be involved with people in their ordinary lives as well as in the social dimensions of life. It was nominated for twelve Academy Awards in 1954 and won eight, including Oscars for Best Film, Best Director, Best Actor, and Best Supporting Actress. The screenplay was by Budd Schulberg, who based the story on the Pulitzer Prize-winning series of newspaper articles by Malcolm Johnson.

Marlon Brando became a successful Broadway actor while still in his twenties. His first starring role in a film was in *The Men* in 1950. For five years his screen reputation soared with movies like *A Streetcar Named Desire, Viva Zapata,* and as Mark Anthony in *Julius Caesar.* His movie choices over the next fifty years were erratic, although he is now immortal as Don Corleone, *The Godfather.* Rod Steiger and Eva Marie Saint were to have long careers as well. The always dependable Karl Malden is impressive as Fr. Barry. Leonard Bernstein's score gave audiences a foretaste of the abilities that would make him a household name with *West Side Story.*

Elia Kazan, who had already tackled American social issues like anti-Semitism in his Oscar-winning *Gentleman's Agreement* (1947) and black-white prejudice in *Pinky* (1949), directed *On the Waterfront.*

DIALOGUE WITH THE GOSPEL

Focus: In the Gospel, Jesus warns his disciples against doing good deeds just so others can see and admire them. Terry Molloy is presented as a waterfront Christ-figure who experiences a Lenten journey of repentance and conversion. He follows his conscience and is prepared to suffer for his convictions.

Over the years, some theologians have viewed *On the Waterfront* as a twentieth-century passion play. Fr. Barry's sermon to the longshoremen in the union hall seems to justify this belief. The priest tells the workers that if some people think that Jesus' death took place only on Calvary, they had better "wise up." Every time workingmen are oppressed, it is a crucifixion. For the longshoremen who were murdered because they spoke to the crime investigators, it was another Calvary. He condemns those who stand around quietly and do nothing. They are worse than the Roman soldiers who pierced the flesh of Christ.

On the Waterfront is a fine film with which to begin Lent, a traditional time for conversion. The film portrays Terry Molloy's conversion, from his repentance for being the unwitting decoy for Joey Doyle's death, to his "confessions" to Edie and Fr. Barry, to standing up to his brother Charlie and testifying before the commission, thus defying Johnny Friendly. Terry's behavior and that of the community of waterfront workers reflect the reading from Joel: change is possible. Paul's statement that we are ambassadors of Christ can also pertain to Terry. When Fr. Barry confronts the men after the murder in the hold of the ship, he tells them that Jesus is standing beside them when they are picked or rejected for work, and while they are at work. If a cup of cold water is given, then it is given to him. When the greedy union racketeers brutalize them, it is done to Christ. When Terry is beaten for his convictions, he is another Christ, an ambassador for his message of reconciliation. And the men follow him back to work.

Johnny Friendly is the waterfront hypocrite, parading his power, his "goodness" to the men he professes to help and in the way he encourages Terry. Friendly is finally unmasked and left isolated, ranting against the men.

Because of the screenplay's allusions to the Gospel and to the passion story, this film can contribute to our lenten preparations for Holy Week. Edie's demands for the truth about her brother's death and her love for Terry make her one of the catalysts for his conversion. So is Charlie, especially in the classic taxi sequence where Terry tells Charlie that he has really betrayed him, and later, when Terry finds Charlie/Judas hanging on the wall. But it is Fr. Barry who shows what Christianity can mean on the waterfront. When he tells Edie that he will be in church and she taunts him, "you never heard of a saint hiding in a church," he declares the waterfront his parish, encourages meetings in the church hall, helps transform Terry, and stands by him in his Via Dolorosa at the end of the movie. Terry Molloy is willing to die, but as he stumbles toward the dock, he has already risen.

KEY SCENES AND THEMES

- Terry as the decoy, patronized by Friendly, challenged by Edie, attracted to her, going to the church, telling the truth to her and to Fr. Barry; Terry's encounters with the investigators, the "I could have been a contender" conversation in the taxi with Charlie, testifying against Friendly.

- Edie demanding the truth, her attraction to Terry, her being upset at his role in her brother's death, his confession to her, her support of him when he makes difficult decisions.

- Fr. Barry not hiding in the church, administering last rites, the meeting in the church hall, his sermon about Calvary; his telling the men that Jesus was present with them on the waterfront; his support of Terry on his final and painful walk.

FOR REFLECTION AND CONVERSATION

1. Christ-figures abound in film. Some contemporary examples are found in the movies *Erin Brockovich, E.T: the Extraterrestrial, Edward Scissorhands, Jesus of Montreal, The Mighty, Simon Birch, Babette's Feast, Lilies of the Field*, and so forth. When *On the Waterfront* is interpreted theologically, it works very well as a re-imagining of

aspects of the life of Christ. Trace and talk about the story lines that might indicate this to you. How was Terry willing to go the distance for what he believed was right? He didn't actually start out as a noble character. In fact, at one point he says, "Hey, you wanna hear my philosophy of life? Do it to him before he does it to you." How do circumstances and relationships help him grow and change? What situations and people in your life have helped you to become more Christ-like?

2. If Terry is the Christ-figure, then who might Fr. Barry be? He tells the longshoremen: "Isn't it simple as one, two, three? One. The working conditions are bad. Two. They're bad because the mob does the hiring. And three. The only way we can break the mob is to stop letting them get away with murder." How does Fr. Barry show that everyday life needs faith to help it change for the good of all people? What attributes does Edie have that contribute to Terry's understanding that the world is bigger than he is? How does what she tells her father ("But, Pop, I've seen things that I know are so wrong. Now how can I go back to school and keep my mind on…things that are just in books, that aren't people living?") show that her own social awareness is growing? What are some other quotes from the film that impressed you? Why?

3. *On the Waterfront* has always been considered director Elia Kazan's personal statement about conscience and justification of his decision to testify against associates who were suspected of being communists when he testified to the House Committee on Un-American Activities (HUAC). Kazan followed his conscience,

but many of his colleagues took it as a betrayal. Do you think it is important to understand the context in which a film is produced? Why or why not? Compare *On the Waterfront* as a parallel for what was happening in American history at that time (1940s–1950s) with *Guilty by Suspicion*, a 1991 film about the effects of the Hollywood blacklist on people who worked in the industry. Were both sides "victims" of too much government? What was the role of personal conscience during these times (the HUAC existed in one form or another at first to monitor foreign agents and then to police anti-American sentiment among its citizens from 1938–1975)? Can we separate the historical context in which a film was made from understanding it as a cultural artifact? Why or why not?

Prayer

Lord, as we begin Lent, give us the strength to follow in your steps in suffering and give us the hope that we will share in your resurrection. Amen.

Ralph Fiennes in *Quiz Show.*

FIRST SUNDAY OF LENT
Deuteronomy 26:4–10;
Romans 10:8–13;
Luke 4:1–13

Quiz Show

U.S.A., 1994, 130 minutes
Cast: Ralph Fiennes, John Turturro, Rob Morrow, Paul Scofield,
Mira Sorvino, David Paymer, Hank Azaria, Martin Scorsese,
Alan King, Barry Levinson
Writer: Paul Attanasio
Director: Robert Redford

Quiz Show

Modern Temptations

SYNOPSIS

It is the 1950s and "Twenty-One" is one of the most popular television quiz shows in America. Everybody is watching it. The competitive aspects of the show and the money prizes provide the attraction. However, the show is rigged and Herb Stempel has been the champion for several weeks because the producers are giving him the answers. As they watch the ratings, the producers decide they want a change of contestants. Herb is bought off with a false promise that he will host his own show if he intentionally loses a match.

The producers select Charles Van Doren as the next "champion." His father, Mark, is an award-winning poet and academic. At first Van Doren goes along with the deception with reluctance, but then begins to relish the fame and popularity. An embittered Herb blows the whistle and Dick Goodwin, a skilled young lawyer, investigates the quiz shows as a basis for a Senate hearing into media fraud. Dick befriends Van Doren, even visiting his home, but cannot persuade him to tell the truth.

Ultimately there is a hearing where Van Doren confesses. However, sponsors, producers, and network managers escape punishment, and show business continues as usual.

COMMENTARY

Robert Redford directs *Quiz Show* with great sensitivity. Paul Attanasio (*Disclosure*) has written an insightful screenplay based on the book *Remembering America: A Voice from the Sixties* by Richard Goodwin. Redford has only directed a few movies, but they always have something to say about values and are elegantly crafted: *The Milagro Beanfield War, A River Runs Through It, The Horse Whisperer, The Legend of Bagger Vance,* and his Oscar-winning *Ordinary People.*

The drama has three focal points: the ordinary guy, the Jewish contestant from Brooklyn, Herb Stempel; the ambitious young WASP lawyer; and the aristocratic Van Doren and his academic family. John Turturro stands out as Stempel and Ralph Fiennes shows his versatility as Van Doren; Paul Scofield plays his father with dignity and authority. The supporting cast is excellent with guest appearances by directors Martin Scorsese and Barry Levinson.

DIALOGUE WITH THE GOSPEL

Focus: At the beginning of his public ministry, Jesus was tempted to choose worldly glory rather than trust in God. In Quiz Show, *two men succumb to the temptation to choose celebrity over integrity.*

Quiz Show is a film about succumbing to temptation. Each of the contestants on "Twenty-One" lives in his own "desert." Wonderful opportunities are offered to them as long as they cheat. Herb is trapped in working-class suburbia. He is a gambler and he needs money for his family. Charles Van Doren lives in the shadow of his renowned father, trying to make something of himself in his own right. New York and the media world make a glitzy "desert" for him. Both Herb and Charles struggle with temptation. Both of them compromise their consciences and yield to temptation.

The characters who are the "Satans" of the film are worth considering. Among them are the hirelings who produce the show. They palm off contestants with empty promises and with financial bonuses because it is in their power to do so. They adapt their spiel to every newcomer, only admitting the truth when they are found out. They lie during the investigation. The arrogant president of the television network is a friend of the high and mighty of the land. Perhaps the most sinister "Satan" is the suave and conniving sponsor, who tries to buy off the investigating lawyer as well.

It is easy to establish parallels with the temptations Jesus experienced: the hunger for money (the contemporary bread); the temptation to presumption because the producers think that the contestants will be saved from disaster; the allure of power, glamour, fame, and success. The short excerpt from Paul to the Romans in the second reading serves as a complementary statement about integrity: keeping the word of truth near you—in your heart and in your mouth—will lead ultimately to salvation.

KEY SCENES AND THEMES

- The opening scene: the lawyer tempted to buy a car he cannot afford followed by the collage of "Twenty-One," the contestant, the audiences, the home viewers, the producers, the sponsors, and the aura of glamour, greed, and success.

- The producer asking Herb Stempel to make a mistake and get the answer wrong, his discussion with his wife, the actual making of the error; the producers making the proposal to Charles Van Doren and showing him how the deception works.

- Confessions: Charles Van Doren's confessing to his father; Herb Stempel's testimony at the hearing and descriptions of how the contestants were trained to behave on the show; Charles Van Doren's public acknowledgment of his guilt at the hearing, the applause and commendations; the critique of the senator who reminded him that he was merely telling the truth.

FOR REFLECTION AND CONVERSATION

1. Talk about some of the dialogue from *Quiz Show,* such as: "Why fix them? Why not just make the questions easier? The audience doesn't want to see the contestants—they want to see the money." "It isn't like we're hardened criminals here—we're in show business." What do you think of this "philosophy"? What does it say about the media, about the people who were involved in media fifty years ago, and about what they thought of the audience? Where is human dignity to be found in this film? Are quiz shows more difficult or easier now? Do they respect learning and intelligence? Do you think quiz shows today continue to "tempt" people? If so, in what ways?

2. Knowing what you now know about what went on behind the scenes of the quiz show, what would you have done if you had been in the place of Charles, Herb, the government lawyer, the executive, and the sponsors? Name some of the "virtues" or "habits of good" in this movie (e.g., integrity, truth, honesty, humility). Compare it with other films about similar themes, such as *The Emperor's Club, Wall Street,* or *The Insider.* How difficult is it to say no to temptation in your own life? How do you handle temptations, especially the kind where "nobody gets hurt" or there is little chance you'll get caught? Is Charles Van Doren the perpetrator or the victim? Explain your response.

3. There are some issues of interest to media literacy education in *Quiz Show,* such as the fact that all media are constructed realities and businesses with commercial interests. Another issue is that of racial and cultural representation and social class. Why does Herb's popularity endure for so long? What are the executives' motives for setting him up so they can remove

him from the show? How are Herb and Charles different yet the same? Do you think the executives used issues of race, religion, culture, and social class on purpose when they chose contestants? Why? Do you think this kind of manipulation still happens today in game shows or other forms of popular entertainment? If so, give some examples and talk about the consequences.

Prayer

Jesus, we are surrounded by temptation. Share with us your wisdom so that we can discern between good and evil. Give us your strength to make the right choices. Amen.

SECOND SUNDAY OF LENT

Genesis 15:5–12, 17–18;
Philippians 3:17—4:1;
Luke 9:28b–36

Close Encounters of the Third Kind
U.S.A., 1977, 152 minutes
Cast: Richard Dreyfuss, Francois Truffaut,
Melinda Dillon, Teri Garr, Bob Balaban
Writer: Steven Spielberg
Director: Steven Spielberg

Close Encounters of the Third Kind

Glory on a Mountain

SYNOPSIS

Government officials examine a site in Mexico that is suspected of being a landing place for a UFO. They hear a series of five musical notes and realize it is a code. They also find a plane that has been missing since World War II. French scientific expert Dr. Lacombe believes that aliens are trying to make contact with humans. His translator, a cartographer, guesses correctly that the musical code corresponds to geographic coordinates. They identify the site as Devil's Mountain in Wyoming. The government orders an evacuation of the area on the pretext that dangerous chemicals have been spilled there. The military moves in.

Meanwhile in Indiana, Jillian is woken by a shuddering of her house and finds that her young son, Barry, has gone outside looking for something. She follows him. Roy Neary works for the electric company and his house is also shaken. He is called out to help investigate the reasons for a power outage. Seeing the spacecraft, he follows it and finds a number of other people who share the encounter, including Jillian and Barry.

Roy loses his job and begins to act strangely at home. His wife and children are upset and eventually leave. Roy is struggling with a sense of a "call," and "sees" a vision of a mound. He eventually builds a model of Devil's Mountain, and then recognizes it on television. Jillian has been drawing it, especially after Barry disappears. The aliens have taken him.

Roy and Jillian each travel to Wyoming and meet near the mountain. Together they break through the restrictive fences and witness the landing of the spacecraft and the musical conversation that takes place between the scientists, the military, and the UFO. Many military personnel who had disappeared at the end of the war come out of the spacecraft. Barry also returns. An alien descends from the spacecraft, followed by others who seem like children. Finally Roy is embraced by them and invited to be part of the group that enters the craft to travel into space.

COMMENTARY

Steven Spielberg's *Close Encounters of the Third Kind* was released in 1977, the same year as his friend George Lucas's *Star Wars (Star Wars: Episode IV—A New Hope)*. These movies transformed the way audiences thought about science fiction and science fantasy movies. They drew on the archetypal dimensions of the human imagination. For Western culture, which was becoming less and less committed to organized religion and churches, these movies offered alternate "mythologies" for human aspirations beyond the humdrum of daily life.

Close Encounters of the Third Kind also gave a new credibility to UFO stories. The movie draws on several traditions, including Christian, about someone coming from "up there" or "out there," someone who offers some kind of salvation. Roy Neary, played by Richard Dreyfuss who appeared in *Jaws* and *Always*, is an "everyman" character, an ordinary citizen who is offered the call of a lifetime and shares in this extraordinary moment of "salvation."

The movie was nominated for nine Oscars in 1977, and won two: for cinematography and a Special Achievement Award for special-effects sound editing.

Focus: Peter, James, and John are invited by Jesus to go up the mountain and experience a "close encounter" with God. Roy Neary, in a more postmodern setting, experiences a close encounter with aliens, hoping for some answers and salvation.

There are some evocative phrases in the Genesis reading about the skies, light, darkness, a sense of vocation, revelation, and the experience of a covenant. Abraham, ratifying his sacrifice to God, receives God's promise of blessing.

Paul reminds the Philippians that heaven is the Christian homeland. From heaven the savior comes. When he comes, he will transfigure those who are faithful. Paul uses the language of transforming "glory."

Close Encounters of the Third Kind is not a parallel of the transfiguration story. However, its themes of salvation coming from beyond the world, of people who hear or sense a "call" to go to a mountain where their lives will be transformed and transfigured, has some interesting points of intersection with today's Gospel.

Roy Neary has a vision that takes possession of him. In following his "call," he leaves family, home, everything. He experiences this call with anticipation, enthusiasm, and curiosity, almost as a transforming "grace." He wants only the fulfillment of his vision, to find answers, to share in a new life beyond this world, a world of glory. His experience is akin to that of Peter, James, and John, who have been specially chosen by Jesus to come up the mountain. They enter into the transforming mystery of his glory. Peter is so moved that he wants to stay on the mountain.

The transfiguration anticipates the resurrection of Jesus, which is the culmination of Lent. Roy Neary's experience is reminiscent of the ascension, because he goes up to a gloriously mysterious new life. Both today's Scripture and the movie highlight extraordinary occurrences that point to something beyond. For Christians, the glory shining on Christ's face is a pledge of our own future transformation.

- The UFO site in Mexico, the message of the five musical notes, the World War II plane appearing in the sandstorm; the effect of the spacecraft flying over Indiana, the lights going out, the homes shuddering; the joyful effect on those who experienced it; the use of music to communicate at Devil's Mountain, and the response of the aliens.

- Barry's "call"; Roy's disturbing behavior, building the model of the mountain; Jillian's drawings; their journey to Wyoming.

- The craft landing, the missing personnel returning, Barry rejoining Jillian; Roy being accepted by the team to go into space; the aliens welcoming Roy into the craft, its departure.

1. During about half of the Cold War (1947–1969), the U.S. Air Force investigated UFO sightings. The Air Force concluded that no UFOs were found to be a threat to national security. In 1997, the CIA admitted that the Air Force investigations had been an attempt to mislead the public about the use of spy planes—sightings of which amounted to about half of those reported during those years. On the other hand, the Air Force was not able to explain 700 of the more than 12,500 reported sightings. What do you think of science fiction, science fantasy, or, better yet, speculative fiction (storytelling that presents a scenario based on enough science to make it at least plausible)? Do you think that life is possible in other universes? Why or why not? What would this mean in terms of salvation history?

2. All the readings today have a cosmic tone to them because they reference things beyond the earth and

what we know through the immediacy of our senses: the stars, the universe, heaven, glorified bodies, a cloud from which a "voice" spoke. How do the readings help us "go beyond" the everyday to consider realities that can transform us, that give us a reason for living? Is the film a visual metaphor for modern seekers of the divine? Indeed, what are the first and second kinds of encounters if the landing of the alien ship with its "crew" is the third kind? What other visual motifs in the film remind you of themes that have appeared in Spielberg movies (e.g., the panic of the people to get on the train)?

3. *Close Encounters of the Third Kind* gave new credibility to UFO stories, showing aliens as friendly creatures and scientists; the military and ordinary people seem interested in them and willing to communicate with them. How does this treatment of aliens differ in other science or speculative fiction films? Do you think Spielberg was more interested in exploring cosmic possibilities or relationships between people—or both? Why or why not? What does it mean when Roy shows his scepticism about the Frenchman, Dr. Lacombe, as he questions his expertise because, after all, he isn't even an American? Is this intolerance, arrogance, or ignorance? Why or why not?

Prayer

Lord, you invite us into the mystery of your glory. May our lives be transfigured by your grace so that after sharing in your sufferings, we may share in your new life. Amen.

THIRD SUNDAY OF LENT

Exodus 3:1–8a, 13–15;
1 Corinthians 10:1–6, 10–12;
Luke 13:1–9

Bringing Out the Dead
U.S.A., 1999, 122 minutes
Cast: Nicolas Cage, Patricia Arquette, John Goodman,
Ving Rhames, Tom Sizemore, Martin Scorsese, Queen Latifah,
Mary Beth Hurt, Marc Anthony, Cliff Curtis, Cynthia Roman
Writer: Paul Schrader
Director: Martin Scorsese

Bringing Out the Dead

Disasters and Depression

SYNOPSIS

Frank is a burnt-out New York City ambulance driver whose life we follow for three days and nights. His desperation comes from feeling more and more responsible for not being able to save the lives of the people he attends. The ghost of a young asthmatic woman named Rose, who failed to respond to his treatment and died, haunts him. He tries to get himself fired. However, the dispatcher continually asks him to fill in for drivers who don't show up for work. Frank drinks, cannot sleep, and has love/hate relationships with his fellow drivers.

Frank is called to the home of a man who is dying. His daughter is a recovering drug addict named Mary who follows the ambulance to the hospital. Frank keeps trying to revive the man every time he returns from a call. Frank also meets Mary each time this happens and they become friendly. Frank comes to rely on Mary's dealer for drugs to help him sleep and later saves the dealer from falling from a balcony. Mary's father keeps telling Frank to let him go, so finally Frank stops reviving him.

Frank comes to the aid of a number of people, especially an addict whom his partner almost beats to death. Frank wonders where God is in his work. He also wonders about his own place in the misery of the streets.

COMMENTARY

Director Martin Scorsese is well known for his portrayal of the "mean streets" of New York City. These mean streets reappear in *Taxi Driver, Goodfellas,* and in these glimpses of a good-willed but exhausted EMT driver. The audience is drawn into sharing the anguish and despair of the hero, Frank, who seeks redemption on his nightly rounds, played with depth by Nicolas Cage. Cage's former wife, Patricia Arquette, plays Mary.

The screenplay is by Scorsese's longtime collaborator, Paul Schrader, himself a director of distinction. Schrader is from a Calvinist background and his religious concerns are given prominence in Frank's discussions about the place of God and his own role in the lives of marginalized people. This is a very somber film that takes its audience into the depths of those who cry for help.

DIALOGUE WITH THE GOSPEL

Focus: The tower fell on its victims at Siloam. Bringing Out the Dead *is a movie about rescuing victims of sin, accidents, and crime. It is also about trying to find how God fits into our painful and sometimes desperate experiences.*

The Gospel for the Third Sunday of Lent is an unusually severe Gospel from Luke, highlighting massacres and death by accident as well as expressing concern about responsibilities for evil and for repentance. The image of the cursed fig tree that bears no fruit is also challenging. *Bringing Out the Dead* shares the same somber mood in the face of human suffering.

The reading from Exodus describes the revelation of God in the burning bush. It is a solemn reminder that even in the harshest of circumstances, in exile and in the desert, God can come and reveal the divine. Indeed, God does this by communicating his personal name, Yahweh, I AM. God pledges fidelity to the Chosen People.

In First Corinthians Paul takes up this Exodus theme: God is always faithful. However, if the people turn from God, they will suffer death by the destroyer.

Bringing Out the Dead is also a grim warning about the fate that befalls so many helpless people in the city streets: the poor, the drug dependent, the mentally disturbed, those in need of discovering where God might be in their lives. They are like those crushed by the tower at Siloam.

Frank is a kind of savior-figure—but a burnt-out savior who is becoming as much a victim as the people he rescues. He has a mission that seems secular, but for the victims, it is a mission of grace and salvation. Like them, Frank is in need of redemption himself. He is in danger of becoming like the fig tree, unable to produce any fruit. He even wants to cut himself down. The people he encounters give him a new sense of purpose—and he gets one more chance. As we pray in the Creed, Jesus descended into hell before the resurrection. The mean and grim streets of New York City are symbols of Lent, a glimpse of that descent into hell before Easter. And yet even to that hell, Jesus comes to save.

KEY SCENES AND THEMES

- Frank's appearance and exhaustion, his growing recklessness, the effect of having to be at the beck and call of so many suffering people and of harassed hospital staffs; the ghost of the girl he could not save, her continued reappearances, her face on the various people in the street.

- Mary and her family, her dying father and her alienation from him; her desire to be reconciled; her conversations with Frank; taking him to her dealer.

• The co-drivers, concerned about eating, playing brutal games with victims; Marcus, with his evangelistic tone and his orchestrating miracles, his Jesus-and-healing language; Frank's saving Cy who is impaled on the balcony, rescuing Noel; Frank continuing to serve; the ghost of the girl absolving him from blame; letting Mary's father die.

FOR REFLECTION AND CONVERSATION

1. *Bringing Out the Dead* is a combination of several film genres: film noir, road movie, religious drama, and even a little horror. Nicolas Cage plays Frank Pierce with the face of a "distressed El Greco painting" of the Christ (Kevin Jackson, *Sight and Sound,* January 2000, p. 44). Using this metaphor, it would seem that if Pierce has the face of an El Greco, his persona is placed on one long-playing Caravaggio canvas because the film is so dark. Does Frank Pierce seem like a Christ-figure to you? Why or why not? What do you think is the significance of the final scene of the movie?

2. Some film critics parallel the three days and nights in the film with the Easter Triduum: Holy Thursday, Good Friday, and Holy Saturday. What scenes in the film might indicate this? Martin Scorsese plays the role of the dispatcher. Pierce continually asks to have his cup of suffering removed by asking the man to fire him. But his boss says, "...maybe tomorrow, but tonight I need you out there." What do you think this means for Frank? How does Frank, and in turn, how can we, bear witness—even when life is so difficult we can hardly bear it?

3. The responsorial psalm refrain is: "The Lord is kind and merciful." This film has images of fire, light, and

hope, as well as destruction and God's displeasure with humanity. At one point, Frank says about suffering, "You learn to sort of block it out, you know, like cops fence off a crime scene. But then something good will happen and everything will just glow." Where is the "light" in this film? How are the readings a promise of good amidst suffering and despair?

Prayer

Lord, you know that there is often so much desperation in our lives. You yourself experienced the same kind of hardships. Look on us with compassion on our lenten journey. Amen.

FOURTH SUNDAY OF LENT
Joshua 5:9a, 10–12;
2 Corinthians 5:17–21;
Luke 15:1–3, 11–32

A River Runs Through It
U.S.A., 1992, 128 minutes
Cast: Brad Pitt, Craig Sheffer, Tom Skerritt,
Brenda Blethyn, Emily Lloyd
Writer: Richard Friedenberg
Director: Robert Redford

A River Runs Through It

A Memoir of Two Sons

SYNOPSIS

Norman and Paul are the two sons of a Presbyterian minister and his wife who live in Montana before World War I. Theirs is a devout household. The boys' father introduces them to the art and skill of fly-fishing in the rivers around mountainous Missoula. While Norman is the studious son, Paul is the wild one, though he excels at the art of fishing.

Norman goes East to study while Paul becomes a local journalist. Norman returns home after six years and waits to hear if one of the universities to which he has applied will hire him as a lecturer in literature. The brothers' bonds are still strong, even though Paul is a gambler and in debt to local thugs.

Paul is involved with a Native American woman and this upsets the townspeople. Norman is attracted to Jessie Burns. Her family suggests that he take her brother, Neal, who is home from California, fishing one day. Norman doesn't like Neal, and asks Paul to come along, too. Norman falls afoul of Jessie's family, however, when Neal is severely sunburned while cavorting with a woman instead of fishing.

Father and sons go on an expedition together and Paul catches the fish of his life. Later, he is found dead in the

90

streets, murdered because of his debts. Years later, Norman, his wife, and children attend a service at his father's church where he preaches on life and his son.

A River Runs Through It is the third movie directed by Robert Redford, who also provides the uncredited voice for Norman's voice-over commentary. Redford has directed five other films so far: his Oscar-winning *Ordinary People, The Milagro Beanfield War, Quiz Show, The Horse Whisperer,* and *The Legend of Bagger Vance.* This movie demonstrates the same sensitivity toward issues such as the environment, the beauty of nature, and family relationships. The screenplay is based on Norman MacLean's 1976 novella about his own experience of growing up in Montana.

COMMENTARY

Tom Skerrit portrays the Presbyterian minister in a precise yet warmly nuanced performance. Rev. MacLean's love for fly-fishing transforms it into a symbol for talent, skill, art, and the means of showing God's grace.

Craig Sheffer is serious as Norman, while the energy of the movie is in Brad Pitt's performance as the younger brother, Paul. British actress Brenda Blethyn gets the American accent just right and shows her versatility by playing a minister's wife who lives in the background with quiet feeling. The movie hearkens back to a past that was not perfect but had the potential for the possibility that a humane American dream could be fulfilled.

Focus: In today's Gospel, a father had two sons, one who led a dissolute life and the other who did as the father expected. A River Runs Through It *is the story of a preacher who had two sons. One worked hard and succeeded in life. The other was a beautiful soul who led a dissipated life.*

DIALOGUE WITH THE GOSPEL

A River Runs Through It does not parallel the parable of the prodigal son in all its detail, but it offers stimulating comparisons. The devout preacher is a father who loves his sons.

He wants a successful life for them with enriching careers. He allows them to make their own choices and is able to let them go their different ways.

The reading from Second Corinthians speaks of homecoming, that is, reconciliation. Paul says that Christ makes God's reconciliation present in the world and "the old things have passed away; behold, new things have come." The way the father reveres religion and creation and welcomes his sons home is a model of Christ's presence in the world.

The principal focus of the film is the two sons. Both Norman and Paul are brought up well by their parents, which is symbolized by their father's teaching them the graceful art of fly-fishing. Norman, the older, more serious son, takes after his father. He studies and obtains a degree that will lead to a career as a writer and as a respectable professor of literature. The younger son, Paul, has his strong qualities too, especially loyalty and love. He has a sense of justice that is seen in his response to the racist treatment of his Indian girlfriend. However, Paul goes his own way in life. He takes up journalism, but also wastes his money and energy in constant gambling, falling hopelessly into debt and marking himself as the prodigal.

As the prodigal in the Gospel came back to his father, Paul offers a gesture of love and reconciliation before he dies: he agrees to go fly-fishing with his brother and father and catches the fish of a lifetime, even as he tenaciously clings to the rod and is washed downstream. This becomes a farewell gift of art, achievement, and grace that he gives to his family before he is brutally murdered.

The older son, more gracious and tolerant than the brother of the parable, preserves his younger brother's memory and the lesson of love and reconciliation he left as his legacy.

- The boys and their father's fly-fishing; the skills, art, beauty, grace, and sense of achievement in fly-fishing; the life of the preacher and his family, supervising his son's studies, his sermons, his relationship with his wife and boys.

- The relationship between the two boys, their love for one another, comparisons between them, their friends; Paul's taking the boat over the rapids, getting in trouble, Norman helping him and fighting for him; Norman going away to college, his degree, career, and teaching; his parents' pride in him; Norman trying to save Paul; Paul's lifestyle, his writing, gambling, defying the prejudice shown toward his girlfriend.

- The final day's fishing and Paul's success in catching the fish; the bonds between father and sons, the bond between the brothers, the sadness of Paul's violent death; grief and memories.

KEY SCENES AND THEMES

1. In Christian asceticism (living a way of life consistent with Christ's example and teaching) and tradition (long-established customs and beliefs), four main "ways" have been identified that characterize a way to respond to God's call or to seek God. These "ways" are subjective and are based on a person's image of God as one, true, good, or beautiful. Which of these "ways" can be found in the film *A River Runs Through It?* What did the minister say about oneness, goodness, and beauty? Was there "truth" in the film? If so, how was it expressed? What was the minister's image of God? What is his image of the human person? Are

FOR REFLECTION AND CONVERSATION

these images consistent with each other? What is your image of God and of the person? Which path(s) do you take to find God? Do these ways to God ever converge in the film, in its characters, and in your own life?

2. Water is a dominant theme in the films chosen for our consideration of the gospels and culture (other films are *The Spitfire Grill, Titanic, The Mighty, Angela's Ashes*). Water is mentioned or referred to over six hundred times in the Bible. It symbolizes a cosmic force that only God can control, a source of life and a means of purification. How is each of these three ways of symbolizing water present in *A River Runs Through It*? Why does water haunt Norman?

3. Talk about the kinds of love expressed in the film and what they might mean. Compare the father in the Gospel with the father in the movie and how they each embodied love. The mother is not mentioned in today's Gospel, but the film presents us with a woman who stays in the background, and is so humble she is almost invisible. Was she a person of dignity, or had she given that up? Explain your views. How did she love? Was her love any less real because of her humility? Although the parents worked so diligently to prepare their sons to live the Christian life in the world, the boys went their own ways. How does this film bear witness to parenting, to families, and to growing up in today's world? How does it witness to hope?

Prayer

Lord, you love all of us as your children. Reach out in love to those who have turned their backs on you and draw them to yourself. Amen.

Geena Davis and Susan Sarandon star in *Thelma and Louise*.

Thelma and Louise

U.S.A., 1991, 138 minutes
Cast: Susan Sarandon, Geena Davis, Harvey Keitel,
Christopher McDonald, Michael Madsen, Brad Pitt
Writer: Callie Khouri
Director: Ridley Scott

Thelma and Louise

Casting the First Stone

SYNOPSIS

Thelma and Louise are friends. Louise, who is a few years older than Thelma, works in a diner, while Thelma takes care of her immature, self-centered, and chauvinist husband. The women decide to go away for a holiday weekend together.

On the road, they experience a sense of exhilaration and freedom. They stop at a roadside diner for supper. When a local man interprets Thelma's behavior as a come-on, he makes sexual advances toward her, almost raping her. Terrible memories flood Louise's mind and she shoots him. The women decide that nobody will believe what happened because Thelma had danced with the man most of the evening.

As they flee, Louise contacts her boyfriend for money. Thelma rings her bewildered husband. On the way, they pick up a young hitchhiker who has a liaison with Thelma and then robs her.

Meanwhile, the police investigate the killing. The chief detective, Slocombe, is sympathetic to the women; when they call home, he tries to convince them to come in.

Thelma and Louise continue to drive west. When they are harassed by a truck driver, they shoot up his truck, causing it to explode. A patrolman stops them for speeding and they force him into the trunk of his car. Convinced that there will be no justice for them, they make a pact. Pursued by police, they drive over the side of the Grand Canyon. The final frame of the movie is frozen as they are suspended in mid-air over the chasm below.

COMMENTARY

Thelma and Louise was one of the most talked about films of 1991. The two women are good friends whose holiday weekend turns into a wild journey through the West of *Butch Cassidy and the Sundance Kid*, where they go out in a blaze of glory.

The movie is also an allegory of the relationships between men and women in twentieth-century American society. Most of the men are caricatured or, deservedly, lampooned. The ending was considered controversial. Could or should Thelma and Louise emulate Butch and Sundance's finale?

Geena Davis *(The Accidental Tourist, A League of Their Own, Stuart Little I* and *II)* and Susan Sarandon *(Bull Durham, Lorenzo's Oil, The Client, Dead Man Walking)* play Thelma and Louise most persuasively. The screenplay is by Callie Khouri, who also wrote *Something to Talk About* and wrote and directed *Divine Secrets of the Ya-Ya Sisterhood* in 2002. She was praised and criticized by both feminists and nonfeminists for this film. Englishman Ridley Scott *(Duellists, Alien, Blade Runner, Legend, Black Rain, G.I. Jane, Gladiator, Hannibal, Black Hawk Down)* directed the film. Harvey Keitel plays the compassionate Detective Slocombe well, but as with all the men in *Thelma and Louise*, he is flawed and not equal to the task.

DIALOGUE WITH THE GOSPEL

Focus: The malicious accusations of the authorities become the occasion for Jesus to make known his compassionate attitude toward those who have sinned. Thelma and Louise have stones cast at them and there is only one man who is willing to give them the benefit of the doubt.

The story of the woman taken in adultery is one of the most quoted of gospel stories: "Let the one who is among you who is without sin be the first to throw a stone at her." The compassionate Jesus does not condone what the woman has done nor does he condemn her. This is a powerful pastoral image, especially when we see it contrasted with the self-righteousness of official religious leaders. This sequence is dramatized in most biblical movies but is quite striking in both *The Greatest Story Ever Told* as well as in Martin Scorsese's *Last Temptation of Christ.*

In today's film, there is more to Thelma's character than being trapped in sexual conflict at home, in the diner, and in her adultery with the hitchhiker. Ultimately, Thelma's issue is that of justice. She feels that no one will believe her, that she will not find justice in a society where the law favors men and judges women harshly. Louise's experience in Texas supports this. Both women feel they are the victims of authorities who are all too eager to cast the first stone. There is no one like Jesus to help them, although the audience knows that the detective would be compassionate toward them if the women would trust him.

The ultimate self-assertion of Thelma and Louise in death is a tragic symbol of violence against women who feel that they have no voice and no life options in a world dominated by men. In today's Gospel, Jesus teaches that everyone has sinned and all deserve the mercy that he so generously offers. This is the lenten lesson the world still needs to learn.

- Thelma at home, Darryl's criticism, her fear of telling him about the trip, leaving a note and a microwave meal; Louise at work, pleasant, talking to people, leaving her house neat and clean; the audience becoming aware that something happened in her past.

KEY SCENES AND THEMES

- Thelma's excitement at the diner, Louise's more re-strained response; the attempted rape; Louise, the gun, her shooting Harlan; facing the dilemma of whether to trust the police or not, deciding not to trust the law, the conversations with the detective, flee-ing.

- The transformations of Thelma and of Louise, evad-ing the police, the cars and the helicopter, the sud-den coming to the cliff and the possibility of going over the edge; their reflection on what had happened to them, going out in the blaze of glory, the final freeze-frame.

FOR REFLECTION AND CONVERSATION

1. Thelma and Louise poised to go over the cliff is the film's most telling scene and visually reminiscent of the woman caught in adultery. Arrayed around the women in a semi-circle, from a distance, are police cars full of men with guns. Not one woman is there to talk or negotiate with them. Only one man rushes forth to offer help, but he is too late. What do you think of the film? Do you agree that it can be consid-ered a fable about the situation of women in society today? (In Pennsylvania today it is still a more serious offense to steal $500.00 than it is to commit rape.) Do you think they would have received justice if they had turned themselves in? What would be the mean-ing of the story if Thelma and Louise had decided to trust the law?

2. *Le Femme Nikita, The Silence of the Lambs, Sleeping with the Enemy,* and *Terminator 2: Judgment Day* are a few of the films released in 1991 along with *Thelma and Louise* that showed women committing acts of violence, even killing. 1991 was also the year of the Gulf War and

U.S. women took part in combat for the first time. How does the film *Thelma and Louise* fit into the feminism of 1991 and of today? Is their story valid? Were Thelma and Louise out of options, or in their case and within the fable genre, was the final pact a valid option? Do you think they really crashed and died? Why or why not? Do you think that the story of the woman caught in adultery has something to say to feminism today, and if so, what?

3. Like today's Scripture readings, *Thelma and Louise* is a movie full of vivid images. The first reading from Isaiah presents us with a vision of a way opening through the sea, of chariots and horsemen and a powerful army, of wastelands and rivers and water in the desert. Paul's Letter to the Philippians is about leaving behind rubbish to choose the prize that is Christ. In the Gospel, Jesus bends down to write in the ground near the Temple area and speaks of throwing stones. What are the images in *Thelma and Louise* that impressed you the most (the use of the car mirror, the wide open spaces, Monument Valley, the traditional male wilderness of Western movies, the car as the symbol of masculinity, the endless roads, the Grand Canyon, etc.)? Why? Were the women moving from slavery to a liberated space? Why or why not? Is there such a thing as Christian feminism, and if so, how do you define it and apply it to a film like *Thelma and Louise*?

Prayer

Jesus, during this time of lenten renewal, we pray that we may learn and live according to your example of total compassion, especially for women who are attacked and abused. Amen.

PALM SUNDAY
Isaiah 50:4–7;
Philippians 2:6–11;
Luke 19:28–40
(Gospel for the blessing of palms)

Mad City

U.S.A., 1997, 114 minutes
Cast: John Travolta, Dustin Hoffman, Alan Alda,
Mia Kirshner, Blythe Danner, Ted Levine,
Raymond J. Barry, Bill Nunn, Robert Prosky
Writer: Tom Matthews
Director: Constantin Costa-Gavras

 *Mad City*

"The Public Is Fickle"

SYNOPSIS

Max Brackett is a tough local television reporter who has been ousted from a top network. While covering a financial crisis at a museum, he witnesses Sam Baily, a security guard who has been fired, approach the director, Mrs. Banks, about getting his job back. She won't listen and he takes over the museum with a rifle and explosives. Sam holds children and their teacher as hostages. In the initial scuffle, his rifle goes off and accidentally but fatally wounds his fellow security guard.

Max takes charge of the crisis, persuading Sam to go on TV to plead his cause and to gain public sympathy. Max negotiates with the network and with the police. Later the FBI arrive, and they are intent on bringing the siege to a quick and, if necessary, violent end. For quite a while, Max is able to maintain public sympathy for Sam. Kevin Hollander, Max's nemesis and a star national news presenter, also arrives. At first he wants to take Max's place as the lead reporter when the siege goes national, but realizes he's too late for that. So he stages a media coup by reporting on the reporter who will do anything for the ratings, from manipulating interviews to advising Sam on how to win his cause via television.

Three days pass and public sympathy for Sam wanes. The parents want their children home. Max continues to assist Sam as well as to promote his own return to the networks. At a certain point, though, Max realizes that Sam is truly a gentle soul who only wants to get his job back and provide for his family. They share a moment of friendship and humanity. Max comes to admire Sam and his cause and wants to protect him from violence.

Sam speaks to Larry King on his CNN show, but continues to lose television audience support when he shoots the gun again. The FBI demands the children be released. Sam does this and promises to come out. He then locks the doors and sets off the dynamite. Max accuses himself, the media, and the crowds of killing Sam.

COMMENTARY

Costa-Gavras began directing strong social-minded movies in the 1960s. He gained international recognition and an Oscar for Best Foreign Language Film in 1969 for *Z*. His film version of Rolf Hochhutz's play, *The Deputy*, was called *Amen* and was critical of the silence of Pius XII concerning the fate of the Jews during World War II. It was released in 2002 and caused controversy in various countries.

Mad City appeared in 1997, the year before a number of movies were released that had media, especially television, as their theme and as the subject of their criticism: *The Truman Show, EdTV, Holy Man, Pleusantville*.

John Travolta gives one of his most persuasive performances as Sam Baily, an average sort of man. This role compares with Travolta's character in the little-seen *White Man's Burden*, where he is, again, a man who has been fired and seeks redress and justice.

Dustin Hoffman is also excellent as the manipulative reporter who gradually learns to respect Sam. Alan Alda leads the supporting cast as a suave but relentlessly ambitious anchorman.

The story may not be new or the message subtle, but it does offer food for thought.

Focus: The crowds welcomed Jesus. Later, they turned against him. Sam Baily is a victim in a mad city. He feels the sympathy of the audience and then feels despair as he experiences his own passion.

Sam Baily is a working-guy "everyman" figure. His life is hard. It has its joys and it has its suffering, and, to some extent, Sam Baily is life's victim. This is the pattern of life suggested in the first reading from Isaiah from the third of the "Servant Songs," in which the prophet details his transition from happiness to suffering to becoming a victim who seeks some kind of vindication: "I set my face like flint, knowing that I shall not be put to shame."

According to Paul's Letter to the Philippians, Jesus shared human experiences with us, from being born a human being to the final humiliation of death that awaits all of us.

Sam begins in desperation but suddenly finds himself in a mad situation, becoming a man holding hostages in a siege. The media make it all public and at first he experiences the acclaim and sympathy of the crowd. But public opinion soon turns on Sam. The authorities want to kill him. Finally, his blood is on their hands as he takes his life.

Throughout his Gospel, Luke presents Jesus as a king, from his birth to his triumphal entry into Jerusalem. We know what happens, though. The crowd and the disciples are fickle, and they abandon him. Sam is not as good an example of a Christ-figure as other cinematic characters are, but he knows acclaim and disdain. He knows suffering and feels abandoned by God and others, which first humbles and then destroys him. Jesus holds out the promise of God's compassion as a reward for trust. This is what he shows the criminal who was crucified with him: hope in God is stronger than any desperate situation, any sin. Sam experiences his Palm Sunday as his Good Friday. For ourselves, our hope is that the darkness of the cross will lead to the coming resurrection.

- Max Brackett and the news media, pleading for a better assignment, willing to "cross the line" to get a good story; using Sam, negotiating for him, instructing him how to act, understanding him, and gradually appreciating him.

- Sam's desperation, arguing with Mrs. Banks, accidentally shooting Cliff, his remorse; how he treats the children and their response to him; Sam as an angry innocent being manipulated by Max; Sam watching the television reports and interviews, succumbing to the lure of the media; his interviews, giving up, taking his own life.

- Kevin's ego and ambition, his clashes with Max; taking over the story by changing the focus, using Laurie and how she follows him without question, doing anything to get the interview with Max; Max's final accusations.

1. *Mad City* dramatizes the way the news media manipulate events and the public as well as how they create their own reality. How does *Mad City* show the human element in news media? Does anyone have a conscience? Who? How does the conversation between Lou and Max about "crossing the line" carry through from the beginning of the film to the end? Do some research on the Nielsen ratings and how they and other audience ratings systems are linked into the economy, politics, the legal system, etc. How can media education, critical-thinking skills that question

information and entertainment media, help create thoughtful media consumers and producers of tomorrow? Visit *www.medialit.org* for more information on media literacy education.

2. It is not easy to like the characters in *Mad City*, although Sam and news director Lou have qualities we can empathize with. Almost everyone else is a caricature of all that is wrong with the news media. Does this "technique" deepen your appreciation of the story? Why or why not? What's the point or the moral of the story for you? Kevin, the most amoral of the characters, says about Sam: "This guy's a poster child for the disenfranchised." If sociology is the study of human societies and how people behave in them, what does Kevin's statement mean from the perspective of society's role in Sam's life? How responsible is Sam for what he is doing? Why does he bring the guns? In a post-Columbine and post-September 11, 2001 era, how do you interpret this 1997 film? (If you have seen *Falling Down*, written by Ebbe Roe Smith, one of the actors in *Mad City*, compare the films on the level of society, male identity, freedom, and responsibility.)

3. Today is Passion or Palm Sunday. The people hail Jesus, and in a few days, he will be condemned to death and abandoned. To a man like Sam, what does Jesus' passion and death mean? In today's Gospel, Jesus showed compassion to the "good thief." How can we grow in compassion during this Holy Week, especially to those who are fragile? At least eight of the films included in the movie lectionary this year touch on the issue of suicide. What are the causes of suicide? Identify some ways we can help ourselves when tempted to despair, and, in turn, help others.

Prayer

Jesus, you emptied yourself to share all our experiences with us. You know what pain and despair are like. Help those who are depressed and those who are victims so that they may learn to hope in your resurrection. Amen.

HOLY THURSDAY
Exodus 12:1–8, 11–14;
1 Corinthians 11:23–26;
John 13:1–15

The Shipping News
U.S.A., 2001, 115 minutes
Cast: Kevin Spacey, Julianne Moore, Judi Dench,
Cate Blanchett, Scott Glenn, Rhys Ifans, Pete Postlethwaite
Writer: Robert Nelson Jacobs
Director: Lasse Hallstrom

The Shipping News

I Am Not a Water Person

SYNOPSIS

Quoyle is a middle-aged man whose life has not amounted to much. He feels worthless because his father taunted him when he was a boy, especially when he could not dog paddle after he was thrown into a swimming pool. While working as an ink setter, he meets the impulsive Petal, marries her, and they have a daughter, Bunny. Petal soon tires of Quoyle. When Bunny is six, Petal leaves home with Bunny and another man. She sells Bunny to some people and she and her lover are then killed in a car accident.

Quoyle receives word that his parents have killed themselves. His father's sister, Quoyle's Aunt Agnis, comes to visit, then stays on to help Quoyle when Bunny returns home. Agnis persuades Quoyle to travel to Newfoundland, where the family originated. They set up house in the old family home, unoccupied for almost fifty years. Jack, the local newspaper owner, hires Quoyle to write the shipping news. Fellow reporters Nuttbeam and Bill Pretty befriend him, but he falls afoul of the fiercely critical Terk Card. Jack is impressed by Quoyle's honesty and offers him a regular column to write that Card tries to sabotage.

Bunny attends a childcare center run by Wavey, whose small son suffered from lack of oxygen to the brain at his birth. Wavey and Quoyle become friends, although Quoyle is passionately devoted to Petal's memory. When he goes to an island cemetery with Bill Pretty, he learns the bloodthirsty history of his ancestors. He finds out that they were cruel and greedy pirates who looted the ships they caused to founder by shifting the shore lights. Forced out, the earlier Quoyle family dragged their house across the ice to its present site overlooking the ocean.

Quoyle tries to overcome his fear of water by buying a boat. One day he comes across a headless corpse in the sea. When he panics, the boat sinks. Jack rescues him.

When Quoyle taunts Wavey for not telling the truth about her bad marriage, she tells him that her husband left her, so she wrecked his boat to make it look as if he has died. On a stormy night, Quoyle goes to Wavey and, as they make love, Quoyle's family house is blown away. During the storm, Jack drowns. At his wake, he suddenly spits water and recovers. Bunny is able, at last, to accept her mother's death. Agnis reveals her own sad story and the families are free at last to begin a new life.

COMMENTARY

Novelist E. Annie Proulx won a Pulitzer Prize for *The Shipping News*, the book on which the film is based. The movie was filmed on the coast of Newfoundland where the story is set.

After his international success with *My Life as a Dog*, Swedish director Lasse Hallstrom moved to the United States, where he made successful films like *What's Eating Gilbert Grape?* and *Chocolat*.

The versatile Kevin Spacey plays Quoyle as a "broken man." In a film with seemingly small roles about seemingly insignificant people, Julianne Moore as Wavey and the Oscar-winning actress Judi Dench as Aunt Agnis bring realism and dignity to their characters. Cate Blanchett proves once again that she can play any role with credibility.

Hallstrom uses the symbol of water extensively in the film. We see Quoyle almost drowning as a boy; the opening sequence begins with the young Quoyle in the pool and the scene is transformed into the adult Quoyle working his various jobs but still seen as if he is drowning. Later, a bed is suddenly submerged in water and the rain never seems to stop. Quoyle is always floating, marooned at sea. With the harsh history of the Quoyle family, it is as if he is possessed by an original sin from which he must be cleansed, as if he has to acknowledge his roots so that the "broken man" can be healed.

DIALOGUE WITH THE GOSPEL

Focus: Jesus uses symbols of water and washing to illustrate his complete service to others and his new commandment of love. Quoyle needs the healing of water to overcome fear and grow in love.

While the focus of the celebration tonight is on the Eucharist, the Gospel is that of Jesus' washing his disciples' feet and commanding the disciples to wash one another's feet as he has done. This "mandate" was the meaning behind the old name for today, "Maundy" Thursday ("Maundy" from the English "mandate"). As the presider washes the feet of the community, it is a celebration of water, cleansing, and love.

The reading from Exodus reminds us that the Chosen People were migrants, setting out into the unknown to find a promised land, just as Quoyle and Bunny left their home and sorrowful memories for Newfoundland.

The Gospel themes of water and washing will be taken up again during the Easter Vigil and linked with the baptismal themes of regeneration and new life.

The setting for Jesus' symbolic action is his last Passover meal. He loves his own, "and he loved them to the end." At this moment, Jesus' self-emptying love urges him to offer his followers the cleansing touch of water. But for Quoyle, water is not cleansing, healing, or nourishing. Instead, when faced with water, he remembers how he almost drowned as a child. He now experiences his humdrum life as a kind of drowning. In Newfoundland, he finds opportunities to face his fears and the sea even though he claims that he is not "a water person." His accident brings him close to drowning again. Quoyle's uncertainties and self-doubts remind us of Peter the apostle, who at first does not understand the need to be cleansed with water. Later, despite being washed, Peter will further demonstrate his confusion and weakness when he denies Jesus.

Quoyle has to come to terms with his heritage—its violence, its predatory greed, and its sexual abuse. After the Newfoundland waters heal him, he must learn to love. He is blessed because he is able to love Bunny, Agnis, Wavey, and her son Harry. The love that he has learned, he has to give to others— a reminder that this night we celebrate Jesus' new commandment of love: "Love others as I have loved you."

KEY SCENES AND THEMES

- Quoyle's father pushing him into the pool and his sense of drowning in his life; Quoyle not being "a water person"; themes of the sea, rain and storms, especially on the night he goes to Wavey's house and the family home blows away; his venture on the sea; the discovery of the headless corpse and his own near-drowning.

- Quoyle's relationships with the women in his life, his love for them; Petal, despite her neglect of him; Bunny wishing her mother was alive; Aunt Agnis and Quoyle's shame and compassion for her past; Wavey and their friendship that grew into love.

- Quoyle's brokenness, his experience of being humiliated by his father, by Petal, even by Bunny and Terk Card; the difference when he experiences Agnis's support, the friendship of the newspaper staff, Jack's trust, and Wavey's love.

FOR REFLECTION AND CONVERSATION

1. If this evening's readings from Exodus, First Corinthians, and the Gospel are about "remembering," then *The Shipping News* fits the liturgical mood very well. How do each of the principle characters in the film, from Quoyle to Nuttbeam, "remember" their lives and their dreams? How do they tell their stories? Do they edit them as they go? When and why do we finally find out the truth? How did remembering help transform these characters? How can remembering the scriptures transform us?

2. Jesus washes the feet of his disciples and, depending on pastoral circumstances, the washing of the feet may be part of this evening's liturgy after the homily. Why did Jesus wash the feet of the disciples? Why do you think water is such a powerful and common symbol in Scripture? What does the symbol of water mean in the Bible and what does water mean for Quoyle? If you were to list symbols that exemplify your life story, what would they be, and why? If your life story were a movie, what Scripture readings would add meaning to it? Can you identify with any of the characters in the film, their experiences or dilemmas? If so, what does this evening, which remembers the "Last Supper" and celebrates the institution of the Eucharist, mean for your life?

3. This evening's liturgy commemorates the institution of the Eucharist and the priesthood and reminds us of Christ's commandment that we love and serve one another. How do the characters in the film do this as individuals and as a community? Do you think the characters are "salvation" for one another? How so? Do you think that fact that Quoyle moves "back" to "Newfoundland" is a metaphor for his own personal life? How so?

Prayer

Jesus, you showed your love for your disciples when you washed their feet. Help us to live your commandment of love, serving and loving one another as you first loved us. Amen.

GOOD FRIDAY

Isaiah 52:13—53:12;
Hebrews 4:14–16; 5:7–9;
John 18:1—19:42

Changing Lanes

U.S.A., 2002, 98 minutes
Cast: Ben Affleck, Samuel L. Jackson, Toni Collette,
Sidney Pollack, Richard Jenkins, Kim Staunton,
Dylan Baker, Amanda Peet
Writers: Chip Taylor, Michael Tolkin
Director: Roger Michell

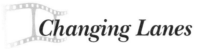 *Changing Lanes*

Rage and Redemption

SYNOPSIS

Lawyer Gavin Banek attends a performance by children assisted by the Dunn foundation, which Gavin's partners administer. Dunn's granddaughter, Mina, is contesting the probate of her grandfather's will because she suspects fraudulent influence by the law firm.

Insurance salesman Doyle Gipson secures a loan to buy a house for his estranged wife, Valerie, and their sons. He also attends an Alcoholic Anonymous meeting.

The next day, Good Friday, both hurry to court. When Gavin changes lanes on the FDR Drive in Manhattan, they crash. Gavin's car is dented, but Doyle's has a flat tire. Gavin has no time to exchange insurance information. Doyle is late for his custody hearing but wants to follow the right procedure. Gavin throws a blank check at Doyle and drives off saying, "Better luck next time." Doyle gets to court late, and loses the custody appeal. Gavin discovers that he has lost the power-of-attorney file he needed at court. Doyle found it, however, on the hood of the car when Gavin drove away, and has bitterly thrown it away. Gavin realizes that Doyle must have the file and tracks him down. Doyle defies Gavin, but tries to recover the documents.

Gavin, with the help of his assistant, Michelle, tries to force Doyle to return the file by hiring a hacker to render Doyle bankrupt. This causes Doyle to lose his option on the house. Doyle, who almost begins to drink again, intends to return the file, but when he learns what Gavin has done, leads him on a chase where one of Gavin's tires falls off and he crashes. Gavin passes a church and goes into the Good Friday service during the veneration of the cross. He desperately asks a priest to explain the meaning of the world. Gavin then creates a situation at the school where Doyle's children attend that results in Doyle's arrest. Gavin has second thoughts as he sees the upset Valerie and the boys.

In the meantime, Gavin's partners have forged a new document. When Doyle is released on bail, he returns the file. Both men are at rock bottom and apologize. Gavin has dinner with his wife and discovers that she is as manipulative as her father. Later Gavin decides to keep the file as evidence in order to make the firm honest. He also arranges for Doyle to buy the house so that he can be reconciled with his family.

COMMENTARY

Changing Lanes, with its grim picture of human failings, might seem an unusual selection for the Catholics in Media Award for 2002, but the way it resolves the consequences of those flaws is what makes the film an outstanding choice. Roger Michell *(Persuasion, Notting Hill)* directed *Changing Lanes,* and Michael Tolkin, author of the novel and screenplay *The Player*, and Chap Taylor, a former production assistant, wrote the script.

The characters are not particularly sympathetic, though several are well developed. Most show the "shadow" side of all of us. Ben Affleck is very credible as an upwardly mobile lawyer who is not particularly concerned with ethics. Samuel L. Jackson plays the recovering alcoholic insurance adjuster, who is separated from his wife and sons, right on the edge. On Good Friday morning, both are hurrying to court. The lawyer changes lanes and they crash. The physical crash leads to a spiritual crash where both have to "change lanes" for the better.

Focus: Changing Lanes *shows two men who struggle with their sinfulness—how it affects those around them and how they ultimately find redemption. The Gospel for Good Friday recounts how Christ suffered and died to atone for our sins— redemption.*

During World War II, British spiritual writer Caryll Houselander wrote "This War is the Passion." She meant that, in view of the resurrection, the struggles and horrors of war are one way of experiencing the passion of Jesus. This can also be true of the more mundane, petty and bitter wars that we engage in daily—exactly what *Changing Lanes* is all about. The story is set on Good Friday. Both Gavin Banek and Doyle Gipson initiate the "war" and employ vicious tactics of pre-emptive vengeance and retaliation. They each have their Judas antagonists: Gavin's father-in-law and partner, the other fraudulent lawyers, and his own wife; and for Doyle, the destructive computer hacker who bankrupted him and the bank manager.

One might like to follow through on some of the day's events and the parallels they present with the story of Jesus' passion: Doyle's Holy Thursday A.A. meeting, his testimony about champagne and being alive, and the children's recital that Gavin attends, fronting for the fraud his company is perpetrating; Friday's struggles for both men: the agonies, the court appearances, the sense of being abandoned, the "death" to their old selves, their conversations with their wives, their reconciliation with each other. Both have their "Gethsemane angels" who tell them the truth and guide them to redemptive action: Gavin has the priest and Doyle his A.A. counselor as well as his wife and children.

Good Friday is followed by a time of reparation and a sense of new life, of some kind of resurrection for both men. Saying "sorry" was not enough for Gavin, because he had destroyed Doyle's means of caring for his family. In a kind of Jesus gesture, he atones for his sin by restoring a home and sense of dignity to Doyle.

- Doyle's hopes for the house, the accident, being late for court and his outburst; his anger at Gavin when he wants to do the right thing but Gavin drives away; Doyle almost drinking but bashing the men in the bar, his murderous luring of Gavin into his car and fixing the tire to fall off; his anger at the school and at being arrested; his counselor telling him that he is "addicted to chaos," "hooked on disaster," and that he has broken his A.A. covenant.

- Gavin's insensitive attitude toward Mina Dunne, his performance in court, realizing that he has been used by the partners; hiring the hacker and then trying to rectify the situation; the crash, his cruel setting up of Doyle in the school; the visit to the church contrasting with the words of his wife.

- Changing lanes and the crash, the behavior and attitudes that led to the "sinful" actions of both men; each reaching rock bottom; their being able to repent, forgive, and make reparation; the Easter hymn that says that the sin of Adam was a "happy fault" because it led to redemption.

KEY SCENES AND THEMES

1. We live in an era of rage, and in the United States, road rage is an everyday occurrence. One study shows that three out of four people are driving more ag-

FOR REFLECTION AND CONVERSATION

gressively in 2003 than they were a few years ago. Other statistics say that eighty percent of people driving are angry for one reason or another the whole time they are driving. In *Changing Lanes,* what begins with an accident caused by distraction and anxiety escalates into road rage. It then becomes out and out war as two grown men indulge in meanness and cruelty under the intense pressure of their personal problems. How do the struggles of the two men remind us of our own struggles to control our animosities and anger? How do their wives and other associates challenge Gavin and Doyle to reflect on who they are and on the integrity that ought to be essential in their lives? Compare Valerie and Cynthia. How do they define integrity and how do the men they married define it? Which characters grow and change?

2. Doyle's A.A. sponsor says, "You know, booze isn't really your drug of choice anyway. You're addicted to chaos. For some of us, it's coke. For some of us, it's bourbon. But you? You got hooked on disaster!" What is Gavin addicted to? Is there anything in our lives that we are addicted to? Addiction (to drugs, food, alcohol, sex, smoking, stealing, lying, disaster, and anger) keeps us in a comfort zone because it has become familiar to us. What will it take for us to make a change in our lives? How do the passion, death, and resurrection of Jesus give us the strength to change? What is the role of faith in the lives of these characters? Stephen Delano, Gavin's boss and father-in-law, tells him, "I can live with myself because at the end of the day I think I do more good than harm...what other standard have I got to judge by?" On Good Friday or

on any other day, is this answer good enough for people of faith?

3. The movie has a number of specifically Catholic icons to remind us of the spiritual meaning of Good Friday: nuns at the opening recital, a picture of the Sacred Heart when Doyle meets Valerie, a rosary in a taxi, the stained-glass window, and, most importantly, the crucifix, though it is veiled above the altar during the ceremony of the veneration of the cross. Add to this Gavin's verbal struggle with the priest in the confessional. Were you ever in a "place" like Gavin's? What would you have told him if you were the priest? (If you have the DVD, watch the deleted scenes of the confession sequence; do you think the editors should have left it as it was scripted? Why or why not?) How can we live so that when we are put to the test, as Gavin and Doyle were, we will do the right thing?

Prayer

Lord, you died for us sinners. Help us to be more aware of our capacities for sin so that we may live according to your example and teaching. Allow us to repent and experience your forgiveness. Amen.

EASTER VIGIL
Romans 6:3–11;
Luke 24:1–12

Green Dragon

U.S.A., 2002, 112 minutes
Actors: Don Duong, Patrick Swayze, Forest Whitaker,
Trung Nguyen, Hiep Thi Le, Jennifer Tran
Writers: Timothy Linh Bui, Tony Bui
Director: Timothy Linh Bui

Green Dragon

Do Not Stay Among the Dead

SYNOPSIS

In 1975, on the verge of the fall of Saigon, 134,000 Vietnamese refugees fled Vietnam for the United States. Many of them were initially brought to Camp Pendleton, California, where they awaited sponsors. Tai has escaped with his little nephew, Minh, and his small niece, Anh. Minh searches the camp continually for his mother while the English-speaking Tai is asked to become a camp manager by the military commander, Jim Lance. While Tai helps Duc, an ambitious young man and the camp's wheeler and dealer, he also cares for a despairing general and his daughters. Others in the camp include a businessman, his obnoxious pregnant first wife, and his young second wife, who had been in love with Duc in Vietnam; some former soldiers who feel that they were betrayed by the general; and a patriotic man who wants to return home despite his wife's pleas.

One of the camp's cooks, Addie, befriends Minh. The cook enlists Minh's aid in painting a mural on an old wall in the storage room. Addie is terminally ill and dies. The news on the radio about Saigon is not good, and the general takes his life. Later, Tai marries one of the general's daughters and soon after, his brother arrives in camp with the news of their sister's death (Minh and Anh's mother). Lance bids farewell to Tai and his extended family as they venture out to make their lives in America.

Tony Bui directed a poignant film about Vietnam called *Three Seasons*, which won three prizes at the Sundance Film Festival in 1999, including the Audience and Grand Jury awards. Here he joins his brother, Timothy Linh Bui, to co-write *Green Dragon* about the experiences of the refugees who fled Vietnam as Saigon fell. This film, about the refugee experience both before and after the April 29–30 fall of Saigon, won a Humanitas Award.

Acclaimed Vietnamese actor Don Duong brings a sympathetic gravity to the role of Tai, who is a good and wise man. Patrick Swayze is the commander who tries to learn, even from his mistakes. Forest Whitaker, whose production company released the film, plays Addie, the cook.

The movie was made more than twenty-five years after the events they portray and by a first-generation Vietnamese who grew up in the United States. *Green Dragon* is both a memoir and a search for understanding about how the refugees responded in the dark times of 1975. The Buis have chosen to make their central characters both Catholic and Buddhist, offering a religious dimension to the realities of joy, suffering, and death.

Focus: Like the passing through the waters of the Red Sea and the baptism described in the readings, the Vietnamese refugees experienced a passing over from one country to another, a "baptism," death, and a kind of burial at Camp Pendleton. After a time, they experienced a resurrection as they went out to their new life.

Green Dragon opens with images of death and destruction. These themes permeate the movie as they do so many of the readings for the Easter Vigil, especially the reading from

Romans. Many of the film's characters die: Minh's father is killed in battle, his mother wastes away on the refugee boat, the old general kills himself in shame, the life-giving Addie dies. Those who survive the war are transported to Camp Pendleton, a dying to their land and their culture, where they are immersed in an uncertain "place" for a time of waiting. Yet, the ultimate theme of the movie, like that of tonight's celebration, is hope and a new life. As the Gospel shows us Jesus rising from the dead, so the Vietnamese eventually leave what must have seemed like a tomb—the refugee camp—and emerge into a new and fruitful life in a promised land.

Tai places a crucifix on the wall near his bed and this places the passion symbolism and the religious faith of this group of refugees in our minds during the movie. The resurrection symbolism is present in the use of water, especially the shower scenes with the women. The symbolism of covenant is present through the rite of Tai's marriage. The continual contemplation of death and dying pervades the entire film, for example, when Tai's brother arrives with the sad news of their sister's death. The dying Addie gives life and hope to Minh, who never gives up the hope that he will find his mother. The family is never meant to stay permanently at the camp. As the Easter angel says, they will not stay "among the dead" but will go on to a new life.

Paul's words on death and resurrection are so rich, it might be best to ponder them slowly after the film in order to see how the characters fulfill them as they experience death and new life.

KEY SCENES AND THEMES

- The opening credits showing the destruction in Saigon, the use of symbols like the crucifix, the showers, the drawings, the wedding ceremony.

- Tai and his story and nightmares, his care for Minh and Anh, his respect for the general, love for the daughter; the general's suicide, comforting the young woman, the courtship and marriage; Tai's friendship with Jim Lance and his concern for the people in the camp; Tai's clash with Lance when the woman is dragged out of the hut and Lance's taking him to see what America is like.

- Minh's search for his mother, with Anh, adapting to life in the camp; Minh's friendship with Addie, the comics and drawings; Addie talking and Minh not understanding the words, the growth in friendship, painting the wall, Minh receiving Addie's drawings; Minh accepting his situation but still hoping against hope.

1. One Vietnamese woman who actually lived at Camp Pendleton during the time depicted in the film said that yes, it was like that, but it's not possible to capture the extent of the sadness and insecurity. When asked why her family left Vietnam for the United States, the woman said that her mother had two reasons: educational opportunity and freedom of religion for her children. Do you think the film portrayed the refugee experience well? How do you think you would react if you were ever to become a refugee for political or religious reasons and had to rely on the kindness of strangers? Do you know anyone who has "passed through the water" and come to our country? In what ways have you welcomed them? Do you or your family have an immigrant or refugee story? How does it parallel the stories told in *Green Dragon*?

2. The popular religious character of Vietnam is made up primarily of a mixture of Buddhist, Taoist, Confucian, and animist beliefs, as well as the Catholicism that began in pre-colonial Vietnam but spread in the

FOR REFLECTION AND CONVERSATION

north during the nineteenth century. How does the film present and respect the interreligious character of the Vietnamese people? How does the diversity among the Vietnamese refugees mirror the religious, racial, and cultural reality of the United States and other countries that have opened their borders to immigrants seeking human and civil rights? What did you think when the Vietnamese refugees were presented with artifacts of "real" American culture that were "things" rather than values? What about their conviction that a guaranteed minimum wage would resolve their anxieties and let them live the American dream? For that matter, what is the "American dream," and why do so many long for it? Do you think most people find that dream?

3. Network television's attempt to represent cultural diversity in ways that respect those cultures is rare and, at best, often forced. However, through mainstream movies and art films, the effort to explore other cultures is often more successful. What do you think the benefits are to fair and wide representation of cultures, religion, gender, age, and social class in entertainment and information media? How is the human family brought closer together through the telling of one another's stories? How can understanding cultures that differ from our own contribute to dialogue, justice, and peace?

Prayer

In our times, Lord, so many refugees have experienced suffering and death. On this night of promise of new life, bless those who are tempted to despair and give them hope for a new life. Amen.

Jeff Bridges stars in *Fearless*.

Fearless

U.S.A., 1993, 118 minutes
Cast: Jeff Bridges, Isabella Rossellini, Rosie Perez,
Tom Hulce, John Turturro, Benicio Del Toro
Writer: Rafael Yglesias
Director: Peter Weir

Fearless

Sharing Risen Life

SYNOPSIS

Architect Max Klein emerges from an airplane crash carrying a baby and leading a young boy by the hand. He is a hero and called a "Good Samaritan" because he led people to safety from the wreckage. He feels numb but elated and begins to review his life. He is able to eat fruit he used to have violent reactions to. Back home, he feels distanced from his wife and son. A post-trauma psychiatrist annoys him and he clashes with a smart, money-chasing lawyer.

The psychiatrist asks Max to visit a young mother, Carla, who is still in shock because her two-year-old son "Bubble" died in the crash. He goes to a church with her, discusses God's will, and is overwhelmed by a profound love for her. They become friends. This further puzzles his wife, a ballet teacher. He secludes himself in his study and draws and collects paintings of his near-death experience.

At night he dreams of the crash and remembers seeing a light and losing all fear. He recalls leaving the side of his business partner to go and sit with a boy who is traveling unaccompanied. During the day, the lawyer's schemes to get money for his partner's family exasperate Max. Meanwhile,

127

his marriage is suffering and Max and his wife speak of separating. One day at work, Max goes screaming to the roof of the building and "dances" with how far he can go to the edge without falling. He is fearless.

Max and Carla go shopping for Christmas gifts for Bubble and his father, even though they are dead. When Carla breaks down and tells him she thinks it is her fault that Bubble died because she could not hold on to him during the crash, he simulates the speed and force of the accident's impact by crashing his car into a wall. Carla is unhurt, but Max is seriously injured. He asks his wife to save him. He almost dies when he eats a strawberry that he is allergic to, and she revives him. Now they can start a new life together.

COMMENTARY

Rafael Yglesias, who wrote the novel of the same title, wrote the screenplay for *Fearless*. Direction is by Peter Weir, whose films include *Picnic at Hanging Rock, Gallipoli, The Year of Living Dangerously, Witness, Dead Poets Society,* and *The Truman Show. Fearless* is a fine vehicle for Jeff Bridges as Max Klein, the survivor of an air crash, and for Rosie Perez, who received an Oscar nomination for her role as the distraught mother, Carla. Isabella Rossellini is the bewildered wife, while John Turturro and Tom Hulce are effective as the psychiatrist and the lawyer.

Fearless is unusual because it does not fit into mainstream romanticized Hollywood entertainment. Instead, it is a thoughtful film that deals with harsh situations that make us uncomfortable and fearful. The film tries to imagine and explore the reality of suffering, pain, and the arbitrariness of accidents and death in our contemporary age. The movie continues its unusual path because it also contemplates the role of religious faith and God's presence in a world where bad things happen to good people who seem to be in the wrong place at the wrong time.

Focus: When Max has a near-death experience and a resurrection, he becomes fearless. The women find Jesus' tomb empty and run to tell Peter and the disciples. What is it to have a new life and to share it with those are still fearful?

DIALOGUE WITH THE GOSPEL

Fearless is a contemporary parable about a man who has had a near-death experience and who feels that he has risen from the dead.

Today's Gospel is the beginning of John's account of Jesus' resurrection and post-resurrection appearances. More gripping stories about Jesus' rising from the dead will follow when we hear about his encounter with Thomas and their breakfast at the Sea of Galilee. Here, it is the familiar narrative about the disciples who believe that Jesus is dead and have no inkling that he would rise. The women, on the other hand, make the effort to go to the tomb; it is because of their words that the Apostles take action. Peter and the other disciple run to the tomb and are amazed. They believe even though they do not understand.

When people learn that Max Klein has survived the plane crash, they are amazed and bewildered. The psychiatrist who specializes in post-traumatic stress wants to help him and enlists his aid to help others; the lawyer wants to get maximum compensation for damages; people who followed the sound of Max's voice to safety are grateful. His son and the young boy he saved see Max as a hero.

Max has literally seen "the light." He has also lost his fears and anxieties, and is now calm and seemingly peaceful so that he can now assist others in their suffering. Like the Good Samaritan, he has led people to new life and safety. He can now do more for others because he has indeed "risen." He is overwhelmed with a kind of love for Carla because he now knows the "sincerity and truth" of the meaning of death.

But his risen or new life still bewilders him. He overcomes allergies and phobias of the past, risks falling from a tall building, and contemplates his near-death experience through art. He can discuss God with Carla, go with her to church, and comfort her. Then, by almost dying again, he enables Carla to accept the fact that she is not responsible for her son's death. But Max is not Jesus. His resurrection to new life is not complete. He has to surrender to the reality of his love for his wife and allow her to save him so that he can fully live again. Although he was spared actual death, Max still needs salvation, which ultimately comes to us through the risen Jesus that we celebrate today.

KEY SCENES AND THEMES

- The experience of the crash; Max's fears, his response to his partner Gordon, his seeing the light and growing calm; assisting the boy and leading people to the light, carrying the child to safety, the Good Samaritan; Max's option to die or to live, wanting his wife to save him, her love and his coming back, his rising again.

- Max's incomplete resurrection; his nightmares about the crash; his alienation from his wife and son; the pictures of tunnels and light in his study; the challenge of the psychiatrist and the lawyer who wants him to lie for others.

- The support group and the reactions of those who resented it, those who were helped, the mother who wanted information about her son; Carla and her isolation, going with Max to church and praying; Max driving into the wall so she can learn that she did not kill her child.

FOR REFLECTION AND CONVERSATION

1. Corn stalks have become Hollywood shorthand for the supernatural. Films such as *Field of Dreams*, *X-Files*, and *Signs* all feature cornfields, because they help to create a sense of being lost or being in some kind of

transformed state. What function does the field of corn serve in *Fearless*? What about the roadways that were so long and so different from each other? Recall other recurring symbols (the art, the scrapbook, the religious statuary, the prayers, the Volvo, the strawberries) as well as the music and talk about how these elements contributed to what the film meant to you or how it made you feel. Did you like *Fearless*? Why or why not?

2. The last line of today's Gospel says, "… and he saw and believed. For they did not yet understand the scriptures that he had to rise again." Although Peter and the other disciple did not yet understand, they saw and believed. During a conversation that Max and Carla have about God, she said, "He hurt me so much. He hurt me forever. But I still believe in him." Max responds that it's not so much that you choose to believe but because we choose not to believe in nothing. How do Max and Carla experience and express faith? Has there been anything in your life that lets you identify with Max, Carla, the wife, or the children in the film? Is this a film about fear or faith, hope and/or love?

3. Post-traumatic stress disorder was identified and officially named by the American Psychiatric Association in 1980. It means that a person suffers an "extreme reaction to extreme stress." Studies indicate that 14 percent of all people experience symptoms of post-traumatic stress at one time or another in their lives. Some of these are anxiety, nightmares, numbness, flashbacks, irritability, depression, etc. There are various remedies such as psychotherapy and medication. Recall the part of the film about the meeting of the

survivors with the psychiatrist. What did you think of how he led the people through the session? Did he empathize with their suffering? Did Carla and Max suffer from this syndrome? How did their faith in God and humanity help them through it? How were the various characters salvation for each other? Would you call this a religious film? Why or why not?

Prayer

On this Easter day, Lord, when we have risen with you, show us how to share your risen life with those who are still searching for new life. Amen.

SECOND SUNDAY OF EASTER

Acts 5:12–16;
Revelation 1:9–11a, 12–13, 17–19;
John 20:19–31

Wit

U.S.A./U.K., 2001, 100 minutes
Cast: Emma Thompson, Christopher Lloyd, Eileen Atkins,
Audra McDonald, Jonathan M. Woodward, Harold Pinter
Writers: Emma Thompson, Mike Nichols
Director: Mike Nichols

Wit

Death Be Not Proud

SYNOPSIS

Professor Vivian Bearing has been diagnosed with advanced ovarian cancer. She is forty-eight and unmarried. At the hospital, research expert Dr. Kelekian recommends an eight-month course of chemotherapy at the maximum dosage. He tells her that it is an experimental procedure. Because Vivian believes she has a strong spirit, she agrees to the treatment.

Vivian's field of research was the seventeenth-century Metaphysical poets, particularly John Donne, who wrote about the themes of death and immortality. Her favorite poem is the sonnet "Death Be Not Proud," especially the comma in the last line which signifies a gentle pause between life and eternal life.

The interminable tests and side effects take their toll on Vivian, who finds herself focused more and more on the present and on her ailing body. The chemotherapy does not bring about the hoped-for cure. However, Dr. Kelekian and his young assistant, Jason Posner, who attended one of Vivian's courses on Donne at the university, are pleased with the results of their research.

During her illness Vivian remembers her childhood discovery of words with her father and her discussions with her tutor, Evelyn Ashford. Vivian also recalls how strict she was with her own students and how she delivered her lectures. She begins to realize that she had despised kindness but now desires it. She discovers compassion through her gentle ward nurse, Susie. Just before Vivian dies, Evelyn visits her. She lies beside her, reads her a children's book, and kisses her before she departs. Vivian dies. Jason tries to revive her but Susie prevails because Vivian has asked not to be resuscitated. With her picture on screen, we hear her recite, "Death be not proud..." from Donne's *Holy Sonnets*.

COMMENTARY

Mike Nichols and Emma Thompson adapted Margaret Edson's thoughtful play for this successful HBO film. *Wit* is one of the most powerful screen depictions of terminal illness and death ever made. Emma Thompson's performance as the academic Vivian Bearing is superb. Her confiding directly in the audience, making clever jokes, and offering wry ironic comments is a device that lets the audience share intimately in her illness and in her treatment, which is cold, clinical, and yet sometimes kind.

Christopher Lloyd plays the doctor who is ultimately more interested in research than in his patients. Jonathan M. Woodward as Jason serves as a mirror image of both Dr. Kelekian and Vivian because of his dedication to knowledge.

Audra McDonald as Susie brings human kindness to the movie. Eileen Atkins also brings final warmth and love as Professor Ashford. Playwright Harold Pinter has a brief scene as Vivian's father.

DIALOGUE WITH THE GOSPEL

Focus: Locked into a room after Jesus' crucifixion and death, the disciples were full of fear. Experiencing the wounds of the risen Jesus helped Thomas believe. Wit *shows us human fears, the agony of dying, overcoming death, and the image of God's saving love.*

Today's readings highlight the joy of the resurrection as well as the curing of the sick and of "those disturbed by unclean spirits" in Acts. The vision of John in the second reading is a mystical vision of eternal life. The climax is Thomas's response to the risen Jesus, "My Lord and my God."

By reflecting on *Wit* for this Sunday, we are invited to go back to the days before Easter, as the disciples might have done, to the experience of Jesus' passion and death. The Gospel highlights how the disciples were terrified after the crucifixion. In a very real sense, they were experiencing their own loss as well as the bleak loneliness that Jesus must have felt at his death.

Wit, though obviously a Holy Week kind of film, reminds us of Jesus' agony and prolonged death. Our very familiarity with the passion story and its images may lead us to sometimes miss the deeper experience of Jesus' suffering. In *Wit*, we are allowed to walk Vivian's *via crucis* with her. We can feel her anguish, humiliation, and fear. The disciples' fear in the present is tied to their recent memory of Jesus' passion and death. *Wit* helps us appreciate what the disciples were going through after Jesus' death. This is so especially for Thomas, who could not bring himself to believe the testimony of those who had seen Jesus risen and alive again. Because we have journeyed with Vivian to her final moment, we feel the loss and we grieve for a wonderful woman who has suffered terribly and has died too soon.

By its use of John Donne's *Holy Sonnets*, *Wit* moves us to go beyond the limits of our everyday existence to ponder eternal life and immortality. Jason tells Susie that Vivian lectured on Donne's themes of sin, forgiveness, and salvation, which Jason attributed to Donne's "salvation anxiety." The screenplay dwells on the tenth sonnet, "Death Be Not Proud." After Vivian's death, we hear her voice-over, reading the sonnet and pausing at the comma in the line of the poem before finishing it: "And death shall be no more; death, thou shalt die." This pause represents the seemingly insurmountable barrier between this life and the next. We know, however, like Vivian and the disciples, that we *can* move from life to eternal life. For Jesus, for the disciples, and for us, *this* is the resurrection.

KEY SCENES AND THEMES

- Vivian's diagnosis and the doctor's explaining that she will undergo the most aggressive form of chemotherapy; her courage in handling the tests, the poking and prodding, the humiliation of the intimate examinations, the side effects of hair loss and nausea, the collapse of her immune system, the isolation; the final awareness that she will not be cured, the options for resuscitation; a long experience of pain and agony; her protracted death.

- The Metaphysical poets and themes of mortality and immortality, the seemingly insurmountable barrier between this life and eternal life; John Donne's *Holy Sonnets* and the themes of forgiveness, the assurance of salvation, and that death can be conquered; Sonnet 10: "Death be not proud."

- The academic world; Vivian's speaking about understanding poetry in the abstract; Dr. Kelekian and Jason, their love for research and their neglect of "bedside manner"; Susie helping Vivian to realize that kindness is important, their sharing stories and simple pleasures like the popsicle; Evelyn's visit, reading the story and kissing Vivian; the storybook, the poem, and the final image of Vivian.

FOR REFLECTION AND CONVERSATION

1. As Christians and believers, we live a paradox. We strive to live as long as we can, to choose life, to support it, and to never cause harm to another. Yet, as the say-

ings go, we live to die, to live well is to die well, to live a holy life is to prepare for a holy death. We celebrate the martyrs but we do not seek out martyrdom; we learn to accept suffering and pain as Vivian did because it is a sign of life. How do we, as believers, reconcile living and dying? How did Vivian and the other characters reconcile life and death? How can we best explain this paradox to a society that often has such difficulty understanding that to choose life is to prepare well for death and eternity?

2. Human dignity is a theme that recurs many times in the films chosen for *Lights, Camera…Faith! A Movie Lectionary*. Which characters understand human dignity in the film? How do they express this in their words and actions? Talk about the end of the film when Jason calls for a "Code Blue." Suzy screams, "She's a DNR!" ("Do not resuscitate") and Jason screams back, "She's research!" Re-read today's scriptures and focus on the various kinds of relationships in them. What are the links between the readings, the dignity of the human person, and the film (empathy, care, concern, kindness, gentleness, peace, presence, etc.—and the lack thereof)? How does *Wit* compare with other films about sick people and the medical establishment such as *Patch Adams, The Doctor, Regarding Henry, John Q.*, etc.?

3. Although it does not start out that way, *Wit* is a religious film. Why is this so? How do the images of light and the music help create religious meaning? Watch the film's last moments when Evelyn Ashford visits Vivian until the end when Dr. Ashford leaves. She speaks to Vivian as a dear friend, and tells her, "Don't be afraid." She then lays down beside Vivian, embraces

her, and reads to her from *The Runaway Bunny,* a story about a little rabbit that keeps telling its mother he's going to run away and turn into another animal; the mother bunny says she will become that animal, too, and find her little bunny. Dr. Ashford proclaims, "What a wonderful allegory of the soul! Wherever it hides, God will find it!" What does this mean? How is the presence of Dr. Ashford and her reading the story like a double metaphor? Who might she represent to Vivian and to the audience? (Their names are also of interest: Vivian = life and Evelyn = Eve, the mother of all the living.)

Prayer

"And death shall be no more; death, thou shalt die." Be with us, Lord, to strengthen our faith in your resurrection. Amen.

THIRD SUNDAY OF EASTER

Acts 5:27–32, 40b–41;
Revelation 5:11–14;
John 21:1–14

Gods and Generals

U.S.A., 2003, 223 minutes
Cast: Jeff Daniels, Robert Duvall, Stephen Lang, C. Thomas
Howell, Mira Sorvino, Kevin Conway, Chris Connor,
Bruce Boxleitner, Mark Nichols, Kali Rocha,
Donzaleigh Abernathy
Writer: Ronald F. Maxwell
Director: Ronald F. Maxwell

Gods and Generals

A Higher Authority

Union General Robert E. Lee is relieved of his command in Texas and ordered to Washington. He meets with Francis Blair, a close acquaintance of President Abraham Lincoln, who offers Lee the position of Major General in the U.S. Army to quell the rebellion in the southern states. Lincoln has decided that self-determination and secession are not options for slave-holding states. Lee declines the commission, stating that though he is opposed to secession, his loyalty lies with the State of Virginia. It is April 15, 1861. Two days later, following the lead of ten other states, Virginia secedes from the Union.

Thomas Jackson, a professor of philosophy and instructor of artillery at the Virginia Military Institute, joins the Confederate army. He is soon given the rank of Brigadier General. He meditates on the scriptures and prays for God's grace and guidance. He takes leave of his precious young wife, Anna.

It is July 21, 1861. Jackson prepares his troops for the first major engagement of the Civil War, the Battle of Bull Run near Manassas, Virginia, at which Jackson is given the name

139

"Stonewall" because his leadership qualities match his physical bearing. The Confederacy wins the battle. The Beale home becomes a hospital first for the Union and then for the Confederates. Jackson befriends the little girl of the family. Martha, their loyal house slave, prays to God for freedom. Irish immigrants, who have fled their homeland because of famine and oppression, fight on both sides of the war.

Joshua Lawrence Chamberlain is a professor at Maine's Bowdoin College. Although a husband and father of young children, he answers the call to arms in June 1862. He joins the Union army and is named a Lieutenant Colonel. He speaks to his wife about God and duty in brief, rational terms.

Soon, the two armies meet at the Battle of Fredericksburg and, though Chamberlain led Maine's troops in a valiant last attack, the Confederacy wins once again. Anna comes to visit Jackson and they conceive a child.

Almost a year later, in May 1863, the two armies engage once again at Chancellorsville, Virginia. Jackson is wounded by his own troops and his arm is amputated. The Confederacy wins this battle as well, but Jackson dies ten days later of pneumonia. General Lee is crestfallen at the news. The Battle of Gettysburg is two months away.

COMMENTARY

Gods and Generals is based on Jeff Shaara's 1996 novel of the same title. His father, Michael Shaara, wrote the Pulitzer Prize-winning novel *The Killer Angels,* on which director Ronald F. Maxwell based his first film of the Civil War, *Gettysburg* (1993). Jeff Shaara wrote *The Last Full Measure* in 1998 to complete the story of the Civil War and Maxwell plans to produce this film as well in the near future.

Stephen Lang as "Stonewall" Jackson gives a strong and credible performance. Jeff Daniels ably and consistently reprises his character of Joshua Chamberlain from *Gettysburg,* and Robert Duvall, taking Martin Sheen's place as Robert E. Lee, is excellent. The original score by Bob Dylan and others is both sweeping and moving. Mira Sorvino is well cast in her too brief role as Chamberlain's wife.

The underlying premise of *Gods and Generals* is that all the players in the Civil War, whether generals, families, soldiers, or slaves, all prayed to the same God for political—and national—victory and deliverance. Unfortunately, the film does not, nor can it, deal with all the dimensions and questions that this premise evokes.

DIALOGUE WITH THE GOSPEL

Focus: Today, we are invited to consider the meaning, consequences, and responsibilities of power, religious and secular. Peter discovers that Gospel leadership is not powerful domination, but is rather love and service unto death. Jackson, too, learns the difficult lesson of what true leadership requires.

In our relationship with God, we experience both God's closeness and "otherworldliness." This is particularly true of Jesus, who shared our human experience with us. As our risen Lord, he is now at the right hand of the Father, the Lamb of God worshipped in today's reading from Revelation.

The Gospel also reminds us that Jesus, though he is the risen Lamb, wants to remain near us. What better instance of simple homeliness is there than cooking an intimate breakfast for friends?

Unfortunately, our lives are not always so simple. Try as we might to do the right thing, we fail. The story of Peter and his threefold denial of Jesus reminds us of failure's possibility. Today, Peter is given the opportunity to confess his belief in Jesus and once again receives his commission to lead. Peter's leadership means dedicated service, suffering (as shown in the reading from Acts), and surrendering to death. These are the true demands of discipleship.

This is the kind of discipleship and leadership asked of Thomas Jackson. He is a devout and prayerful man, with his own strengths and weaknesses. He is a good man—in his relationship with his wife, in his encounters with the Beales, and with Martha. He faithfully takes up his duties and, while courageous and victorious, is like Peter in the Gospel, who will later face an unwanted, even ignominious death. Like Peter, Jackson will be helpless in his death, re-living in his own life the passion of Jesus.

After today's passage the Gospel continues with Jesus telling Peter that he is not to be concerned what happens to the beloved disciple. Peter, Thomas Jackson, and each of us, must accept Jesus' invitation to profess our love and single-mindedly respond to his command, "Follow me."

KEY SCENES AND THEMES

- Blair's meeting with Robert E. Lee to offer him the commission in the Union army; Lee's refusal to accept and his reasons, his loyalty to Virginia, his prayer; Thomas Jackson teaching the cadets, his decision to join the Confederate army, his wife, his relationship to God and Scripture, his faith and prayer; Joshua Chamberlain at home with his wife in Maine, his decision to join the Union army, his faith and prayer.

- The people in Manassas, the town, the families preparing for the invasion of the Union army; the Beale family and Jackson's interaction with them; the visit of Anna with the baby; the slave Martha and her family, her prayer.

- The three battles, the victories and losses, the Irish regiments fighting on both sides; the dead, the friendly fire, and Jackson's injury; the debates among the Union generals and bad decisions that result in so many deaths; Jackson's death; General Lee's response.

1. The American Civil War was a war between brothers, as many families had soldiers on both sides of the conflict. Ostensibly, the Civil War portrayed in *Gods and Generals* (and in *Gettysburg*) was fought over slavery. In actuality, the war was based on economic need and the relentless expansion of the United States across the North American continent. The eleven southern states formed the Confederacy to protect the rights of states versus the rights of the central, federal government. The institution of slavery, because it did not fit into the emerging overall economic system of the country, was a divisive issue, but not the only one. Given all this, how was slavery a moral issue beyond any political or economic consideration? How are the effects of slavery still affecting our culture today? How are slavery and racism linked? What are the historical roots of racism in our culture and what is a Christian response to racism of any kind?

2. *Gods and Generals* shows many of the characters, especially General Thomas "Stonewall" Jackson, praying to God for help and victory. Stephen Lang, who portrays Jackson in the film, said, "Jackson was a man of absolute heroic stature. He was both complex and contradictory—an Old Testament warrior with New Testament faith." If soldiers, slaves, and everyone else engaged in the Civil War prayed to the same God, what does this say about religious faith and God's presence in our lives? How is it that good people, who are willing to fight each other for freedom of self-determination, can believe in and pray to the same God? How do current world events reflect this paradox—

that at least half the world believes in the same one, true God (Christians, Jews, and Muslims), yet we cannot get along? How can interreligious dialogue further peace? What role does justice play in peacemaking?

3. All three readings today are about power. Notice how the characters in the readings from Acts, the writer of Revelation, and Jesus and his disciples (especially Peter) understand the dynamic between secular and religious authority and power. The responsorial psalm refrain says, "I will praise you Lord, for you have rescued me." With what focus might each of the characters in *Gods and Generals* have prayed this psalm? What does it mean for us as we face the challenge of integrating faith and citizenship in a county and in a world that still neglect and deny basic human rights? How did *Gods and Generals* make you feel about war as a solution to problems? What other solution does the film (and Christian teaching) offer to resolve conflict?

Prayer

Lord, though we have failed you, you still ask us to profess our love for you. Help us to take responsibility and be faithful in our commitment to whatever you ask us to do. Amen.

Henry Fonda and Jane Darwell in *The Grapes of Wrath*.

The Grapes of Wrath
U.S.A., 1940, 129 minutes
Cast: Henry Fonda, Jane Darwell, John Carradine,
Charley Grapewin, Russell Simpson, Ward Bond
Writer: Nunnally Johnson
Director: John Ford

The Grapes of Wrath

"We're the People!"

SYNOPSIS

When Tom Joad is released from an Oklahoma state prison, he rejoins his family, who are trying to eke out a living in the Mid-western dust bowl during the Depression. He meets a former preacher named Casy and confides that he killed a man in a drunken brawl.

A friend, Muley, explains that the banks have foreclosed and everybody has to get out. Ma, Granpa, and the others are preparing to set out for California because they have seen flyers advertising for workers. They have lost all their possessions that cannot be put in the truck.

Granpa dies on the way. Gas station attendants and others who watch the family pass look down on them as poor "Okies" and less than human. The camp they move into is ugly; the children already there are hungry. Ma's response is to feed them all. They learn that there are too many migrants for all the jobs advertised on the flyers. They discover that the foremen are really con men who promise work but then withhold wages as payment for rent and force the workers to pay high prices at the company store. The Joads experience the conflict between workers and scab laborers who break the union lines.

The family is in trouble. They find jobs but are beaten down with high prices and low pay for their work. They live in a camp with guards. Tom goes for a walk one night and finds Casy. In the dark, violent scuffles break out between the strikers and the "tin sheriffs." Casy is killed and Tom kills his attacker in turn. The family has to move on. They find a well-organized Department of Agriculture camp where people are respected and allowed to run things for themselves. Police come looking for Tom and he is forced to go on the run, hoping to help fix social ills. Tom kisses his mother goodbye and the Joads move on to another camp.

COMMENTARY

John Steinbeck's portrait of the people has become a literary classic and made Steinbeck a Nobel Prize winner. In the aftermath of the Depression, the book touched a chord in the American heart. Its place in between the economic depression in the United States and the rise of totalitarianism in Europe with Stalin, Hitler, and Mussolini, offered filmgoers a look at socialism. It was a portrait of poverty and oppression, not outside the United States, but within. To make a movie of this novel in 1940 was a huge box-office risk.

Director John Ford was already an established filmmaker with a vision of American society and its past as well as a master of his craft, especially Westerns. He was awarded his second Oscar for Best Director for *The Grapes of Wrath* in 1940. He had already won an Oscar for *The Informer* in 1935 and had just made his classic western, *Stagecoach*, *Young Mr. Lincoln*, and *Drums along the Mohawk* in 1939. He was to win another Best Film Oscar in 1941 for *How Green Was My Valley*, and a fourth in 1952 for *The Quiet Man*.

Henry Fonda gives the performance of a lifetime, although he was not recognized by the Academy until forty years later when he won an Oscar for *On Golden Pond*. Jane Darwell won the Oscar for Best Supporting Actress. The cast consists of many character actors who were regulars in John

Ford's movies. The screenplay was by Nunnally Johnson, who wrote dozens of scripts in his lifetime, including *Tobacco Road*, also directed by John Ford.

> *Focus: Jesus the Good Shepherd knows his own, leads them with kindness, and offers them hope. Tom Joad is an American "everyman." Despite his poverty, he was able to offer moral leadership to his oppressed family and neighbors.*

DIALOGUE WITH THE GOSPEL

During the liturgies of the Easter season, the image of Jesus as the Good Shepherd is offered as a model of leadership. While Tom Joad is no saint, he tries to do his best. His family and his neighbors and friends listen to his voice and follow him. He tries to give them some sense of life in the world in which they are struggling to exist. In a sense, he has been entrusted with a life-giving mission, just like Jesus the Good Shepherd.

The first and second readings can throw light on the experiences of the Joad family and of the others on the road who search for a place to put down their roots. The onlookers despise them as they pass by. Paul and Barnabas in the Acts of the Apostles, go on their missionary journey, sometimes being listened to, other times being ridiculed and subjected to violence. Some women stir up persecution against them and they are expelled. Paul and Barnabas shake the dust from their feet in protest. The Joads' experience is of dust that they cannot shake off. The Joads are people of faith and Ma is a woman of courage. In a way, the Joads place their hopes in readings like that from Revelation today, "and God will wipe every tear from their eye." They are, finally, "the ones who have survived the time of great distress."

Tom Joad's final speech in the movie is a defiant plea for tolerance and a challenge to respect the marginalized—those who often feel that they are like sheep without a shepherd. Before leaving the family, Tom Joad tells his mother what his life's work will be: "I'll be all around in the dark. I'll be every-where, wherever you can look. Wherever there's a fight so hungry people can eat, I'll be there. Wherever there's a cop beating up a guy, I'll be there. I'll be in the way guys yell when they're mad. I'll be in the way kids laugh and they're hungry and they know supper's ready and when the people are eatin' the stuff they raise, even in the houses they build, I'll be there." His words express the justice of God's king-dom, toward which Jesus the Good Shepherd leads us.

KEY SCENES AND THEMES

- Tom Joad released from prison, riding on the fender of the car, defiant; confessing to Casy, learning of the bank's foreclosure, going home; his relationship with Ma, his father, Granpa, and the rest of the family; their dependence on him.

- The hard journey in the old truck, their few posses-sions, Granpa dying and his funeral; crossing the river and the sense of achievement in getting to Califor-nia; the hardships endured on the way, in the camps, the being swindled, the hard labor, the tension be-tween the workers.

- Tom's supporting the family; the fight, his killing the man, having to move on; the family settled in the De-partment of Agriculture camp and the possibility for a future; Tom on the run and the family moving on in hope.

FOR REFLECTION AND CONVERSATION

1. John Steinbeck's novel and John Ford's film present many themes for us to consider. What are some of the themes presented by the film (man's inhumanity to man, the generative power of goodness, the place of the family in the world and in the American dream, the legitimacy of wrath in the face of injustice, the central role of women in a man's world, etc.)? Why

do you think the presence of these themes have made film critics consider *The Grapes of Wrath* a parable or morality tale? What is the moral of the story? Is it as valid for today's globalized world as it was in 1940? Why or why not?

2. In the Movie Lectionary for Cycle A, the eyebrow-raising Erin Brockovich *(Erin Brockovich)* was the Good Shepherd-figure of leadership in the community at large against a gigantic utilities company. In Cycle B, a fictitious seminarian, Mark Dolson *(Mass Appeal),* is the model for authentic leadership in the Christian community struggling to make sense of the Church and the call to follow Jesus more closely in a time of change. In Cycle C, we have another fictitious figure, Tom Joad, who embodies the courage of Brockovich in the face of grave social ills, and the almost biblical authenticity and idealism of Dolson, so that he can give hope and courage to those who follow him. Does Tom Joad have something to say to the faith community today in the United States or in other "first-world" countries? If so, what do you think he would say? Why?

3. This classic black-and-white film uses lighting to create much of its emotional meaning. There is also a lot of preaching or "moralizing." There is talk of the universal human family, of clarity of vision, of water. How did the film work for you? How did it make you feel? What did you think of Casy's remarks at the beginning of the film, Ma's speech about the differences between men and women, and, finally, Tom's vision of himself as an advocate of justice? Was the film really universal in that it represented the perspectives of men, women, and children everywhere, regardless of creed, culture, age, gender, or social class? Why or

why not? What did Rose of Sharon's pregnancy mean and how did it function as a symbol in the film? What did it mean for the future?

Prayer

Lord, you had compassion on those who were like sheep without a shepherd. May your people, your flock, hear your voice, follow you, and find a new life with you. Amen.

Schindler's List
U.S.A., 1993, 187 minutes
Cast: Liam Neeson, Ben Kingsley, Ralph Fiennes,
Embeth Davidtz, Caroline Goodall
Writer: Steven Zaillian
Director: Steven Spielberg

Schindler's List

Life, Death, Love

SYNOPSIS

It is 1939 and the Jews in Krakow are being pressured, hassled, and tormented by the Nazis. Oskar Schindler, a thirty-one-year-old Czech-born German businessman, womanizer, con man, and lapsed Catholic, arrives to persuade the Nazi military, with charm and bribes, to allow him to manufacture pots and pans, and so bring great profit to himself and to them. He hires accountant Itzhak Stern to manage his factory. Schindler employs the Jews because they work cheap. By March 1941, the Jews are forced into a ghetto, but those who are employed by Schindler get to leave every day to go to work because it is a protected industry. Meanwhile, Schindler lives a life of luxury.

Krakow commandant Amon Goeth is cruel and arbitrarily kills prisoners for "sport." He oversees the destruction of the ghetto and the transfer of all Jews to the Plaszow Forced Labor Camp. Schindler's factory continues to thrive. However, Schindler has witnessed great cruelty during the liquidation of the ghetto. When he realizes that his workers are destined for the camps, he makes a deal with Goeth to "buy" them for work in a new factory in Czechoslovakia. With the help of

Itzhak Stern, he compiles a list of people to be saved. The men arrive at their destination, but the train with the women goes to Auschwitz. Schindler rescues them.

The factory makes munitions during the war's final months but Schindler makes sure they are unusable. As the war ends, he lets the workers as well as the German soldiers go. He is now viewed as a criminal because he has profited from the war. The workers he saved give him letters of recommendation and a gold ring so that he can start a new life. He regrets he did not save more Jews. In modern Israel, the Schindler survivors and the actors portraying them place memorial stones on Schindler's grave.

COMMENTARY

With *Schindler's List*, Steven Spielberg combined his considerable cinema talents with the acknowledgment of his Jewish heritage. While feted for his exclusively entertaining films like the *Indiana Jones* trilogy, *E.T.: The Extra-Terrestrial,* and the *Jurassic Park* movies, Spielberg has consistently shown a serious side to his movie-making with films such as *Duel, The Color Purple, Empire of the Sun, Saving Private Ryan, Amistad, Minority Report,* and even *Catch Me If You Can. Schindler's List* won Oscars for Best Film, Director, Cinematography, Musical Score, and Screenplay, which was based on Australian novelist Thomas Keneally's Booker Award-winning book, *Schindler's Ark.*

Screenwriter Steven Zaillian *(Searching for Bobby Fischer, A Civil Action)* has written a powerful Holocaust story. Liam Neeson has the role of a lifetime as Oskar Schindler. Ben Kingsley is intelligent and subtle as Stern. Ralph Fiennes gives a tour-de-force portrayal of all that was evil in Nazi superiority and cruelty.

The black-and-white photography makes the movie more striking because audiences perceive the film as historical, almost a documentary. However, color is used sparingly and with great effect.

Focus: During the horrors of the Holocaust, Oskar Schindler learns to forego his ambitions and greed and to embody Jesus' new commandment that we love one another.

DIALOGUE WITH THE GOSPEL

Schindler's List is rich with themes. For today, the focus is on Oskar Schindler himself and his spiritual journey. Even while Steven Spielberg has immersed his audiences in the experiences of the Jews during the war, he has also given us a portrait of an ordinary man, both sinful and good, who underwent a conversion experience from selfishness to understanding and living the commandment of love from his seemingly forgotten Catholic upbringing. Oskar Schindler, perhaps without knowing it, actually put Jesus' "new" commandment into practice. The commandment of love needs to be renewed in every generation. Schindler is often referred to as a "good man." By saving twelve hundred Jews, he left a legacy that showed he was a disciple.

Oskar Schindler was the embodiment of the "worldly man" and a member of the Nazi party. He was self-confident, even arrogant. He was a smooth and shrewd operator, a womanizer who loved luxury. He was an entrepreneur who told his wife that he wanted to make as much money as he could from the opportunity provided by the war. Indeed, he exploited it. While Schindler employed Jews and treated them humanely, his purpose was initially business success. But when he witnessed the liquidation of the Krakow ghetto, his heart and conscience were so moved that he could never be the same again. He had to do something to help the Jews survive.

The movie shows the steps in his transformation, beginning with his disgust at Goeth's cruelty and his attempt to teach Goeth about power and pardoning. He had laid down his life for the Jews, and, in the end, was sorry he had not done more.

The reading from the Acts of the Apostles speaks of hardships experienced by Paul and Barnabas. Hardship and persecution have been the hallmark of Jewish history. *Schindler's List* is a powerful reminder of the consequences of hatred and scapegoating. The reading from Revelation, however, says that suffering will pass away and that a new Jerusalem will be built where God will make all things new. Decades later, the Holocaust survivors from Schindler's list visit his grave to pay tribute to his memory. Our Easter faith reminds us that resurrection—a life where all is new—is promised to us all.

KEY SCENES AND THEMES

- Oskar Schindler, man of the world, his strategies to obtain permits for his factory, negotiating with Itzhak Stern and the Jews; his production line, employing the Jews and the infirm; his interactions with Goeth, trying to teach him the power of pardon; Schindler's concern for Helen, kissing the Jewish girl at his party, saving the aged parents, and getting Stern off the train.

- The Jewish register in Krakow, forcing the Jews into the ghetto, their humiliation and suffering, their work in the factory; the liquidation of the ghetto, the little girl in the red dress, the arbitrary shootings by the soldiers and Goeth; the stories of the camps and the women taken to Auschwitz and into the showers.

- Schindler's watching the destruction of the ghetto, his decision to use his money to pay Goeth for the Jews, the making of the list, including Stern and Helen; the new factory and his benign management, the celebration of Sabbath; the end of the war, his fleeing, the gift of the gold ring; the aftermath and his failures; Schindler being named a "Righteous Gentile" and the tribute at his grave.

1. Steven Spielberg has made a film about the extermination of six million Jews and about the life of one "Righteous Gentile," who was a failure before the war, a hero during it, and alas, by human standards, a failure after. To be honored as a "Righteous Gentile" in Yad Vashem, Jerusalem's Holocaust memorial, the person must be known for "extending help in saving a life; endangering one's own life; absence of reward, monetary and otherwise, and similar considerations which make the rescuer's deeds stand out above and beyond what can be termed ordinary help." Talk about how Oskar Schindler fulfilled these requirements (his gentle concern for Helen Hirsch and her treatment by Goeth; employing the aged and the crippled; his hosing down the train carriages to cool the stifled Jews; his decision to buy the Jews from Goeth; the making of the list; encouraging the Sabbath prayer; sabotaging his manufactured munitions; going bankrupt but regretting not saving more Jewish people from death). What can account for what he did to save the twelve hundred Jews when it was so out of character for him? What might you have done?

2. Today's Gospel tells us to love one another as Jesus loved us. The story of the Holocaust stays with us still, and so it must, so that nothing like it will ever happen again to humanity—by humanity. Television public-service announcements advise us not to tell jokes, especially to children, that ridicule people's race, color, religion, culture, gender, body size, handicap, or age, because to do so is to teach hate, not love. How does your use of language socialize the people with whom you live, work, and share faith? List at least three prac-

tical ways that you can create a culture of love that promotes human dignity without distinction through language, whether verbal or physical.

3. As a filmmaker, Spielberg is an artist and storyteller of the first order. How does his use of the black-and-white "documentary" style work to create emotional meaning for the story? Spielberg is known for making movies about or that include "lonely" children. What are some of these lonely child characters, and why do you think they are important for Spielberg? Who is the lonely child in *Schindler's List*? What does she symbolize? How does the candle that is lit and then extinguished, its smoke turning into chimney smoke, convey meaning? What are some other symbols in the film and how did these images and the music contribute to your understanding of the meaning of the film? What is your response to the film? Silence? Prayer? Transformation of your own life into one of love?

Prayer

Lord, you knew suffering and you offered loving forgiveness. Help us, even in the most tragic of world or personal events, to know and live the meaning of your commandment to love. Amen.

SIXTH SUNDAY OF EASTER
Acts 15:1–2, 22–29;
Revelation 21:10–14, 22–23;
John 14:23–29

Star Wars
(*Star Wars: Episode IV—A New Hope*)

U.S.A., 1977 (special edition re-issue, re-mastered 1997), 125 minutes
Cast: Mark Hamill, Harrison Ford, Carrie Fisher, Alec Guinness, Peter
Cushing, James Earl Jones, Anthony Daniels, Kenny Baker
Writer: George Lucas
Director: George Lucas

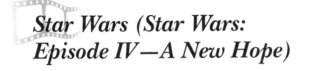

Star Wars (Star Wars: Episode IV—A New Hope)

The Spirit Is the "Force" of Jesus

SYNOPSIS

A long time ago, in a galaxy far, far away, a tyrannical empire has replaced a benevolent republic. Princess Leia, a republican rebel, is captured after stealing plans of the Empire's new Death Star, a weapon able to destroy planets. Her two robots or droids, C 3PO and R2-D2, find themselves on a barren planet, sold to a farmer. The farmer's nephew is Luke Skywalker.

R2-D2 delivers a message from Leia to Obi-Wan Kenobi, a Jedi knight, asking him to get the plans hidden in the droid to the rebels. Obi-Wan tells Luke that he is the son of a Jedi. The Jedi believe in a mystical power, the Force, which binds the universe together. When invaders sent from the renegade Jedi, Darth Vader, kill Luke's uncle and aunt, Luke begins a mission of avenging his family.

Meanwhile, Jabba the Hut pursues a mercenary pilot, Han Solo, who has a companion, Chewbacca. Luke hires Han Solo and they fly to Princess Leia's planet, and find that it has been destroyed. When Luke rescues Leia, Darth Vader kills

Obi-Wan Kenobi. However, he lives on in the Force and is able to hand on his wisdom to Luke.

Han Solo assists Luke in the attack on the Death Star. Luke also taps into the Force and completes his mission.

COMMENTARY

What more can be said about *Star Wars?* First released in 1977, this engaging adventure has more than stood the test of time. As the prequels (and sequels) are being produced, *Star Wars* is becoming known as George Lucas envisioned it: *Star Wars: Episode IV—A New Hope.*

Why such a phenomenon? By the mid-1970s, the United States experienced a cultural shift away from acceptance of authority to disillusionment with politicians and political structures. *Star Wars* was in pre-production at the time of the Watergate scandal and the resignation of Richard Nixon in 1974. The United States was losing the war in Vietnam. There was also a movement away from organized religion, accompanied by confusion about religious teaching and authority. This revealed a basic need for role models, for storytelling, and for the creation of a myth that would stir the imagination, organize existence, and dramatize values in ways that would resonate with people. The need for a mythic legend like *Star Wars* was almost urgent. The cosmic scope of the film and its reliance on the tradition of heroism and chivalry, characterized by the struggle between good and evil, met these desires of the 1970s. And continues to do so today.

DIALOGUE WITH THE GOSPEL

Focus: The Last Discourse was the occasion for Jesus' revelation to the disciples that he is the source of our peace as he sends the force of his Spirit into our world. The Jedi knights serve the Force that unifies the universe in Star Wars.

In his excellent little book, *The Gospel from Outer Space,* Robert L. Short refers to the "Gospel According to Lucas," because of the parallels between the *Star Wars* trilogy and the

Gospel story. Robert Jewett's excellent book that encourages dialogue between the New Testament and cinema, *Saint Paul at the Movies* includes a chapter that offers a gospel challenge to understanding an even deeper "Force" than that of the *Star Wars* mythology.

However, for more than a quarter of a century, millions of people around the world have found an entry into thinking in more mythical and transcendent ways through the *Star Wars* movies. While some "rationalists" decry the seeming addiction of so many people to *Star Wars* and its eccentrically symbolic world, the second reading for this Sunday of Easter has an excerpt from the book of Revelation whose cosmic apocalyptic symbolism is not alien to a *Star Wars* mentality.

St. John's presentation of Jesus' Last Discourse in today's Gospel is full of a mystical promise of truth, love, and peace. Jesus says that he will send an Advocate, a Paraclete, an unseen Spirit that is gift of God but is a power binding the world together. Why? Because this Spirit will remind the followers of Jesus of all the things he taught them. We are invited to live on in Jesus' love and to be one in his Spirit. The Spirit is one of wisdom—and audiences can recognize echoes of Jesus' words in the wisdom and the sayings of Obi-Wan Kenobi, such as, "The Force surrounds and penetrates us. It binds the galaxy together."

The confrontation between good and evil in *Star Wars* is reminiscent of the similar transcendent and real struggle in the gospels; to many people this parallel indicates a shared theology between the two.

Star Wars, however, offers popular culture a limited and sometimes vengeful version of the "Force" or God. This consideration of the image of God in both film and today's Gospel offers an opportunity and a challenge for audiences and believers to dialogue about these themes ever more deeply, moving from cinema and the realities of life to the message of Jesus, who promises to be with us until the end of time.

**KEY SCENES
AND THEMES**

- The evil Empire in the galaxy; the Emperor, the Death Star, the renegade Jedi and the will to possess power; the Grand Moff Tarkin; Princess Leia and the rebels, the battle, and her being taken prisoner; Leia's robots escaping and being sold to the farmer.

- Luke Skywalker and his "hidden life" with his uncle and aunt on the farm; the revelation that he is the son of a Jedi knight and his being chosen by Obi-Wan Kenobi; Han Solo as the mercenary on the run; the contrast between Han and Luke.

- The battle against the Death Star, Luke and the Force, Han Solo covering him, the death of the Grand Moff Tarkin; the final celebration with Princess Leia.

**FOR REFLECTION
AND
CONVERSATION**

1. While the *Star Wars* movies are not Christian allegory per se, they do get people thinking about God, as filmmaker George Lucas thought they would. People interpret films according to what they "bring" to it, so it is understandable that a Christian might infer that Obi-Wan Kenobi is a Christ-figure and Luke Skywalker a disciple. Although the original *Star Wars* was released in 1977, it was both the heir and forerunner of many films with a popular adventure hero as a kind of Christ-figure, such as Jericho Cane in the apocalyptic *End of Days.* Lloyd Baugh lists some of them in his book *Imaging the Divine: Jesus and Christ-figures in Film:* Luke in *Cool Hand Luke,* Father Barry in *On the Waterfront,* and Randle Patrick McMurphy in *One Flew Over the Cuckoo's Nest.* Do you see *Star Wars* as a movie with religious potential, as entertainment, or both? Why?

2. How old were you when you first saw *Star Wars*? Did the film and its successors form part of your consciousness when you were growing up? If not, what popular

films play a part in your memory? Where do they fit in with your recollections of life at school, church, scouts, or other organizations, and with your memories of current events in the larger world? Does *Star Wars* (or another film) have a nostalgic quality that comforts you? Why might this be so? What accounts for the influence of storytelling and myth on our psyche? What stories from the Bible do you recall from your early years? How did these become part of who you are? How do you think Jesus' words in today's Gospel (as well as the imagery from Revelation) helped create visual "images" that Christians have maintained throughout history?

3. When film was first invented (c. 1895), science fiction was already on its way out as a popular genre, despite the best efforts of H. G. Wells. Perhaps the invention of photography had something to do with attracting popular taste toward "realism" versus make-believe, at least until Stanley Kubrick's *2001: A Space Odyssey* in 1968. The Lumiere Brothers made the first "reality" films in France, and beginning in 1896, magician Georges Méliès made hundreds of short, fantasy, futuristic films that combined animation and real footage, notably *Le Voyage dans la lune* in 1902 and *Le Voyage à travers l'impossible* in 1904. But audiences wanted "reality" and Méliès style was seldom seen for decades. What do you think accounts for the long "pause" in popular speculative fiction in the history of film? Why would people prefer "reality" for so long, and then opt for science fiction? Now, retro fantasy is "in" with Peter Jackson's Lord of the Rings Trilogy. What accounts for people's fascination with myth—that overarching attempt to explain existence, the human

condition, the reality of good versus evil, and the gray areas in between? What are your genre preferences? Why?

Prayer

In these days of Easter, Jesus, we recognize your power and wisdom as our risen Lord. May your "force" be always with us, especially in the gift of your Holy Spirit's love and peace. Amen.

Chariots of Fire

U.K., 1981, 124 minutes
Cast: Ian Charleson, Ben Cross, Nigel Havers, Nicholas Farrell,
Ian Holm, John Gielgud, Lindsay Anderson, Cheryl Campbell,
Alice Krige, Brad Davis, Dennis Christopher, Nigel Davenport
Writer: Colin Welland
Director: Hugh Hudson

Chariots of Fire

Running the Good Race

In 1919, Harold Abrahams goes to Cambridge to study law. He is a secular Jew whose family came from Lithuania and he feels the need to prove himself to be a true Englishman. Abrahams is a sprinter and sets his sights on the Paris Olympic Games of 1924. His friends and fellow athletes, Aubrey Montague and Andrew Lindsay, support him. The masters of Trinity and Caius College are wary of him and voice their anti-Semitic attitudes when they criticize him for employing a professional coach, Sam Mussabini (who happens to be of Italian Arab parentage), instead of training in the traditional way as an amateur. Harold is very fond of Gilbert and Sullivan operettas that embody so much of his British ideals. He meets and falls in love with an actress, Sybil Gordon.

Meanwhile in Scotland, champion rugby player and sprinter Eric Liddell is persuaded to train to run in the Olympics. He was born in China to a missionary family. His sister, Jennie, applies emotional pressure on him to return to the mission rather than "waste" his time running. Liddell, however, sees his talent for winning races as God's gift that in

SYNOPSIS

turn gives God pleasure. When he competes with Abrahams for the 100-meter sprint, Eric easily beats him and Abrahams is devastated. Sybil persuades Abrahams to take a more mature attitude toward his compulsions.

Abrahams, Liddell, and fellow athlete Lindsay are all selected for the British Olympic team to go to Paris. Liddell finds his first heat for the 100 meters is scheduled for a Sunday and he cannot, in principle, run on the Sabbath. The British committee, including the Prince of Wales, try to persuade him, but the situation is saved only by Lindsay's arranging to change days for his heat. Lindsay comes in second in the hurdles, Abrahams wins gold in the 100 meters and Liddell in the 400 meters—a race for which he has not even trained. It is a golden era for British athletics.

COMMENTARY

When released in 1981, *Chariots of Fire* was a surprising commercial hit. While its picture of Britain in the 1920s might have seemed narrow and excessively patriotic, this story of two significant athletes appealed across cultures and the movie eventually won four Oscars: for Best Picture and Costume Design, for Colin Welland's original screenplay and for Vangelis's stirring and memorable score.

Colin Welland's screenplay and Hugh Hudson's direction recreate the elitist atmosphere of Cambridge as well as the plain and ordinary world of Scotland. Ben Cross is both edgy and jovial as Abrahams. Ian Holm plays Sam Mussabini in an Oscar-nominated performance. The late Ian Charleson as Liddell convinces us that the young runner is a good, grounded, sincere, and principled evangelical Christian. John Gielgud and Lindsay Anderson (who directed *The Whales of August*) are the Cambridge masters who, in their brief scenes, create a narrow, elitist, exclusive, even archaic England.

Chariots of Fire, whose title comes from Blake's hymn "Jerusalem," blends religious and secular themes into a powerful and moving drama. Harold Abraham's keen sensitivity to racism and anti-Semitism in British society and Eric Liddell's authentic and unselfconscious Christian faith are compared and contrasted as the two men train for the games. The movie is a portrait of a man of faith and convictions, as well as of a man searching for purpose and dignity.

> *Focus: Jesus prays that we may be one with him in faith and then in glory. Eric Liddell, in* Chariots of Fire, *is a good man who acknowledges his faith and his giftedness.*

Though all of today's readings are in the form of prayers or contain them, a sense of great triumph is also evident: Stephen's vision of Jesus as he dies; John's ultimate vision of Jesus as the Alpha and the Omega; and from John's Gospel, the conclusion of Jesus' prayer that his disciples be united with him as he is with his Father. *Chariots of Fire* is a movie about commitment, discipline, achievement, and triumph.

With Eric Liddell, we see a man who fulfills these scriptural texts. With Harold Abrahams, we see a man who is searching for meaning through excellence. Harold's experience represents the struggles of the Jewish people over the centuries and his awareness of his heritage compels him to succeed—especially in the face of the elitist prejudice he encounters at Cambridge University. Eric Liddell is a devout and humble man whose inner convictions about his God enable him to follow his principles. He cannot run on the Sabbath because he believes to do so would be contrary to God's law. The members of the British Olympic committee fail to really understand this. However, we have seen Liddell fulfill the "priestly" prayer that Jesus offers after the Last Supper: "Righteous Father, the world does not know you, but I know you." Because of his religious background, Liddell is able to speak freely about God in his life. Eric acknowledges the gifts he has received: his swiftness and that he gives God pleasure by running his best and winning. He is shown praying in his church, quoting Jewish Scripture about the unimportance of nations in God's eyes. He preaches gently about how running can be a metaphor for faith. Like Stephen, we find out that he gives his life to his mission and dies at the end of World War II in occupied China.

Jesus prayed that all should be one. *Chariots of Fire* shows how Abrahams and Liddell, who come from two different religions, two different strata of society, join together in the honorable quest for Olympic victory. They share things that matter on a deeper level as each of them matures and comes to a better understanding of himself.

KEY SCENES AND THEMES

• Harold Abrahams at Cambridge; his record run and his friends; the prejudice of the masters; his driving ambition and his love for Sybil; being coached by Sam; his awe of Liddell and being beaten by him, his having to mature, and winning the gold medal.

• Eric Liddell, his missionary background, his love for his sister, Jennie, and her pressure on him to give up running, his studies; known and admired in Scotland, his gift for running; his faith, preaching, prayer; the contrast with Abrahams.

• Liddell's stance concerning running on the Sabbath, the committee, Lindsay's solution; his race and victory; Harold's race and victory.

FOR REFLECTION AND CONVERSATION

1. Sports movies, many of which are based on true stories, are often presented as metaphors for life: *The Legend of Bagger Vance, Remember the Titans, Field of Dreams, Slap Shot I* and *II, Brian's Song, The Hurricane, Love and Basketball, Rudy, Hoosiers, Hoop Dreams, A League of Their Own, Wind, Cool Runnings. Chariots of Fire* is no less a metaphor for its being about real people and telling about the struggles the characters faced in life—how they did the best they could and

won. Sam tells Abrahams that the 100 meters is run on nerves, a race for neurotics, and that the longer-distance races demand a calmer approach, something from the inner depths. How do the two main characters express this "inner depth"? Is Sam's observation true for other sports films you have seen? How so? What does Eric mean when he says: "Then where does the power come from, to see the race to its end? From within."

2. List some of the ways that the film compares and contrasts Abrahams and Liddell. How were they similar and how were they different? How does each man view God? Have you ever experienced a contemplative moment in your relationship with God that let you express what Eric does about the gifts God has given you: "I believe God made me for a purpose, but he also made me fast. And when I run I feel His pleasure." Describe those moments and insights. How do today's readings resonate with Eric's statement?

3. The Catholic Church has set the Seventh Sunday of Easter aside since 1964 as World Communications Day (though some Bishops' conferences designate another day for pastoral reasons). Today's commemoration of "communications" is to raise our awareness about the role of mass media in our lives and about its potential for good, and to ask for our support for the Church's pastoral efforts in the field of communications. Two areas that the Church in the United States and in other countries is interested and involved in are cinema and media literacy education. The Church has long considered cinema as an art form, though in the United States it is often thought of primarily in commercial terms. Media literacy education

promotes critical thinking and production skills about information and entertainment media. What makes a film like *Chariots of Fire* "art"? What is art and entertainment? Can they coexist? How are some of the principles of media literacy education applied to *Chariots of Fire* (e.g., issues of how human dignity, race, social class, gender, age are represented)? Is the film fair? Why or why not? How can communication help the world become one, as Jesus prayed?

Prayer

Lord, be with us today and always that we may we give you glory as we run our course in life. Amen.

Tom Hanks and Paul Newman in *Road to Perdition*.

Road to Perdition

U.S.A., 2002, 132 minutes
Cast: Tom Hanks, Paul Newman, Jude Law, Tyler Hoechlin,
Daniel Craig, Stanley Tucci, Jennifer Jason Leigh,
Ciaran Hinds, Anthony LaPaglia
Writer: David Self
Director: Sam Mendes

Road to Perdition

Dead Because of Sin but Alive in the Spirit

Mike Sullivan is a mob enforcer for his surrogate father, John Rooney, who has provided him with a home and security for his family. When Mike's older son, Michael, witnesses a slaying, Rooney's irresponsible son, Connor, murders Mike's wife and younger son, Peter. Mike goes to the Chicago boss, Frank Nitti, for protection, but Nitti has already been bought by the Rooneys. John Rooney sanctions the killing of Mike but not of his son Michael. Nitti also hires a hit man: Maguire, a press photographer whose specialty is victims of crime.

SYNOPSIS

Mike and his son go on the road and are almost killed by Maguire. They decide to put pressure on the Chicago mob by robbing the banks that are storing the mob's laundered funds. Mike also obtains evidence that Connor has been robbing his father. When he confronts John Rooney, he finds that Rooney already knew of his son's guilt. Mike ambushes Rooney and guns him down and with Nitti's permission he then kills Connor.

When Mike and his son arrive at a safe cottage in Perdition, Maguire, who has been wounded in a shootout with Mike, shoots him. Maguire turns his gun on Michael, who is unable to fire. His father saves Michael but dies in his arms.

Michael then starts a new life with an elderly farming couple that had cared for him previously when his father was convalescing after the earlier shootout with Maguire.

COMMENTARY

Road to Perdition obviously denotes hell, although it is also the name of the town that Tom Hanks, playing a hit man on the run, is trying to reach for his safety and that of his son. In fact, the movie is more a study of the relationships between fathers and sons than a simple gangster movie.

The film's Irish-Catholic families are very clannish, with lives centered on the church. *Road to Perdition* portrays individual criminals who were often personally devout and who presented themselves as pillars of the Church. In fact, in the graphic novel by Max Allan Collins and Richard Piers Rayner on which the movie is based, Mike Sullivan goes to confession every time he kills someone. At the end of the novel, readers learn that his son is a priest. Director Sam Mendes *(American Beauty)* said that he filmed a confession sequence but that including it in the film made its significance too explicit and that movie audiences would have found the boy's becoming a priest too much. Paul Newman received an Oscar nomination for his role as John Rooney.

Road to Perdition powerfully dramatizes the perennial themes of sin, repentance, and redemption.

DIALOGUE WITH THE GOSPEL

Focus: Road to Perdition *shows us a world of people who, though they know better, choose sin and died because of it. The Gospel proclaims the peace of Christ and assures us that the Holy Spirit has the power to forgive—and retain—sin.*

The Pentecost story from Acts reminds us that membership in the Church is universal. The disciples of Jesus are many and diverse. The Church is a communion of saints and sinners.

The reading from the Letter to the Romans highlights our sinfulness, "those who are in the flesh cannot please God."

It is only when the Spirit of God dwells in us that the body, which is dead because of sin, can be filled with the life of the Spirit. Paul reminds us that if we live according to the flesh, we will die. Paul Newman, as patriarch John Rooney, says this about his gangster empire, "This is the life we have chosen and there is no guarantee except that none of us will reach heaven." Soon after, he and his bodyguards are gunned down. Those who live by the sword or gun will die by the sword or gun.

However, Mike Sullivan tells Rooney, his surrogate father who has decreed his death, that "Michael can" make it to heaven. His son, the innocent witness to this world of evil, need not be corrupted. Mike Sullivan has fought so that his son does not have to follow his footsteps and can live in freedom. When Mike dies in his son's arms, he says three times, "I'm sorry." These are Irish-American gangsters who should know better; they say prayers, light candles, and receive Holy Communion. The movie asks whether forgiveness and redemption are possible for them.

The celebration of Pentecost invites us to look at how God's gift of the Spirit can enliven those whose faith is weak, because the Spirit did indeed fill Peter with powerful words that he did not know he could utter. The Spirit can forgive and remove the spirit of slavery so that we can "put to death the deeds of the body" and live. Jesus breathes on his disciples—giving them the Spirit of peace—and speaks of the forgiveness of sins.

A movie like *Road to Perdition*, with its wintry landscapes, its steely interiors, its empire of greed and violence, portrays for us of a world of sin. We can live and die unrepentant or we can acknowledge our sinfulness and ask forgiveness, moved by the Spirit of Jesus.

- The plot of the movie and the characters; Mike's choices, his wife, the elderly couple who care for him;

KEY SCENES AND THEMES

going against John Rooney, running away, running the banks, the final confrontation, and death.

- Michael and the movie's focus on his eyes: all that he saw at home, at the murder scene, at John Rooney's; his innocence and his dilemma about his father's good and his evil; his father protecting him; his love for his father yet his inability to shoot Maguire; his father dying in his arms and his return to the farm, never holding a gun; leading the life his father wanted for him.

- Fathers and sons: Mike Sullivan and his distance from his children, his grief at Peter's death, his protection of Michael; John Rooney's love for Mike and Mike's gratitude for being his foster father; John Rooney's knowledge that Connor was guilty but choosing to protect him, despite knowing this will mean condemning Mike to death.

FOR REFLECTION AND CONVERSATION

1. The use of iconography throughout the movie creates the atmosphere of an Irish-Catholic religious world: signs of the cross, grace at meals, wakes and prayers, funeral rituals, nuns at school, churches with altars and candles, Mass and Communion. How deep is the religion of the Rooneys and the Sullivans? Or is it merely nominal? How is the religious culture expressed in the film similar or different from that of *The Godfather* or *Angela's Ashes*? How does the Catholic faith really influence or impact the lives of the characters? What explains the choices they make? How does your religious faith influence the choices you make? Does it?

2. The characters in *Road to Perdition* know that they are doing wrong and that they need God's forgiveness

and forgiveness from each other. Do they seem to have free will? Roger Ebert said in his review of the film, "Choice, a luxury of the Corleones *(The Godfather),* is denied to the Sullivans and Rooneys, and choice or its absence is the difference between Sophocles and Shakespeare. I prefer Shakespeare." Do you agree? Why or why not? Is *Road to Perdition* a drama or a tragedy? Is the virtue of hope, as promised by the coming of the Holy Spirit on Pentecost, present in the film? If so, how? If not, why? What challenges faith, hope, and love in this story? How does the cinematography create a visceral "hell" for the audience?

3. There are three sets of father-son relationships in the film. between Mike and his son Michael, between John and Conner, and between foster father and son, John and Mike. John and Mike were very close, as illustrated by their piano duet. What brought them together and ultimately tore them apart? How are the gifts of the Holy Spirit (wisdom, understanding, counsel, fortitude, knowledge, piety, and fear of the Lord) shown in the film? How might they be said to form a framework for it? How can these gifts bring fathers and sons, indeed, all family members, closer together as we journey toward salvation?

Prayer

Lord, send us your Spirit so that our bodies, which are dead because of sin, can be filled with life and your forgiveness. Amen.

Contact

U.S.A., 1997, 160 minutes
Cast: Jodie Foster, Matthew McConaughey, Tom Skerritt,
James Woods, Angela Bassett, David Morse, John Hurt,
Rob Lowe, Jake Busey, Jena Malone
Writer: Michael Goldenberg
Director: Robert Zemeckis

Contact

Making Contact with the Transcendent

SYNOPSIS

Ellie Arroway had a loving father who encouraged her interest and research into extraterrestrial communication. He died when she was just nine years old. As an adult she pursues this interest as a career. She becomes Dr. Ellie, a radio astronomer for SETI—the Institute for the Search for Extraterrestrial Intelligence. Ellie scans the heavens for messages. When government support for her work is withdrawn, she receives help from a reclusive millionaire, S. R. Hadden. She moves from Puerto Rico, where she has been working (and where she has met and fallen in love with the religious adviser to the president of the United States), to New Mexico, and soon identifies a signal from space.

When the message from the large-magnitude star, Vega, is deciphered, it indicates that a giant spaceship should be built for further exploration. When it is ready, her hostile government adviser, Dr. Drumlin, is chosen to go into space instead of Ellie. When he is killed in an accident, Hadden puts up the money for an alternate spaceship and Ellie is chosen to be the astronaut.

Ellie is interrogated by the approval team about her suitability to make contact, especially about her belief in God.

178

They say that if she does not believe in God, then, as an unbeliever, she would not represent the beliefs of the majority of Americans. Ultimately, she leaves on her mission and experiences a transcendent illumination. She also meets her father, who is in a transformed state. However, there is no record of what transpires during her journey. All that remains is eighteen hours of static on the video. Humiliated by politicians, she retires to the desert to do research and teach but still searches the skies for signs of contact.

COMMENTARY

Carl Sagan (1934–1996) was an astronomer who popularized science through his writings and on television to make it more accessible to people. The film was in production when he died and is largely based on his novel of the same title. The director is Robert Zemeckis (*Back to the Future* series, *Forrest Gump, What Lies Beneath, Cast Away*).

As the scientist Dr. Arroway, Jodie Foster gives an intelligent performance that people can identify with. Most of the other actors create stereotypes (James Woods as the gung-ho political adviser) and fail to convince (Matthew McConaughey as the philosopher and presidential religious adviser). Footage of President Clinton is frequently included to give the film the feel of the 1990s. However, the movie does come together in a satisfying way at the end, when the viewer does not know where the plot is going, how the contact will be made, and what will be the consequences for us humans. As the screenplay and Sagan say: If there is no life out there in such vastness of space, what a waste!

DIALOGUE WITH THE GOSPEL

Focus: Dr. Ellie Arroway is searching for intelligent life beyond our world. The readings reveal God's vast creation, loving wisdom, hope that does not disappoint, and Jesus' promise to send the Spirit into our world.

The reading from Proverbs introduce a cosmic theme, that God, the Creator is greater than we are, that the world is greater than we imagine, and that God is eternal and not confined to a specific place.

St. Paul's Letter to the Romans reminds us that though we suffer, "affliction produces endurance, and endurance, proven character, and proven character, hope, and hope does not disappoint...." This could be a description of Ellie's journey, from the death of her father to her encounter with him and the final scenes of the film as she is grilled by Kitz, the National Security Advisor.

In the Gospel Jesus speaks of further revealing the mystery of God to his disciples: "I have much more to tell you, but you cannot bear it now." Jesus promises the fullness of revelation, the complete truth, which will be given to them by the Spirit of God whom Jesus will send.

Today's readings present, in symbols and language, the aspirations of people who share the Judeo-Christian faith tradition and of those who do not. These themes form the basis of the questions that Ellie Arroway confronts in *Contact*. She has a yearning for the transcendent inspired by her father, who eventually will reveal the truth of the universe to her. She searches, suffers, endures, and perseveres in humility and hope. Unsure of her beliefs, she is cross-examined and must declare herself to hardheaded government pragmatists as well as to Joss, the religious adviser to the president.

Whatever the mystic import of her space odyssey, she has been contacted and has made contact with the faith within her and with whatever is beyond this earth.

KEY SCENES AND THEMES

- Carl Sagan's comment (mentioned three times) that if there were no intelligent life in the universe, it would be a waste of space.

- Young Ellie, her skills, her relationship with her father; the mature Ellie and the flashbacks; her quest; hearing the message, deciphering the numbers, building the machine; the test and the disaster, the new flight and her space odyssey; her return to the reality of earth, the aftermath of the hearings, and her continued work; the chance encounter with Palmer, his studying for the ministry, celibacy, religious ideas, social ideas; giving her the compass and her treasuring it.

- Ellie and her hopes; issues about science and religion; Palmer Joss's questions; Ellie's inability to say that she believed in God; the way she presents herself as a scientist looking for proof; Ellie's voyage and the recording of static; the visual odyssey and Ellie's response to the beauty of space and to her mystical experience; her humility and the humiliation at the press conference, arguing about her experience and not having any proof for it; meeting with the school children and contemplating creation.

1. A dictum of the medieval theologian/philosopher William of Occam (c. 1285–1349) is repeated over and over in the film. It is known as "Occam's Razor": "one should not increase, beyond what is necessary, the number of entities required to explain anything." The "razor" means that scientists can (and should) "shave off" whatever is unnecessary to explain a phenomenon. How well does this principle work for the arguments made in the film? Do you think this principle can be applied to theology? Why or why not? Research Occam's Razor and how this truism has influenced modern science. Does this principle "permit" a role for religion in scientific research? What function did the principle serve in the film?

2. Michael Kitz, the national security advisor, tells Ellie that revealing news of a message received from outer

FOR REFLECTION AND CONVERSATION

space may constitute a breach of national security. She responds, "This isn't a person-to-person call. You can't possibly think that a civilization sending this kind of message would intend it just for Americans." Most films about outer space deal with unfriendly aliens, for example, *Independence Day* and more recently, *Signs*. *Contact*, like *E.T.: The Extra-Terrestrial* and *Close Encounters of the Third Kind* (both Spielberg films) show us "aliens" who are intelligent and "friendly." In a world and culture so concerned with the "aliens" among us, how might *Contact* be an important metaphor for how people of one nation or culture perceive and welcome people from a different culture? How does national centrism create the perception that all non-citizens are to be feared? Why is it risky for one country to perceive itself as the center of the universe, above others?

3. Ellie testifies at the government hearing: "I had an experience I can't prove and can't explain, but everything that I know as a human being tells me that it was real. I was given something wonderful that changed me forever. A vision of the universe that tells us undeniably that we belong to something that is greater than ourselves, and that none of us are alone." Was this a profession of faith on Ellie's part? Do you think this is where science and faith meet? Talk about some of the symbolism in the film, for example, at the end, when Ellie reaches from the car for Palmer's hand. Are science and faith compatible? Why or why not? How do you interpret the last scenes from the film, from Ellie talking to the children about life in the universe to her contemplating creation. How did these moments in the film make you feel? What might

the difference be between Ellie's faith, Palmer's religion, and your own?

Prayer
Lord, as we celebrate the very life of God, we pray for those who do not share our faith but who are searching for life's meaning and for you. Amen.

BODY AND BLOOD OF CHRIST
Genesis 14:18–20;
1 Corinthians 11:23–26;
Luke 9:11b–17

Eat Drink Man Woman
Taiwan, 1994, 124 minutes
Cast: Sihung Lung, Sylvia Chan, Yang Kuei-Mei,
Wang Yu-Wen, Winston Chao
Writers: Ang Lee, James Schamus, Wang Hui-Ling
Director: Ang Lee

Eat Drink Man Woman

Banquets

SYNOPSIS

A retired master chef, affectionately called Uncle Chu, lives with his three daughters and has lost his sense of taste. He is a widower of sixteen years and enjoys cooking for his family. There is a crisis at the restaurant where he worked and he is called back to supervise a major banquet before it becomes a disaster. He saves the day but will not return to work full time.

Although Uncle Chu lives with his daughters, they have grown apart, especially Chu and Jia-Chen, the middle daughter. The young women have begun to make their own lives. The older sister, Jia-Jen, is a Christian and rather prim. She teaches chemistry and is harassed by pupils who write her anonymous love letters. However, she is attracted to the new sports coach and suddenly marries him. Jia-Chen works as an executive for the airlines but delights in cooking. She has uneasy relationships with men. She has a liason with an art gallery owner who marries someone else but wants her to remain his "friend." She then strikes up a friendship with a co-worker who has a wife and child in America. The youngest daughter, Jia-Ning, works in a fast-food restaurant. She

184

befriends a young man whom she meets while he waits for another girl to get off work. She becomes pregnant and they marry. All three girls are friends with a young woman, Jin-Rong, who is in the process of getting a divorce. She lives next door and has a young daughter named Rachel. Uncle Chu fixes the little girl lunch every day and takes it to her at school.

Madam Liang, the mother of Jin-Rong and grandmother to Rachel, returns from America and pursues the available Uncle Chu. But Chu startles her and his own daughters by telling them he wants to marry Jin-Rong instead. He decides to sell his house to Jia-Chen when he marries. Time passes. His young wife is pregnant. The couples are busy with their own affairs. The middle daughter is still at home and her father visits her for a meal and discovers his taste has returned. They are reconciled.

COMMENTARY

Director and co-writer Ang Lee offers an arresting visual portrait of a Taiwanese family in *Eat Drink Man Woman*. He gives audiences a feel for life in Taipei and in Taiwan with a focus on food as love, sharing, delight, artistry, and communication. Other "food movies" include *Babette's Feast, Like Water for Chocolate, Big Night, Chocolat, Simply Irresistible, What's Cooking,* and *Dinner Rush.* In 2001, an American remake with a Latino flavor was released, *Tortilla Soup. Eat Drink Man Woman* was nominated for several awards, including the Oscar for Best Foreign Film in 1995.

Eat Drink Man Woman is a story of family and its strained relationships, of young women finding partners and roles in life, and of an aging man's past and future. The film treats its characters with irony and is at times funny, at other times melancholic. The recurring images of food and cooking give it a sensual texture that brings the emotional issues down to earth.

Focus: Meals are signs of sharing food in blessing and joy. This is the spirit of the feast of Corpus Christi and the generosity of Jesus who cares for the crowds. Eat Drink Man Woman *offers lavish images of sharing food, love, and reconciliation.*

The Body and Blood of Christ is a celebration of Jesus as the Bread of Life, the Food of Life. In the first reading from the book of Genesis, the King-Priest, Melchisedek, blesses bread and wine. Through this blessing, bread and wine are shown as symbols of the sacred nature of the food that Jesus will give us. This sacred theme is repeated in the reading from First Corinthians, but this time with the fullness of blessing: the presence of Jesus in the bread and wine. Both sharing Eucharist and sharing food are occasions for the presence of God in our world because both nourish, reconcile, and heal.

Eat Drink Man Woman celebrates the exquisite nature of food and the love that goes into its preparation. While the commemoration of the Lord's Supper is held on Holy Thursday, it is done so in the context of the passion of Jesus. The feast of Corpus Christi comes soon after Eastertide and celebrates the continuing presence of Christ in our midst in the Eucharist.

Those who sit at this Taipei table at the special meal respect the daughter and her new husband, who is a Christian, and she leads them in a prayer of blessing. These are people, like people everywhere, who are seeking their place in the kingdom of God. The Chu family lives amid tension and their relationships are at various times estranged. They, like so many families the world over, are like the crowd in the Gospel because they need healing. The father needs to recover his lost sense of taste, his colleague desires health, and his daughters need healing from disappointments in life.

The numerous cooking and eating sequences in the film are vivid and lavish. They remind us that food is a blessing.

Jesus blessed food and while he had only loaves and fish to feed the crowds, "they all ate and were satisfied" and the leftovers filled twelve baskets. Jesus fed the people abundantly, as did Uncle Chu. Jesus' feeding of the five thousand was an image of the eschatological banquet that will be ours in heaven. *Eat Drink Man Woman* provides rich images of food, feast, and celebration that prefigure the heavenly banquet to come.

KEY SCENES AND THEMES

- The opening meal with the father Chu; the loss of his sense of taste, his care with the preparation of a lavish meal; his daughters around him, estranged by their personal problems and unable to appreciate the food.

- The master chef at work; at home, preparations, herbs and spices, sauces, the cooking; his coming to the rescue at the banquet and the satisfaction of the guests and the staff.

- The daughter who loved cooking and her personal delight in preparing and serving food, but being unwelcome in her father's kitchen; the meals where revelations were made: the daughter leaving home because she is pregnant; the daughter marrying and introducing her husband; the father announcing his marriage and selling the house; the final meal with father and daughter, his criticism and his finding his sense of taste; their calling each other "daughter" and "dad" and their reconciliation.

FOR REFLECTION AND CONVERSATION

1. Of all the food movies, *Eat Drink Man Woman* has to be one of the most vividly produced. One reviewer called it "a cinematic dream." This film not only lets us see the beauty of Chinese cuisine, but we can practically taste and smell it as well. What is the significance

of the Sunday meal, even though only one member of the Chu family is Christian? How is this significant for the merging of the cultures of East and West in *Eat Drink Man Woman*? What other cultural contrasts are there (modern transportation versus traditional preparation of food; the roles of men and women; intergenerational relationships; notions of love and marriage; the ways that the fast-food restaurant compares to Uncle Chu's careful and beautiful presentation of food; a bad investment in a housing scheme versus living at home)? How does food connect the older generation to mainland China (might this be a subtext of the film)? What is the role of tradition in the culture of various countries today? How does food help a country's culture and values to endure?

2. *Eat Drink Man Woman* is a film that contains many sayings and proverbs about food that comment on friendship, family, and love. One daughter says that they communicate by eating, so what's wrong with karaoke? Another says that all her childhood memories are cooked into her existence. What does Chu's colleague mean when he said, "People die for money and birds die for food"? and "Good sound is not in the ear; good taste is not in the mouth; eat, drink, man, woman—is that all there is to life"? Is this a proverb or a riddle or both? Why? Recall other sayings that impressed you and talk about their "truth" in the context of the film and of your own life. Are memories of your own childhood "cooked" into your existence? If so, talk about some of them and what they mean for you now.

3. Talk about some of the Christian motifs in the film (dialogue, the daughter's demeanor, her choices, the images, etc.). Why do you think the director, Ang Lee,

decided to include a Christian in this movie? What are the other religious images or sequences in the film? How do the basic elements of life, death, love, marriage, children, and religious faith appear in the visual metaphor of preparing food? How often does your family gather together to break bread and communicate around and across the table? Did you ever time your family dinners? How long do they last? Why are they so short or what are the reasons when they last a little longer? Jesus showed great compassion when he fed the people rather than have them go and find their own food. How can compassion be a consistent ingredient in the meals we share with our families? How often do you attend the Sunday Eucharistic celebration or church services together? What characterizes the Eucharist that you share?

Prayer

Lord, you have given us the banquet as the image of heaven. Through our celebrations of the Eucharist may we share your bread of life in a spirit of heavenly joy. Amen.

Meg Ryan and Andy Garcia in *When a Man Loves a Woman*.

Isaiah 62:1–5;
1 Corinthians 12:4–11;
John 2:1–11

When a Man Loves a Woman

U.S.A., 1994, 125 minutes
Cast: Meg Ryan, Andy Garcia, Ellen Burstyn, Tina Majorino,
Philip Seymour Hoffman, Lauren Tom, Mae Whitman
Writer: Ronald Bass, Al Franken
Director: Luis Mandoki

When a Man Loves a Woman

Sign of Joy and Suffering

SYNOPSIS

Michael Green is an airline pilot, happily married to Alice. They have two young daughters and live comfortably in San Francisco.

It emerges that Alice is a secret alcoholic who has been drinking on the sly. She arrives home drunk one day and in a rage hits the older of the two little girls, the child she had with her first husband, whom Michael has now adopted. She collapses and is taken to a clinic to dry out. Michael tries to manage the children at home but finds it increasingly difficult. He cannot communicate with Alice. He visits her at the clinic and is pleased with her progress, but at the same time he senses her estrangement. She has made a number of new friends in this different world.

Alice's mother has been caring for the children. When Alice returns home, her personality seems to have changed. Sober, she is very critical and edgy and Michael does not know how to deal with this Alice. Gary, a friend from the clinic, comes to visit her and Michael finds them deep in conversation. This is the breaking point for Michael and he reacts angrily. Alice asks him to go to a counselor with her. The counselor recommends that he attend Al-Anon meetings for partners of alcoholics.

Michael moves out. When he visits one day, Alice invites him to come to listen to her talk at A.A. to mark her six months of sobriety, but he refuses. However, when she does tell her story to the other members of A.A., Michael is there.

COMMENTARY

The title of the movie comes from Arthur Wright and Calvin Lewis's song of the same name. *When a Man Loves a Woman* has the semblance of romance genre yet at the same time it is quite grim and realistic, thus making it a drama. Luis Mandoki *(White Palace, Born Yesterday, Message in a Bottle)* directed *When a Man Loves a Woman,* and all his films follow a similar theme. They are popular presentations of human dilemmas rather than movie treatises on their subject. When the film was released, some criticized it for its romantic middle-class setting with attractive stars when it should have been a sobering study of a prevalent human problem.

Meg Ryan is simultaneously cast in type as the pretty, suburban wife in a romance, and against type as the alcoholic wife. She has starred in many romantic comedies, such as *When Harry Met Sally, Sleepless in Seattle, I.Q.,* and *You've Got Mail,* and has successfully played more dramatic roles in *Restoration* and *Courage Under Fire.* Andy Garcia is a sympathetic Michael.

DIALOGUE WITH THE GOSPEL

Focus: The story of Cana is a joyful one and it evokes the image and reality of the sacraments of both matrimony and Eucharist. Michael and Alice are united in a marriage marred by alcohol abuse. They need to be transformed into their better selves.

The subtitle for the reading from the book of Isaiah is "The bridegroom rejoices in his bride." The text is a lyrical poem, an allegory about the Lord loving his people despite their having turned against God in the past. God is described as the "bridegroom" and Israel is the "bride." No more will God's people be called "forsaken."

The wedding feast at Cana was a very happy occasion. We see and hear very little from the bride and groom, perhaps because the focus of the Gospel account is on the wine and its joyful (and Eucharistic) symbolism. Mary, the mother of Jesus, is concerned that the celebration will lose its joy if the wine runs out and that the bridal couple will be embarrassed. Jesus, despite some symbolic hesitation, is lavish with the wine he provides and the feast is a success.

This movie's title points to the core of a marriage: the love between husband and wife. The early glimpses of Alice, Michael, and their family are of married happiness and delight. The couple, however, have to work through their problems for better or for worse. Despite Alice's alcoholic illness and Michael's inability to cope, the film seems to promise that they find their married happiness again. The Gospel reminds us that Jesus made the wedding at Cana a truly happy feast. When God is present in a marriage, despite the inevitable difficulties, the marriage is blessed.

Paul reminds us in today's second reading that we are not all the same. God's spirit works differently in each of us and each of us is invited to discern how the Spirit works. The Alcoholics Anonymous meetings portrayed in the film demonstrate in a practical way how each person does indeed have his or her own gifts to use for the good of all.

The Gospel ends with a reminder of the symbolic significance of the Cana story, which is ultimately a story of faith. The miracle at Cana is a glimpse of Jesus' glory, a sign of his grace in the world. An alcoholic who has begun the difficult work of recovery can likewise be a sign of faith, hope, and grace to family, friends, and colleagues.

KEY SCENES AND THEMES

- The portrait of a happy American household, loving mother and father and two daughters, good jobs, comfortable home, security, and happiness.

- The exposure of Alice's drinking, the performance between Alice and Michael at the bar, the seeming playfulness, but the reality of the drinking and its effect on Alice; the destruction of the happy atmosphere in the home, Alice returning drunk, hitting her daughter, the collapse.

- Alice in the clinic, the methods for dealing with alcoholics, her response, unwillingness, change, making friends; Michael's inability to cope at home; his reaction to Alice's irritability on her return and his blowing up when Gary visits; going to the counselor; Michael moving out; Alice's invitation for him to come to the A.A. meeting and hear her speech; his refusal, changing his mind, and hope for reconciliation.

FOR REFLECTION AND CONVERSATION

1. *When a Man Loves a Woman* is a difficult film wrapped in a pretty package with a moving song. It is about the havoc that the disease of alcoholism can wreak on a person, on relationships, on families. No one knows the real cause of alcoholism, but there seem to be genetic, psychological, and social reasons why a person has an uncontrollable craving for alcohol. Do we ever find out the causes for Alice's alcoholism? If so, what do you think they are? Do you agree that alcoholism is a disease? Why or why not?

2. Bill W. and Dr. Bob founded "Alcoholics Anonymous" in Akron, Ohio in 1935. They were able to achieve sobriety when they recognized alcoholism as a disease. Members follow a twelve step program that begins with the acknowledgment that alcoholics are powerless

over alcohol and they surrender themselves to the help of God (or a Higher Power). A.A. is for alcoholics, family members, and children of alcoholics, and the twelve step program has been applied to many other areas of addiction over the years. What are the twelve steps? (See www.alcoholics-anonymous.org.) Talk about what they mean for you in the light of the Scripture readings and the film.

3. Print out the lyrics to "When a Man Loves a Woman" (www.lyrics.com) or play the song from a CD. Talk about Michael's role in the marriage and in the film. Was he an enabler? Do you think he only viewed Alice and their family from his own perspective, for his own comfort? How could he have behaved differently at any point in the film? Would it have made any difference? Would the story be different if the roles were reversed? Do the words of the song describe what it really means for a man to love a woman? Why or why not? How can the mutual love of husband and wife survive alcoholism? What about the children? How can the contemplation of the wedding feast of Cana be put into practice in your life?

Prayer

Lord, the marriage feast at Cana was full of joy. Bless those who suffer any form of alcoholic or addiction illness and enable them to recover their sense of joy. Amen.

Remember the Titans
U.S.A., 2000, 114 minutes
Cast: Denzel Washington, Will Patton, Donald Faison,
Wood Harris, Ryan Hurst, Ethan Suplee,
Kip Pardue, Ryan Gosling
Writer: Gregory Allen Howard
Director: Boaz Yakin

 *Remember the Titans*

Leadership for the Sake of the Team

SYNOPSIS

Herman Boone is a successful African American football coach in South Carolina. In 1971, he is hired to be the head coach of the Titans, the team for the T. C. Williams High School in Alexandria, Virginia, which has recently been racially integrated. There is a tense atmosphere because the previous white coach, the very popular Bill Yoast, was not reappointed. However, Yoast has accepted the position of assistant to Boone.

Boone moves his family to Alexandria where they experience subtle forms of suspicion and hostility from their neighbors.

At training camp Boone puts his coaching methods into practice. His authoritarian manner irks most of the players, especially the white team members. While he makes demands on them, he also devises ways for the players to become aware of their prejudices, to get to know one another, and to meld into an efficient team. Yoast is supportive. A strong friendship develops between Gerry Bertier, the white captain, and Julius Campbell, the black quarterback.

The season's games are a challenge for the team and they become more conscious of the prejudice within the community. The team finally begins to win games; by the end of the season, they are victorious. A major difficulty arises when some of the officials try to get Boone dismissed. In the meantime, Yoast has been proposed for the state Hall of Fame. When he continues to support Boone against dismissal, his nomination is rejected.

As time goes on, the team is successful and the community begins to accept them. The struggles as well as the friendships are reflected among the team members. The undefeated Titans become state champions. There is a crisis when Gerry is paralyzed in a road accident. The film ends in 1981, when everyone assembles for Gerry's funeral.

COMMENTARY

Remember the Titans, based on a true story that took place in 1971, was a huge box-office success, a film that left audiences feeling uplifted and inspired.

Producer Jerry Bruckheimer is best known for his gung-ho action features like *Top Gun, The Rock, Con Air, Armageddon,* and *Pearl Harbor,* so it is surprising to see him back an inspiring sports movie. Director Boaz Yakin's previous work included smaller, independent movies about minorities, such as *Fresh,* a film about African American city-dwellers.

With Oscar winner Denzel Washington as the coach, the film can't be anything but inspirational. Will Patton is the white coach who is passed over but who becomes a true friend to the newcomer.

The film is a mixture of racial drama, sports action, emotional outbursts, reconciliation, and expressions of friendship. It wears its heart on its sleeve.

DIALOGUE WITH THE GOSPEL

Focus: Luke portrays Jesus as a great man, a leader with many qualities. Remember the Titans *presents Herman Boone as a great leader who broke down prejudices and built up not only his team, but also the community.*

Today's Gospel begins with Luke's introduction and explanation of what he was trying to do by narrating his version of Jesus' life and ministry. Like the great Greek and Roman historians, Luke wanted to paint a word portrait of a great and heroic man. He wanted to persuade his readers that Jesus was a great teacher who merited the faith his disciples placed in him.

Remember the Titans is a story of a sports hero, Herman Boone, told in much the same style. The real-life portrait pays homage to what this man stood for and achieved: belief in one's true self, racial equality, human dignity, and a commitment to the ethos of sport—playing for the sake of the game as well as for winning.

In the Gospel, Jesus is presented as the fulfillment of all hopes. Luke quotes the book of Isaiah to reinforce his point that Jesus is a leader and a teacher who is both kind and just and who inspires the best in those around him. Herman Boone is also this kind of man. In another parallel with Jesus' life, circumstances forced Boone to be tough in the way he approached his players as well as the authority figures. Were we to continue reading chapter four of Luke, we would see that Jesus also experienced hostility and suspicion in his own town, as Herman did, and was thrown out. The community in Alexandria offers parallels with the community in Nazareth.

While the Gospel focuses on the heroic leader and teacher, the second reading focuses on the body, the team. Paul describes the Christian community as one in which each member is inspired by the Spirit, but each has his or her own gift and function, each needs the other. There is no division in the body. Rather, says Paul, the parts have the same concern for one another: if one suffers, all suffer; if one is honored, all share the joy. One might say that Paul, who uses other sporting imagery at times, knows how to offer a pep talk to a team.

And the reading from Nehemiah? The whole community listens to the word of truth and then is invited to celebrate. Sports and its culture have led to a more just integration among people, which is a source of joy for all humanity.

- Herman Boone and his family moving to Alexandria and experiencing suspicion as well as overt hostility, especially to his wife and children; the newness of integration at the high school, the students' learning to cope, the football team training and playing together.

- Herman Boone's leadership and authority, a man of courage coming from a marginalized minority; his strict, even authoritarian training methods; his relationship to each team member and how he brings out the best in them; the achievements off the field as well as on; the breaking down of community prejudice.

- Boone's friendship with Bill Yoast; Yoast's having to deal with his own prejudices, issues about coaching, and of being an assistant to Boone; the crisis of his nomination and the plans to oust Boone; Yoast's honor and friendship with Boone.

1. "Civil rights" refers to political and social concepts by which the state (government) guarantees freedom, justice, and equality to all its citizens. This means equal opportunities and equal protection under the law. It also means that the government protects the rights to freedom of speech, religion, due process, and so forth. How do equality and liberty of the individuals and team members in *Remember the Titans* interface? Do you think this movie is realistic? Or does the film

manipulate our emotions? If so, what techniques does it use to do this? Do you think that the emotional experience of any film changes its truth? What is the "truth" of *Remember the Titans?*

2. The events in the film take place more than thirty years ago. Other films such as *Mississippi Burning* (1988), *To Kill a Mockingbird* (1962), and *Lilies of the Field* (1963) have depicted the harsh realities of those times. The films brought attention to the ongoing civil rights movement that eventually made the racial integration at T. C. Williams High School possible. *Cry Freedom* (1987) successfully contributed to the world's awareness of South Africa's apartheid system, which was not that different from the U.S.'s own Jim Crow segregation laws that existed until the 1960s. Racism has been the subject of filmmaking as recently as 1998 with *American History X,* which recounts the story of the legacy of racism passed down from father to son. How can *Remember the Titans* be seen as a film that is good for society?

3. If you were a teacher or pastoral minister, which clips would you select from *Remember the Titans* to illustrate today's Scripture readings? What kind of questions would you ask? How would you respond when children, teens, or adults make racial remarks or tell racist jokes? How can we exercise Christian leadership for the sake of the "body" that is the human family, in the face of racism of any kind?

Prayer

Lord, today you show us qualities of leadership. May we learn these qualities so that each of us contributes to the building up of your body, the church. Amen.

Good Will Hunting
U.S.A., 1997, 126 minutes
Cast: Matt Damon, Robin Williams, Stellan Skarsgård,
Minnie Driver, Ben Affleck
Writers: Ben Affleck, Matt Damon
Director: Gus Van Sant

Good Will Hunting

Overcoming Rejection

SYNOPSIS

Will Hunting works as a janitor at MIT in Boston. His friends are laborers from Boston's working-class South End. Will has incredible mathematical talent. While he is cleaning the floors one night, he secretly solves the theorem that a professor writes on a blackboard in the hallway as part of a contest. The teaching staff and students are amazed.

He is then urged by Professor Lambeau to study mathematics. Meanwhile, Will goes through life hanging out with his buddies and gets into a brawl with the cops that lands him in jail. Lambeau makes a deal with the judge to get Will out of jail. He has to study math and go for therapy. Will, bitter about being an orphan and about the abuse he suffered when he was young, deliberately frustrates the psychiatrists. Finally, one psychiatrist, Sean Maguire, really listens to him and challenges him. Will is difficult and, in turn, challenges the doctor. Maguire is patient and Will comes to a greater understanding of intimacy as he listens to Maguire talk about his loving relationship with his deceased wife.

Will dates a British medical student from Harvard named Skylar but is intimidated by the thought of commitment. He handles all crises with offhanded irony. His friends urge him to move on with his life and pursue his gifts. He thinks about Dr. Maguire's story and finally decides to follow Skylar to California in search of his own life.

COMMENTARY

Good Will Hunting received nine Oscar nominations, including Best Picture. Writers and stars Matt Damon and Ben Affleck won the award for Best Original Screenplay and Robin Williams won Best Actor in a Supporting Role. The movie touched a chord with American audiences and was popular all around the world.

Matt Damon, who starred in *The Rainmaker, Saving Private Ryan, The Talented Mr. Ripley, The Legend of Baggar Vance,* and *The Bourne Identity,* is Will Hunting. Stellan Skarsgård *(Breaking the Waves)* plays the ambitious professor. Robin Williams is the therapist, Sean Maguire. Williams has portrayed an unconventional teacher *(Dead Poets Society)* and unconventional doctors *(Awakenings, Patch Adams).* Here he employs a more subdued approach and has moments of great wisdom and tenderness in his encounters with Will.

Gus Van Sant *(Drugstore Cowboy, My Own Private Idaho, To Die For)* directed this film, as well as *Finding Forrester* in 2000, which revisited several of the themes about human dignity found in *Good Will Hunting.*

DIALOGUE WITH THE GOSPEL

Focus: At first, Jesus won the approval of all. Then those who thought they knew him best rejected him and ousted him from Nazareth. Will Hunting is gifted and has experienced rejection. He now needs to understand love.

The first reading recounts the call of the young and reluctant prophet, Jeremiah. We are reminded that a person's vocation is something that transcends fears and one's sense of inadequacy. It is a summons to be our better selves. Will Hunting is a young man with a strong sense of inadequacy, despite his many talents.

The Gospel takes up the story of Jesus' vocation and the response of the people of Nazareth who knew him. At first they are charmed by his graciousness, and then they turn on him, questioning his right to be who he is since he is only "the son of Joseph," one of them.

Jesus replies that those who think they know him but who in actuality do not understand him reject prophets. Will Hunting has experienced rejection by his family and foster parents and now he suspects that Professor Lambeau wants to use him to boost his own professional standing. Will learns that things can be different through the wisdom of his psychiatrist, the love of Skylar, and the genuine friendship and support of his friends.

At the end of the film, Will, though for reasons different from those of Jesus as he left Nazareth, has to slip through the crowd of those with high expectations and go on his own life's journey. Much of the motivation for this is because he discovers he loves Skylar. He is urged to follow her for the sake of this love, which, as Paul tells us in the second reading, is above all else.

KEY SCENES AND THEMES

- Will Hunting's world: Boston, the neighborhoods, universities, cafés and bars, working-class areas; the contrast with the world of education, lectures, mathematics, solving puzzles, theories and theorems; Will's intellectual ability, the way he defends himself in court, his demeanor at the office of the prospective employer, his arguments with the student in the bar; his poor self-image.

- The montage of visits to the psychiatrists; the encounters with Dr. Maguire, growing trust, the discussions about paintings and Maguire's wife; Dr. Maguire standing up to Will yet listening; his patience with Will;

Maguire's discussions about reading things in books and the contrast with experience, the nature of intimacy; revealing his love for his wife, the story of his missing the historic game because of his love for her.

- Will's self-image: the gradual revelation of his being violently abused as a child, the police records; his encounter with and his love for Skylar and his gradual transformation; Will's friends and the blue-collar life and job; their urging him to move on; his decision to leave because of love for Skylar; finding his own vocation.

FOR REFLECTION AND CONVERSATION

1. Who is a friend? To what extent will friends sacrifice for one another? How do Will's friends try to save him from disaster? Will's friend Chuckie tells him, "You're sitting on a winning lottery ticket. It would be an insult to us if you're still around here in twenty years." What does he mean by this? Who are Will's true friends? Re-read Paul's description of love from First Corinthians. How do Will and his friends live this kind of love? How do St. Paul's and Dr. Maguire's images of love parallel each other?

2. All three readings today depict conflict or a response to conflict, even Paul's description of love. Will lived in inner conflict and created external conflict on his journey to find himself. The readings are also about vocation: following the call. What is yours? Examine any conflict in your own life and see how it might be tied to the call to follow God in love and fidelity. What is Will's "lottery ticket"? How are our gifts linked to our vocation in life?

3. One of the most moving scenes in the film is when Dr. Maguire finally gets Will to admit that the conflict

and abuse he experienced as a child were "not his fault." Perhaps many of us have had similar experiences. And perhaps we blame ourselves for things that happened to our families or to us as children. How did this scene in the film make you feel about Will, about your own life, or about the experiences of people with whom you live or whom you care about? What did the scene have to do with Will's growing in freedom and dignity as a human person?

Prayer

Lord, many men and women feel rejected and lost. They are often unable to see and appreciate their gifts and talents. May they experience the love of friends that gives them confidence in themselves and in you. Amen.

FIFTH SUNDAY OF THE YEAR

Isaiah 6:1–2a, 3–8;
1 Corinthians 15:1–11;
Luke 5:1–11

The Outlaw Josey Wales

U.S.A., 1976, 135 minutes
Cast: Clint Eastwood, Sondra Locke, Chief Dan George,
Sam Bottoms, John Vernon
Writers: Philip Kaufman, Sonia Chernus
Director: Clint Eastwood

The Outlaw Josey Wales

A Call and Its Consequences

SYNOPSIS

Just before the end of the Civil War, Josey Wales farms his spread in Missouri and lives contentedly with his wife and son. When marauding Union soldiers attack, they destroy his house and kill his wife and child. Josey Wales buries them and tries to accept this as God's will. Soon, however, a spirit of revenge takes over.

He joins a group of Confederate soldiers to track down the killers. At the end of the war, the soldiers are urged to take the oath of loyalty to the Union. They start to do so but are betrayed by the Union officers. Josey is suspicious and counters the attack, killing many of the Union soldiers. All but two of his own companions are killed. Josey and a young soldier escape, becoming fugitives. His captain, who is unaware of what really happened, stays with the Union soldiers and vows to track Josey down.

Soon, Josey's companion dies. As he moves through the landscapes of the West, Josey encounters a number of people who are wandering and lost. They attach themselves to him. One is an old Indian, Lone Watie, who says he has been "civilized" and so has "lost his edge" because he can no longer creep up on people unawares. Another is a young woman,

Laura Lee, who seems mentally unstable, and her grand-mother, Sarah.

Josey and Lone Watie head for Mexico and on the way they rescue Laura Lee and the grandmother from attack. The women are traveling to some property in a valley called Santo Rio, "the holy river." The men decide to guide them there. Grandma welcomes everyone to her broken-down home, left to her by her dead son. Josey makes peace with the Indians in the area and they exchange "words of life." When there is a confrontation with bounty hunters looking for him, Josey and his band defend themselves, shooting from the special windows with cruciforms in them. There is a final silent confrontation with his old captain and the town's people protect him. Life has now changed for Josey Wales, making him more human, a man purged of hatred. His journey ends in peace.

COMMENTARY

The Outlaw Josey Wales is a significant movie in Clint Eastwood's exploration of stories of the American West and many think it is his best. The other Westerns he directed are *Bronco Billy, Pale Rider,* the harsh *High Plains Drifter,* and his Oscar-winning movie, the grimmest of them all, *Unforgiven,* made in 1992.

Eastwood was well prepared to pursue these themes of revenge, healing, and peacemaking. His television apprenticeship was served in the popular series *Rawhide.* Sergio Leone turned him into a star in the 1960s as the character "The Man with No Name." Apart from Woody Allen, he is the most prolific of the movie stars turned director, with almost thirty movies to his credit.

The Outlaw Josey Wales is a spectacular action movie, re-creating the lawless post-Civil War period and the West of the pioneers. Relationships between whites and Native Americans are important. Chief Dan George is the old chief who has lost his edge but not his intelligence or sense of humor.

Sondra Locke appears in one of her several roles in Eastwood movies as the young woman, Laura Lee.

The screenplay is based on a book, *Gone to Texas,* by Forrest Carter.

DIALOGUE WITH THE GOSPEL

Focus: Today we listen to the call of Isaiah and to the call of Peter. Josey Wales did not know he was "called," but on his quest for revenge and flight from his pursuers, he discovers the futility of vengeance and leads his followers to a land of peace.

The first reading is that of the call of the prophet Isaiah. While a statesman of great reputation, he is humbled in the awesome presence of God in the Temple. He discovers a profound sense of his own sinfulness. The overwhelming experience leads him to understand and willingly accept that he is to be the instrument and the messenger of God.

Paul writes to the Corinthians about how God's call for messengers is extended to everyone because it is God's grace that makes us who and what we are, even if we have a "past" as Paul did. Paul acknowledges that he is the least of the apostles and testifies to the power of God's grace.

The Gospel offers another example of how God chooses messengers and apostles. Four fishermen on the Sea of Galilee, with no credentials except their skills at their trade, are called by Jesus to follow him. They are destined to be the core of the group that would preach the kingdom of God. Peter, like Isaiah in the Temple, has a sense of overpowering awe and of his own sinfulness. Jesus reassures him when he lowers his net at Jesus' command and had a huge haul of fish. A fine fisherman, now he will even more successfully "fish" for people.

Josey Wales does not hear an immediate call as did Isaiah, Paul, or Peter. His experience of God is gradual and begins with his suffering; "the Lord he gives, the Lord he takes away," he prays as he buries his wife and child. First anger, then the need for revenge, and finally the desire to escape motivate him on his journey through the West.

And yet, he seems to have been called to something higher, to a personal cleansing, like Isaiah, Paul, and Peter; and to achieve this, he must go on a quest for salvation. As he goes on his quest, he becomes somewhat like Jesus, not only as one called but through his leadership, calling others. They follow confidently. We see his rag-tag band of disciples following him until they reach his promised land, Santo Rio, "the holy river."

- Josey Wales working the fields, the sound of the renegade soldiers and their destruction; burying his wife and son with the words, "Ashes to ashes, dust to dust," and the words of Job, "the Lord he gives, the Lord he takes away"; the stick cross falling on his shoulders.

- Setting out on his revenge quest and his being consumed by it; the fight with the soldiers and his escape; the young soldier; the encounters on his journey: the carpetbagger, the Indian chief trying to creep up on him, the attack on the young woman and her grandmother; crossing the river; the image of Josey Wales and his followers on the horizon of the landscape; master and disciples.

- The revenge and the confrontation with the killers and its effect on Josey Wales; the fight to protect the homestead; the decision to leave, then to stay; final confrontation with his old captain and the protection by the town's people.

KEY SCENES AND THEMES

1. *The Outlaw Josey Wales* is considered by some to be Clint Eastwood's best movie. What is the moral of the story for you? Its message? Does it have one? Why or why

FOR REFLECTION AND CONVERSATION

not? Do you think that Josey is a good person? Does he have a conscience? Talk about your responses. Why do the others follow him? The film came out in 1976, just after the end of the Vietnam War. At one point, Josey tells the bounty hunter as they face off with guns, "This isn't necessary. You could just ride on." What happens? Could this film be understood as a statement about war and violence and "men with guns," similar to films such as *Men with Guns, The Magnificent Seven,* and *A Few Good Men?*

2. The film is an interesting "parallel" to the Scripture readings today. What is the "call" that Josey receives? Does it come all at once or is it in the choices he encounters? What is the turning point for him? What is the role of conscience in his transformation? How might the journey of Josey Wales be a metaphor for the inner life? Does he learn humility, and if so, when? How?

3. *The Outlaw Josey Wales* is a finely made film. Eastwood has admitted his admiration for the paintings of Charles M. Russell, the famous artist from Montana who is known for his delicate use of cross light in his portraits of Western landscapes. Eastwood has recreated these scenes in the carefully constructed shots and camera angles. What kind of response do shots like these evoke from the viewer? What is the role of the music in the film? How do sound and image help create the ambiance, the feelings, and ultimately the meaning of the story in this film, or any film? What are your thoughts at the conclusion of the viewing and at hearing the Word of God proclaimed in today's readings?

Prayer

Lord, you have called the messengers of your Gospel in mysterious ways. Continue to call them in our times and give them the courage they need. Amen.

SIXTH SUNDAY OF THE YEAR

Jeremiah 17:5–8;
1 Corinthians 15:12, 16–20;
Luke 6:17, 20–26

Shine

Australia, 1996, 105 minutes
Cast: Geoffrey Rush, Armin Mueller-Stahl, Noah Taylor,
John Gielgud, Lynn Redgrave, Googie Withers, Sonia Todd
Writer: Jan Sardi
Director: Scott Hicks

 *Shine*

Ultimately Blessed

SYNOPSIS

David Helfgott is an Australian child prodigy, a pianist whose father, Peter, instills in him a love for music. Peter, a Polish Jew who survived the Holocaust, has bitter memories of his own violin being smashed by his father and he tightly controls David's musical training. David is successful in local music competitions and even wins a medal. When he wins a scholarship to study in the United States, his father persuades him to turn it down and stay at home.

When David is invited to study at the Royal Academy of Music in London, he defies his father and accepts. Peter is tormented by memories of how the Holocaust tore his family apart and he is determined that nothing will break up his family, not even his son's musical education. But David goes to England just the same. David enjoys studying there with Cecil Parkes and pushes himself to the limit. While playing Rachmaninoff's notoriously difficult Third Concerto in public, he collapses and has a nervous breakdown.

Back in Australia, David is institutionalized and goes many years without seeing his family. His father eventually comes to visit him but walks out, leaving David's gold medal on the table. When David is released, he plays the piano in restaurants in Perth. Sylvia, the manager of one of them, befriends David and takes him on a holiday. She also introduces him to her friend, Gillian the astrologist. Eventually, Gillian and David marry. David gives a performance that is successful, goes on the concert circuit and visits his father's grave.

Shine is based on the life of pianist David Helfgott, born in Australia in 1947 to Jewish migrants. He played "The Flight of the Bumble Bee" live at the Academy Awards ceremony in March 1997, where *Shine* and its director, Scott Hicks *(Snow Falling on Cedars, Hearts in Atlantis)*, were nominated for Oscars.

COMMENTARY

David Helfgott is portrayed with enormous skill by the young Noah Taylor and, later, by Geoffrey Rush *(Elizabeth, Shakespeare in Love, Quills, Lantana, Frida)* in his Oscar-winning performance.

Armin Mueller-Stahl plays Peter Helfgott as a man in such pain that it is frightening.

Focus: The scriptures today contrast the difference between a blessing and a curse. Pianist David Helfgott and his dominating father show us the fruit of blessings and the pain and curse of conflict as a metaphor for the difference between good and evil, hope and despair.

DIALOGUE WITH THE GOSPEL

Both the reading from Jeremiah and the responsorial psalm highlight the contrast between the good and the bad, the blessed and the cursed. The image of the bad man or woman is that of dry scrub (sparse vegetation) in the wasteland and of winnowed chaff (grain separated from its husks). On the other hand, the image of a good person is that of a tree by the water's edge; its leaves never fade and it is fruitful even in drought.

Luke's version of the Beatitudes and of the woes, or "curses" shows Jesus' application of the contrast between good and evil in the human spirit.

David Helfgott suffered a mental breakdown. He is shown as poor, hungry, weeping, and driven out, even by his father. According to the Beatitudes, he would finally laugh and be satisfied. His father, on the other hand, an honorable man who could not see how he was living his own life through his son's talents, rejects his son (and himself) when David does not win the expected awards. When his moments of "glory through his son" diminish, he experiences an unfulfilled hunger for success and weeps, though not with beatitude joy. Peter Helfgott was a man in need of the Beatitudes.

The Beatitudes are not an exact commentary on the lives of David and Peter Helfgott—whose name means "the help of God." *Shine* reminds us of the contrast between the guidance of good spirits and the influence of evil. We need discernment. David Helfgott was blessed that at the age of almost forty, he found friends who supported him and a wife who would love, appreciate, and care for him. He has also learned how to enjoy life and to share his music with others, so that they, too, could experience the gift of beatitude blessing.

KEY SCENES AND THEMES

- David in London: Cecil Parkes and the discussions about Rachmaninoff's Third; learning the notes, then expressing the spirit and the emotion of the piece; the cast of Rachmaninoff's hand and the hopes for David's future; his dazzling performance of Rachmaninoff, his father listening on the radio, the final triumph, his collapse, the close-up on his glazed eye.

- His father reading about him in the newspaper, going to visit him, putting the medal on his neck, wanting to tell his violin story but David's saying he didn't know it; the effect of his father's presence, the empty doorway, and his father walking away.

- David supported by his friends, the meeting with Gillian, their wedding; going with Gillian to visit his father's grave, the reflection on his life, and on the influence of his father.

1. David's father was a secular Jew, contemptuous of religion and the soul in a post-Holocaust world. He worshipped music and his family. To raise funds for his son to go overseas for training, he does permit him to study the scriptures and to make his bar mitzvah. Later, he forbids David to go abroad to study and when David disobeys, he disowns him. What makes Peter Helfgott the way he is? What hope was there for him and his family? What could he have done differently regarding David? Do you think Peter was really a nonbeliever? Why or why not? How are religion, family, and survival mixed together in this film? Do you think the film exaggerates the chasm between David and his father for dramatic effect? Why or why not?

2. A cursory look at *Shine* may lead us to think it is about goodness (David) and evil (Peter, the father). However, what happens if we consider David as the fulfillment of hope in God and the future of humanity and Peter as representing the downtrodden, the victims, the despairing—those in need of a world that lives the Beatitudes? Have you ever met someone you thought was "evil" and later found out that they were "hopeless" instead? Did you discern the situation and change your manner in regard to that person? If so, how?

3. Go through the Beatitudes one by one. How are the Beatitudes "practical"; in other words, how do you think they help us to live the Christian life in con-

crete ways? What is Christian morality ("Living in a way worthy of our dignity as human beings and God's adopted children," *Basic Catechism,* p. 154)? What other films have you seen that demonstrate Christian morality? How and why is morality about the love of God rather than mere conformity to laws? Was David obligated to obey his father? Why or why not? How do the Ten Commandments and the Beatitudes compliment the other? How are love and hope demonstrated in *Shine?*

Prayer

Jesus, you spoke of blessings for those who suffer. May those who are in pain of body or soul feel your comfort and support. Amen.

Cuba Gooding Jr. in *As Good as It Gets*.

As Good As It Gets

U.S.A., 1997, 138 minutes
Cast: Jack Nicholson, Helen Hunt, Greg Kinnear,
Cuba Gooding Jr., Skeet Ulrich, Shirley Knight
Writers: Mark Andrus, James L. Brooks
Director: James L. Brooks

As Good As It Gets

Compassion Is Possible

Melvin Udall is a reclusive writer who lives in New York. He is plagued with obsessive-compulsive phobias and exhibits bigotry toward all minorities. He continually mocks his gay artist neighbor, Simon, and loathes Simon's dog. At the local restaurant where he eats breakfast every day he is dependent on his favorite waitress, Carol, to serve him, because she tolerates his boorish behavior.

SYNOPSIS

When Simon is assaulted by robbers and hospitalized, Melvin is forced to take care of the dog. To his surprise and pleasure, Melvin starts to grow attached to the animal. One day, Carol misses work because her son, who suffers from asthma, gets sick. Because the other waitresses avoid him, Melvin arranges to have a good doctor care for the boy so that Carol can come back to the restaurant. Carol is suspicious of his generosity but accepts it in the end.

Melvin gradually befriends Simon and agrees to drive him to Baltimore to see his parents to ask for financial help. He asks Carol to accompany them because he doesn't want to drive alone with a gay man. Simon rediscovers his painting abilities and does a portrait of Carol. She becomes angry with

Melvin on the trip because he is so obtuse. Melvin listens to Simon's advice. He goes to Carol to express his love for her.

COMMENTARY

This movie is a wry comedy from the writer-director of *Terms of Endearment* and *Broadcast News,* James L. Brooks. He shows sympathy for a wide range of characters, especially those who are annoying and cantankerous and gradually reveal their more humane side.

Jack Nicholson, in an Oscar-winning performance, is Melvin, a rude, prejudiced, obsessive writer. Nicholson relishes the opportunity to be manic. Helen Hunt, star of television's *Mad About You,* also won an Oscar and subsequently starred in several more hits, *Cast Away, What Women Want,* and *Pay It Forward.* Greg Kinnear *(Sabrina, Dear God, We Were Soldiers)* plays the gay artist with humour and pathos.

This trio are not stock cutout characters because Brooks and his cast take us below surface eccentricities. There are some fine scenes where each character gets to make a speech about being a better person for having met the other. When the movie ends, we can believe that there can be life after the final fade-out.

DIALOGUE WITH THE GOSPEL

Focus: Jesus' sermon about loving enemies presents a high ideal, one that sometimes seems too difficult to live up to. When Carol encounters an annoying character like Melvin Udall, this ideal moves beyond difficult to seemingly impossible. Through compassion, the three main characters in this film all learn to love.

Jesus' sayings in today's Gospel form part of Luke's version of the Sermon on the Mount. Jesus elaborates on the theme: "Love your enemies." We are prepared for the Gospel by a rather exciting action story in the first reading, where David has an opportunity to kill Saul but does not do so. It is a very dramatic example of loving one's enemies, of doing good instead of evil.

Melvin Udall is an obnoxious bigot who enjoys offending people, frequently using cutting remarks, especially to get his own way. At the beginning of the movie it seems inconceivable that he will change. But he does. And not only does he change! He begins to put into action the advice that Jesus urges on his listeners—to love not only our neighbors but our enemies as well.

Early in the movie, in the psychiatrist's waiting room, Melvin asks the other patients, "Is this as good as it gets?" It does, in fact, get better. Whatever the motivation is that changes Melvin, he opens up to people he would ordinarily ignore or despise. Even though he initially tossed Simon's dog down the garbage chute, the dog's affection for him influences him for the better. Carol, the waitress, pays attention to Melvin and reprimands him for his bad behavior. This allows him to express his need for help and for love. Although Melvin pays for her son's treatment, it is so that she will be free to wait on him, hardly an unconditional gift at first. But for Melvin it is certainly more than he ordinarily would have done and is beyond what he needed to do.

True change came about for Melvin in regard to his gay neighbor, Simon. After the brutal assault, and despite himself, Melvin acts like the Good Samaritan and discovers a greater capacity for love than he ever could have imagined. When Simon loses his apartment, Melvin offers him a room in his own home, though he can't resist making gibes.

Melvin, Carol, and Simon, each in their own way, show great compassion. Jesus says when we behave with mercy we act like God. By the end of the film, the characters have stopped judging one another and "good measure" is given unto all.

- Melvin at his most phobic and mean, with the dog, mocking Simon and his sexuality, the Jewish custom-

KEY SCENES AND THEMES

ers in the restaurant, with Carol's actress friend, with her sick son, with the Hispanic woman at his door; Melvin's phobias, the locks on his door, cleanliness, cutlery, gloves, the way he packs his suitcase and walks down the street skipping the cracks in the sidewalk.

• Carol and her work, her firmness with Melvin, her control of him by reprimanding him and demanding that he apologize and be honest; her care for her son and her relationship with her mother; Melvin's complimenting Carol that he is a better man because he knows her; his speech about her being a wonderful woman; the authentic generosity of his praise; Carol's ambivalence because of his instability.

• Simon and the assault, the hospital, his disfigurement, his loss of money and his desire to paint; Melvin's taunts; the dog's affection for him; Melvin's mellowing, his being pleasant to Simon and generous to Carol and her son; his unwillingness to be thanked; driving Simon to Baltimore to ask for his parents' help; Simon's sketching Carol and the bond between them; Simon encouraging Melvin to declare his love to Carol.

FOR REFLECTION AND CONVERSATION

1. Obsessive-compulsive disorder is a mental illness that affects 1.5 to 2 percent of adults in the United States. Recurring thoughts that compel the person to engage in certain behaviors, like repeatedly washing one's hands, and rituals that involve repeatedly checking things, such as whether or not the door is locked, characterize the disorder. The roots are often a combination of biological and/or psychological factors. As the film teaches us, psychotherapy and certain

drugs can help people with the anxiety disorder. What do you think of the way Carol responded to Melvin? If you know people like Melvin, what strategies do you use to maintain boundaries yet still respect the dignity of the person? Talk about the challenge to be the kind of Christian Jesus describes in today's Gospel when you find yourself in situations with people who may be living with the burden of mental or emotional illness.

2. One of the filmmakers' accomplishments in *As Good As It Gets* is that the film brings humor to the human condition without ridicule. Yet we see the struggle between the three main characters to respect the other without becoming personal. In fact, Carol with Melvin and Melvin with Simon are guilty of insulting the other and then reminding the other not to descend to the level of rudeness. It's as if they are struggling between what Paul describes as earthly and heavenly. How do they accept "correction" from one another? Is it always easy for them? When relationships are difficult for us, which level of response do we choose?

3. One of the seven principles of Catholic social teaching, if not the main one, is that of human dignity. Talk about how each of the main characters, Carol, Melvin, Simon, Carol's mother, her son and the doctor, embody and express human dignity toward one another. Recall Melvin's remarks to Simon and to the young secretary at the publishing company, to the Jewish customers at the restaurant, to the waitresses. How does he change? Why does he change? Are Melvin's changes permanent, or do you think he will always be a work in progress? Are we ever done striv-

ing to be more Christ-like? How is *As Good As it Gets* a parable of the Christian life (or of any life that seeks to be more fully human)?

Prayer

Even today, Lord, your advice to love our enemies astounds us. Help us to love and to achieve what otherwise seems to be impossible. Amen.

Sirach 24:4–7;
1 Corinthians 15:54–58;
Luke 6:39–45

Amadeus

U.S.A., 1984, 170 minutes (director's cut, 2002, 190 minutes)
Cast: Tom Hulce, F. Murray Abraham, Roy Dotrice,
Elizabeth Berridge, Jeffrey Jones, Charles Kay,
Simon Callow, Kenny Baker, Cynthia Nixon
Writer: Peter Shaffer
Director: Milos Forman

Amadeus

Blind Jealousy

SYNOPSIS

Antonio Salieri is aging, suicidal, and confined to an institution. He reminisces with the chaplain about his life, his career as a musician, and his hatred for Wolfgang Amadeus Mozart. Salieri contemplates his jealousy of Mozart's music and it continues to consume him. He claims that he murdered Mozart.

Salieri's narration flashes back to Vienna in the 1780s. Salieri is composer-in-residence to Joseph, Emperor of Austria, when he encounters the young prodigy, Mozart, at a reception. Salieri cannot understand how Mozart can be capable of composing such glorious music when he is such a frivolous and vulgar character. Mozart, who came from Salzburg and was trained by his father, lives a partly dissolute life while fulfilling the musical composition requirements of a court appointment. He marries Costanza.

Although he is continually short of money, Mozart's career blossoms with a variety of compositions and successful operas, especially *The Marriage of Figaro* and *The Magic Flute*. Salieri, on the other hand, finds only modest and conventional success. He becomes more and more jealous of Mozart.

Mozart, who is haunted by the memory of his father, composes *Don Giovanni.*

Salieri plots Mozart's downfall and death. In disguise, he hires the poverty-stricken Mozart to write a requiem that he will claim as his own and will play at Mozart's funeral. Mozart's wife, disgusted by his inability to provide for the family, takes their young son and leaves him. Mozart collapses at the opening of a "vaudeville" he has written for cash instead of working on the Requiem. Salieri, though he is consumed by envy, takes him home. Salieri knows the Requiem is a masterpiece and offers to write down the remainder of the piece as Mozart dictates it. Mozart dies and is buried in a pauper's grave. Salieri lives out his life lamenting continually to God about his own limitations and about the genius of Mozart.

COMMENTARY

Peter Shaffer's 1979 play, *Amadeus,* was one of the impressive theatrical events of its time. It celebrated Mozart and his music while showing him to be an immature and superficial young man despite his enormous gifts and talents. Milos Forman's 1984 film, with the screenplay by Shaffer, continues to give viewers an inside look at Mozart through Tom Hulce's Oscar-nominated performance as a vigorous, giggling, and vulgar genius. Forman, who won the Best Director Oscar for *One Flew Over the Cuckoo's Nest* in 1975, again won an Oscar for *Amadeus* in 1984. The film garnered the Best Film Oscar that year as well.

Though the film centers around Mozart, it was F. Murray Abraham who won the Oscar for Best Actor in his role as Antonio Salieri. He offers a twofold performance as the middle-aged and as the old Salieri, and he is equally successful with both.

The movie is a "period piece"; its costumes are sumptuous as is the production design. *Amadeus* was filmed in Prague and re-creates the elegance of the eighteenth century. The extensive music repertoire is by Neville Marriner.

Focus: Jesus speaks of blind guides, of the disciple who sees the speck in his brother's eye but not the plank in his own, and of knowing a tree by its fruit. Antonio Salieri is a powerful example of being a blind and jealous master musician and a tree that bears evil fruit.

The reading from Sirach focuses on judging people from what they say, "So too does one's speech disclose the bent of one's mind. Praise no one before they speak, for it is then that people are tested." This is not always true of Wolfgang Amadeus Mozart, because so much of his talk was that of an irresponsible youth. His speech did not reveal his inner abilities. Sirach's words, however, are very true of the portrayal of Salieri. His flaws are instantly apparent and his words betray the depths of his passionate hatred.

The Gospel is proclaimed after a responsorial psalm that begins with a glorification of music. Salieri illustrates Jesus words from "the Sermon on the Plain" because he reveals himself to be a blind guide who is obsessed with seeing the splinters in Mozart's character and behavior, unable to notice the wooden beam of jealousy in his own. At the end of his life, awaiting the "sting of death" because of his sins and confined to a mental institution, he is tormented because he can now see the beam in his own eye.

Jesus says that such a person is a hypocrite. The core of *Amadeus* shows how Salieri lived out his hypocrisy. He made a pact with Jesus on the crucifix as a young man, but even that promise was flawed because Salieri's own glory was one of the conditions. He undermined Mozart at court while pretending to be his patron; he exploited his position with the emperor; he hired the innocent maid to spy on Mozart while pretending to be generous; and, finally, he schemed to steal Mozart's Requiem and pretended to be his friend at the end.

Salieri produces bad fruit because he has sold his soul for success. There is little goodness in his heart for him to draw from; instead, he draws from his store of evil jealousy and rage. He is frustrated by the image he desires for himself and by his inability to fulfill it. The "fullness of his heart" destroys him, even as he sought to destroy Mozart.

KEY SCENES AND THEMES

- Salieri in his old age, demented, destroyed, and consumed by envy; his laments and his grievances as he tells his story to the priest; Salieri in his final private hell; having rejected Jesus, he is alone with himself, his memories, and his madness.

- Salieri's story and his pact with the crucifix; his initial encounters with Mozart; his shock at Mozart's vulgarity, his schoolboy giggles, and his humor; Salieri's irritation at Mozart's unwitting criticism of his welcoming composition; being overwhelmed by Mozart's music while wanting to see himself as the genius; rejecting his covenant with God and railing against him.

- The beauty of Mozart's music in comparison with that of Salieri; music as a gift of God; Mozart's compulsion to compose the Requiem; his inspired genius.

FOR REFLECTION AND CONVERSATION

1. Salieri tells Jesus on the crucifix: "From now on we are enemies, you and I. Because you choose for your instrument a boastful, lustful, smutty, infantile boy and give me only the ability to recognize the incarnation. Because you are unjust, unfair, unkind I will block you, I swear it. I will hinder and harm your creature on Earth as far as I am able. I will ruin your incarnation." What is Salieri's image of God? How is it expressed from his early life on? Compare his vision of God with that of Mozart's. Why do you think the film uses Salieri's relationship with Jesus on the crucifix as its consistent visual and theological theme? How does

the title *Amadeus* (meaning "love God" or "lover of God") create a framework for the story?

2. Do Salieri's and Mozart's relationships with God have anything to do with their relationships with their own fathers? Why or why not? How is *Amadeus* a film about male relationships with God, with fathers, and with one another? In today's Scripture, Jesus describes professional jealousy and we have applied his words to Salieri in today's film. Can Jesus' words be applied to professional relationships today? Why or why not?

3. Lawrence Kohlberg was a moral philosopher and researcher in child development whose work has influenced theology, catechetics, and education around the world. In 1981, he identified what seem to be the stages of consecutive moral development that are universal for all people and then outlined a framework to study them. In brief, stage one is about obeying in order to avoid punishment; the second stage values people only insofar as they are useful and views ethical action in terms of satisfying one's own needs; the third stage says that right behavior is when the individual acts to please others and "sin" is when the social order is breached. Stage four maintains that the individual has a duty toward society to maintain law and order, tradition, and consistency; one rarely, if ever, questions authority figures. This is followed by a transitional stage of morality that says, "Do your own thing." In stage five, the person begins to think on a universal level of justice, and moral principles: society should limit a person's freedom only when it infringes on that of another; at stage six, the person sees and acts from the principle of the equality and dignity of all people because it is the right and just

thing to do in itself. Where do Salieri and Mozart stand in relation to the stages of moral development? Why did they make the choices they did and how did their choices influence others? Did either man ever move beyond the self as the standard for ethical or moral behavior to think of others? Why or why not? How might Jesus' words in the Gospel help us grow from one stage of moral development to another? And finally, did Salieri really kill Mozart, according to the film? How?

Prayer

Jesus, let your powerful words touch our hearts so that we can see beyond our prejudices and appreciate the gifts of our brothers and sisters. Amen.

Ninth Sunday of the Year

1 Kings 8:41–43;
Galatians 1:1–2, 6–10;
Luke 7:1–10

The Green Mile

U.S.A., 1999, 187 minutes
Cast: Tom Hanks, David Morse, Bonnie Hunt, Michael Clarke
Duncan, James Cromwell, Michael Jeter, Sam Rockwell,
Doug Hutchison, Graham Greene, Gary Sinise
Writer: Frank Darabont
Director: Frank Darabont

The Green Mile

Masters, Servants, and Healing

Former Louisiana prison guard Paul Edgecomb becomes upset while watching an old movie, the Fred Astaire film *Top Hat.* The song, "Heaven, I'm in heaven…" makes him cry and run out of the room. The film takes him back to 1935, when he worked as a warden on death row, "the green mile," when an illiterate black prisoner, John Coffey, accused of murdering two little girls, changed his life.

SYNOPSIS

Edgecomb is a man who believes in the prison system although he is personally very compassionate. He is critical of the sadistic Percy Westmore, an inept and cowardly political appointee. As part of their work, Edgecomb and his team supervise the execution of several prisoners.

When Edgecomb suffers from a urinary problem, the prisoner John Coffey, a giant of a man, touches him and seems to take the pain into himself. Coffey also brings a pet mouse back to life for another convict who is later cruelly executed by Westmore.

Edgecomb, along with other guards, conspire to take Coffey to the warden's house to heal his wife—which he does.

Coffey also touches a crazed and cocky convict who, in fact, murdered the little girls whom Coffey was trying to heal when the mob found him. Coffey absorbs the convict's memories and lets Edgecomb witness them. Before his execution, Edgecomb arranges for Coffey to see *Top Hat.* Coffey is put to death but has given long life to Edgecomb who grows old and sad at the loss of his friends and family.

COMMENTARY

The Green Mile is based on a Stephen King novel adapted by Frank Darabont. Darabont also adapted another King prison story for the screen, *The Shawshank Redemption,* in 1994. *The Green Mile* and Michael Clarke Duncan as John Coffey were nominated for Oscars.

With Tom Hanks at the center of the movie, the screenplay highlights basic American decency but shows how it can be compromised by the state and within the prison system.

Michael Clarke Duncan is both a powerful and a childlike giant presence. With those evocative initials, J. C., David Morse leads a strong supporting cast, including Doug Hutchison as the repellent Percy.

At the end of 1999, there were a number of movies that had healings and/or miracles at the center of their plots: *Jesus' Son, The Third Miracle, The End of the Affair, Whatever Happened to Harold Smith. The Green Mile* is about miracles and about a miracle worker who is a marginalized and misjudged man, the object of hatred and prejudice, who is put to death even though he is innocent.

DIALOGUE WITH THE GOSPEL

Focus: In some ways, the two main characters in The Green Mile, *Paul Edgecomb, the death row prison guard, and John Coffey, the prisoner, can be compared to the centurion and the servant who needs healing in today's Gospel. John Coffey is also a Christ-figure who offers healing and salvation to his master, the prison guard.*

The Green Mile offers several parallels with the gospel story of the centurion. The story shows Jesus unexpectedly moved by a man of compassion and faith who was "different." Prison guard Paul Edgecomb can be compared with the centurion because he is in charge of a group of guards and prisoners. John Coffey's character parallels that of the servant who is about to die and needs God's help through Jesus' healing power.

Edgecomb works within a prison system where he says "Go" and subordinates and prisoners move at once; he says "Come," and they come. At first, neither he nor the audience is sure whether Coffey has killed the little girls; after all, he is caught holding their bodies in his arms, weeping. Edgecomb and the audience wonder who he is and they come to believe in his innocence even though he has been judged guilty and convicted. In fact, John Coffey (J. C.), the "servant," has gifts of healing, empathy, and grace.

The centurion asked Jesus to heal his servant. Edgecomb wants to save Coffey but cannot and Coffey gives his "permission" to be executed. Edgecomb, the centurion figure, asks that Coffey, the "servant," perform a healing for him, saying, "Go and heal," and Coffey obeys him.

In *The Green Mile,* it is Coffey who has faith and Edgecomb who learns what faith is. Edgecomb finds that the long life that Coffey miraculously gave him has to be lived in repentance and atonement for what he has allowed to happen.

KEY SCENES AND THEMES

- Life on "the green mile," the guards and their friendship and support; Percy's sadism, the prisoners and their fate and behavior; Paul Edgecomb, his character and role as the death-row guard; the executions, the grim death of Delacroix.

- John Coffey and his size and gentleness; the scenes of the crime and his arrest; the mood of the mob; his capture and condemnation; Coffey touching and healing Edgecomb; how evil physically and symbolically pours out of his mouth.

- The strategies for getting Coffey to the warden's house; Coffey's healing touch; the aftermath; his touching the real killer and communicating this to Edgecomb; Coffey's execution and Edgecomb's long life.

1. *The Green Mile* once again opens up for us the whole question of the death penalty in the United States through film. How does *The Green Mile* compare with films such as *Dead Man Walking, True Crime, The Life of David Gale* (or a play like *The Exonerated* by Jessica Blank and Eric Jensen)? What questions arise about the ethics and morality of the death penalty in our time? Paul Edgecomb pleads with the prisoner Coffey: "On the day of my judgment, when I stand before God, and he asks me why did I kill one of his true miracles, what am I gonna say? That it was my job? My job?" What is the proper course for a person to take when their conscience conflicts with what is legal? Talk about John's response to Edgecomb.

2. How does the dialogue in the film set the stage and explain the situation to us? For example, Paul Edgecomb says: "They usually call death row the last mile, but we called ours the green mile, because the floor was the color of faded limes. We had the electric chair then. Old Sparky, we called it. I've lived a lot of years, Ellie, but 1935 takes the prize. That was the year I had the worst urinary infection of my life. That was also the year of John Coffey and the two dead girls." In terms of storytelling, how does *The Green Mile* compare to other prison films, such as *The Shawshank Redemption, Hurricane*, and others? Are these films telling us stories with a moral? Why or why not? How did *The*

Green Mile make you feel? Are the characters more symbols than human beings? If so, what do they symbolize? Why?

3. In the 1996 movie version of John Grisham's novel, *A Time To Kill*, the overriding question is: Can a black man get a fair trial in America today? Do you think it is possible for a person of a minority race to get a fair trial today? Would it have been possible in 1935, the year of the setting of *The Green Mile?* What role does race play in the U.S. legal system and culture? The centurion of the Gospel was a "foreigner," a non-Jewish person. John Coffey was a black man, a non-white in a state and country dominated by white people. Who was a person of faith in the Gospel? In the film? What role does faith play in human relationships and in societies? What is the Gospel trying to say about equality and justice?

Prayer

Lord, you admired the faith of the centurion. You granted his wish and healed his servant. Help us to see faith in the people with whom we come in contact. Amen.

TENTH SUNDAY OF THE YEAR

1 Kings 17:17–24;
Galatians 1:11–19;
Luke 7:11–17

The Deep End of the Ocean

U.S.A., 1999, 108 minutes
Cast: Michelle Pfeiffer, Treat Williams, Whoopi Goldberg,
Jonathan Jackson, John Kapelos
Writer: Stephen Schiff
Director: Ulu Grosbard

The Deep End of the Ocean

Lost Son, Grieving Mother

SYNOPSIS

Beth Cappadora has three children whom she takes with her to a high-school reunion. As she checks into the hotel, she asks the oldest boy, Vincent, to look after the children, but he lets go of three-year-old Ben's hand and he disappears. Distraught, Beth tries every avenue to find the child. She loses interest in everything else, clashes with Pat, her husband, and gives up her job as a professional photographer. The police try to help but are unsuccessful in finding Ben.

Six years later, the Cappadoras move from Madison, Wisconsin, to Chicago. Beth begins taking photos again. One day, after almost three more years pass, Beth notices the boy who mows the lawn and takes his picture. She becomes convinced that he is her son. He tells her his name is Sam. Beth tells Pat and they notify the authorities. They detain Sam at school and check his fingerprints. They match. When the police go to Sam's house, Beth is with them and they discover the truth about Sam's parents. His "mother" was an old school friend of Beth's who became mentally unbalanced when she lost a baby. She then kidnapped Ben, ran away to Minnesota, and married. At the time, her husband "adopted"

236

the child, not knowing the truth. A few years later, she committed suicide.

Now that his identity has been established, Sam is torn between the memory of the woman he thought was his mother, his generous stepfather, and his birth family. His brother, Vincent, is hostile, acts out, and even ends up in juvenile detention. Sam remains at home with his stepfather. However, Sam visits the Capadorras and he and Vincent reconcile.

COMMENTARY

This is a very emotional movie that plays on the fear of children being abducted and portrays the impact of their disappearance on their families. It also shows the emotional confusion that children who are found can experience because they are torn between two families. This theme was well explored in the television movies *Family of Strangers* (1993) with Patty Duke and Melissa Gilbert and in *The Missing Years* (1989) with Stephen Dorff.

Ulu Grosbard, known for his thirty-year career in theater, directed the film. The screenplay is based on the novel by Jacquelyn Mitchard. The movie is so blatantly emotional that most film reviewers had little patience with it. It also lacks in the area of character development.

Michelle Pfeiffer (in one of her "unglamorous" roles) plays the grieving and embittered mother. Treat Williams is the understanding father who works hard to help his family survive the loss of their son and brother. Whoopi Goldberg adds a sympathetic touch as the detective who helps search for the son.

DIALOGUE WITH THE GOSPEL

Focus: Images and stories of mother and son are strong throughout the scriptures. The widow of Nain loses her son in death. Beth Cappadora does not know whether her son is dead or alive. Both mothers have their sons restored to them.

The story of the widow of Nain and the raising of her son from the dead by a weeping Jesus is one of the most popular tales in the Gospels. The crowd that witnessed Jesus' miracle must have felt the mother's sadness and empathized with her grief at losing an only son, as Jesus did.

All the readings today are about mothers and their sons. The first reading "previews" the story of the widow of Nain. The widow of Zaraphath offered the prophet Elijah food and hospitality during a three-year drought, only to have her son die. Elijah goes through some life-giving rituals and restores the son to his mother. She now realizes that he is truly a prophet and that the word he speaks is from God.

In the second reading, Paul, too, appeals to his awareness of being chosen while he was still in his mother's womb to convince the Galatians of the divine origin of the Gospel and of his mission.

In *The Deep End of the Ocean,* a busy mother loses one of her children. The film asks its audience to try to appreciate the pain and loss, guilt and grief, as a mother is suddenly deprived of her son. With the widow of Nain, there was grief at death. In the movie, the mother is uncertain whether the child is alive or dead. She can only go on desperately searching and hoping that the child is alive.

For the widow, her son's death meant separation, and when he is raised to life, mother and son are reunited. In the movie, when the son does reappear, his mother continues to grieve as he struggles to find his identity and place in the family who brought him up and the family of his birth. They are reunited, but still apart.

Jesus is referred to in the Gospel as the "Lord" who has the power to raise the dead. He is the answer to the mother's unspoken prayer and the crowd glorifies God for this miracle.

KEY SCENES AND THEMES

- The atmosphere of the reunion, friends greeting one another, Beth's friend who seems to have it all, and the irony of her abducting the child; Beth's desperation and frustration, the search, the police, Pat's coming; the reality of losing one's child.

- The passing of time, a new life; Beth and her depression, giving up photography, the clashes with her husband, her attitude toward Vincent; consequences of the abduction.

- Sam's appearance and Beth's reaction; the photos and her hopes, Pat's caution; Sam and his experiences in his home, his dead mother, his love for his stepfather; the intrusion of his birth family into his life and his having to cope; staying with the Cappadoras and arguing with Vincent; hearing the reactions of Beth and Pat; Sam's discussions with his stepfather, his decision, love for all, reconciliation with Vincent, "restored to life."

FOR REFLECTION AND CONVERSATION

1. Kidnapping is a heinous offense that is seldom dealt with on the silver screen, although many television movies have been made about the subject. Do you think that *The Deep End of the Ocean* is more about kidnapping or about the fragility of the relationships that bind us together? What happens to Beth and her relationships with the rest of the family because of Ben's kidnapping? Would you blame her for what happened? Why or why not? What about Vincent's role in the story—how did he handle the guilt of losing his brother, letting go of his hand? Why do we, as human beings, always seek to apportion blame, to self and others? Is it always possible to do this (an issue the film *The Sweet Hereafter* tried to explore)? Why do bad things happen to good people?

2. We do not know anything about the widow in today's Gospel story, except that she was burying her only son. There is no mention of the father or other relatives or even why the son had died. Jesus, however, was moved with pity. Try to imagine the widow's "story" and how you would have felt and behaved if you were she or if you were a member of the crowd and knew more about the son's death than even Jesus apparently did. How would you judge her? Would you be moved with pity, even if it seemed it was her fault the son had died?

3. When Beth rediscovers her son she realizes that he is experiencing an emotional struggle for his identity. How do human beings establish their identity (family, school, church, culture, media)? Of all of these, what do you think is the most important for well-adjusted human growth and development? Why? Is there a difference between self-identity and self-image? Pat says: "I'm not self-righteous, I'm *right*! Kids don't just vanish up in smoke, kids don't just get lost, *people lose them*!" Do you agree? What are other ways that parents can "lose" children to drugs, poverty, and consumer and media culture? What are some positive ways to find them again, so that families can rise again to new life?

Prayer

Jesus, you were the only son of your mother, and you raised the son of the widow of Nain to new life. Bless every mother who grieves at the loss of a child. Amen.

The Accused

U.S.A., 1988, 111 minutes
Cast: Jodie Foster, Kelly McGillis, Bernie Coulson, Leo Rossi
Writer: Tom Topor
Director: Jonathan Kaplan

The Accused

What a Bad Name This Woman Has

Sarah Tobias has a fight with her boyfriend and goes to a bar to unwind. Three young men rape her while the patrons of the bar look on and do nothing to help her. A college student named Ken, a friend of one of the rapists, watches and then calls the police. But it is too late. Sarah runs out and a passerby takes her to the hospital.

SYNOPSIS

Kathryn Murphy is the assistant district attorney appointed to prosecute the accused rapists. At first she seems committed to winning the case against the men. But when faced with the fact that Sarah will not make a sympathetic witness because of her behavior that night when she drank, smoked pot, and dressed and acted provocatively, Kathryn lets the men plea to the lesser charge of "reckless endangerment." The men not only receive a sentence with the chance for early parole, but any reference to a sexual offense is removed from their records.

When Sarah discovers this, she feels betrayed because she never had the chance to tell her story in court. She confronts Kathryn. As she can no longer charge the rapists, Kathryn decides to charge the bystanders for soliciting the crime because they cheered the rapists on. Sarah's friend Sally identifies the men in a line-up. Kathryn finds the name of the student who called the police listed on one of the games in the bar. It is Ken, and when she confronts him with the telephone tape of his 911 call, he is persuaded to give evidence. Despite pressure from his college friend, Bob, now serving time for the "assault," he tells the court the true story of the rape and how the crowd urged the men on. The bystanders are found guilty.

COMMENTARY

Jodie Foster *(Taxi Driver, Little Man Tate, Nell, Silence of the Lambs, Sommersby, Anna and the King)* won her first Academy Award for her performance as Sarah Tobias in *The Accused.* Here, Foster demonstrates her considerable skill as an actress who can play any role she chooses with credibility.

Foster is certainly making a statement in support of rape victims by drawing attention to the false presumptions that the female, no matter what, is somehow responsible for rape and is guilty until proven innocent. Kelly McGillis *(Witness, At First Sight)* plays the assistant district attorney and also gives a persuasive performance.

Jonathan Kaplan is well known as a director of small, tough action movies. He brings these skills to a movie that makes challenging demands on both emotions and consciences. One of the difficulties with this kind of movie is the visualizing of the rape sequence that caused the movie to receive a restricted rating. Kaplan, however, draws a fine, clear line between serious social drama and any possibility for misunderstanding it as an exploitation of sexuality through film.

The Accused is based on actual events that took place in Massachusetts.

DIALOGUE WITH THE GOSPEL

Focus: Sarah Tobias experiences being an outcast. She is vindicated by compassion and by the law. Jesus' encounter with the woman who had a bad name shows his compassion and acceptance.

The Gospel speaks of a woman who had a bad name in the city—she was known as a "sinful woman." Sarah Tobias is a working-class waitress who lives with a man outside of marriage. By today's standards she would not be considered a religious outcast for her lifestyle, but some might consider her a social one. And after the rape and her court ordeal, she is also despised. Although Sarah is not a prostitute like the woman in the Gospel, she enjoys going to bars, having a good time, and flirting. Men interpret this as her wanting their "attention." Today's Gospel and the film are not an exact parallel, but the Gospel informs the social situation presented in the film. Both accounts have everything to do with human dignity.

Jesus highlights the sanctimonious attitudes of the men who despise the "sinful" woman in today's Gospel. They disapprove of Jesus having anything to do with a sinner because they think that he should only associate with people like themselves, who obey the law. Jesus sets them straight by showing that many sins will be forgiven to those whose love is great. Love is what is important, not the quantity of sins. In the film, the district attorney's office only wants to associate with cases they know they can win. They think the jury will judge Sarah on her lifestyle rather than on her humanity, which is exactly what they themselves are doing. Thus, they accede to a double standard, as do the Pharisees of the Gospel.

The second reading from Galatians speaks about a person's inner life, where integrity comes from inner conviction. The Gospel also highlights the woman who grieves at her life and, from inner conviction, wants the reassurance of Jesus' forgiveness, acceptance, and approval. He speaks with deep feeling of her great love and faith.

Sarah Tobias may have a large quantity of various sins on her account, but Jesus teaches that human dignity is for everyone, not only for the righteous. No one deserves sexual violence and/or abuse. Even though both men and women consider her on the edge of "proper" society, Sarah discovers through her ordeal a personal integrity that moves her beyond public opinion to an awareness of female dignity and justice. Because of Sarah's case (and this film), the justice system and the public comes to a greater understanding that no woman ever "deserves" sexual violence and abuse. Jesus receives a woman who is considered to be at the margins of society and vindicates her. Jesus stands by the woman and offers compassion. We can do no less.

KEY SCENES AND THEMES

- The aftermath of Sarah's ordeal at the hospital; its effect on her, her friend Sally, and her boyfriend; her call to her mother; Sarah and Kathryn Murphy, their discussions, the pressure on Murphy, and letting the rapists plea to a lesser charge; Sarah's confrontation with Kathryn Murphy; her pain, humiliation, and self-assertiveness.

- The behavior of the rapists, their backgrounds, that night in the bar, their callous attitudes; Bob Joiner in prison.

- Bob's smug self-assurance and his pressure on Ken not to testify; the rapists' attorneys; Ken's personal dilemmas, his meeting with Sarah, his personal integrity; his testimony through vivid flashbacks showing what really happened: Sarah's ordeal and the role of the men, the bystanders; the role of Cliff; Sarah as victim but her being vindicated in court.

FOR REFLECTION AND CONVERSATION

1. As discussed, the Gospel and the film stories are not parallels, but the narrative elements are: both abound in sinners, sin, victims, victimizers, and double standards. Who are the sinners in each story? How is it that some of the sinners are victims, some of the vic-

timizers are sinners, and some of the victims are sinners, and so on? Were the victimizers also victims? What made them do what they did, whether the rapists or the Gospel's cheering crowd? Do you think the silent bystanders should have been accountable as well as the ones that cheered? Why? What made the woman in the Gospel a sinner? How was she justified? Was Sarah a sinner, a victim, or both? Why? How and why did Sarah finally receive justice? On what was her "justice" based? Was Sarah a heroine?

2. Recent statistics show that rape is still all too prevalent in America. The Rape, Abuse and Incest National Network Website (www.rainn.org) states: "Somewhere in America, a woman is raped every 2 minutes, according to the U.S. Department of Justice. In 1996, 307,000 women were the victim of rape, attempted rape, or sexual assault. Between 1995 and 1996, more than 670,000 women were the victim of rape, attempted rape, or sexual assault." Rape is also described in Scripture, literature, romance fiction, television (e.g., the third season of HBO's *Sopranos* and NBC's *Law and Order: Special Victims Unit*). What do you think about programs and films like these? Have they lost their power to shock or can they be used as a platform to talk about serious social problems like rape? Why? How do you feel about talking about sexual violence and other crimes against women? How did *The Accused* make you feel? What can people of faith do to create a culture that values the dignity of all people, but especially the most vulnerable: women and children? Identify the causes of rape then make a parallel list of practical culture-building ideas and talk about how they can be implemented.

3. The dictionary defines *feminism* as the belief in women's rights (and opportunities) as equal to those of men. Feminism also describes a movement toward securing these rights. Christian feminism is "faith seeking understanding" through the lens of equality between men and women. Feminism could also describe women's friendships. How does Sarah and Kathryn's relationship grow and change in the film? What did you think about Sally? In what ways do some of the shots or scenes help create the meaning of the film, such as Sarah's attempt to bash her car into that of the video-store owner? Could it be said that this sequence is a "picture" of the frustrations of the unequal, the disenfranchised, and the abused? Why or why not?

Prayer

Jesus, you showed compassion to the woman with a bad reputation. You taught the Pharisees that to love is the greatest virtue. May we share your compassion with all we meet. Amen.

Falling Down

U.S.A., 1993, 112 minutes
Cast: Michael Douglas, Robert Duvall, Barbara Hershey,
Tuesday Weld, Rachel Ticotin, Frederic Forrest, D. W. Moffett,
Vondie Curtis-Hall
Writer: Ebbe Roe Smith
Director: Joel Schumacher

Falling Down

"I'm the Bad Guy?"

In L.A., Bill Foster frets in his car in a traffic jam. He is surrounded by noise, heat, and squabbling. His license plate indicates his work, D-FENS. Foster abandons his car in frustration. This begins an urban odyssey in which he crosses the city and becomes ever more paranoid and violent. At the same time Detective Martin Prendergast sits in the same traffic jam and notices the billboards around him. He sees the man walk away from his car. He helps to push it off to the side of the road and notes the vanity license plate.

It is Prendergast's last day on the job because he is retiring. As information comes in about what D-FENS is doing, he begins to make connections and takes on the job of solving the problem, even as he is being processed out of the police department.

Prendergast and another detective visit the scene of D-FENS's first altercation. The detective realizes it is where he saw the man walk away that morning. He runs the plate and goes to the man's home. The mother lets the detectives know that the son has been acting strangely. They learn that Foster lost his job in the defense industry a month before and that he is "overqualified and underskilled, obsolete and not eco-

SYNOPSIS

nomically viable." His wife has divorced him and does not want him to visit for their daughter's birthday.

Foster confronts violent elements in the city and builds up a store of weapons while continually calling his wife on the phone. He inadvertently takes a family hostage on the grounds of a lavish home and explains his desperation to them. He arrives home to find his wife and daughter gone. Finally, he sees them on the Venice pier. Prendergast arrives soon after. In the confrontation, he explains to Prendergast that he has been lied to and victimized. Prendergast tells him he will go to jail, and Bill is surprised. He asks, "I'm the bad guy?" Bill provokes Prendergast into a shootout on the pier so he won't go to jail. He and Prendergast draw their guns. Bill is wielding only a water pistol. He is shot to death and falls into the sea.

COMMENTARY

Falling Down is a sobering look at the situation of middle-aged men in American society who have found that they are redundant and ineffectual in the late twentieth century. The film raised controversy on its first release because some thought it was about vigilantism. Rather, the sociopathic behavior of the central character is a metaphor and a commentary on the change in American male identity in the last decades of the twentieth century.

As Bill Foster, Michael Douglas plays against type in *Falling Down*. Audiences are accustomed to seeing him as a strong hero-character, even when he is in the wrong *(Fatal Attraction)*. Foster's mental, moral, and social disintegration is the focus of the story and it is counterbalanced with the character of Detective Prendergast, played by Robert Duvall.

Barbara Hershey plays Douglas's strong, independent wife, a counterpoint to Tuesday Weld as Duvall's dependent, fragile wife. Direction is by Joel Schumacher, who followed this movie with the more traditional Grisham film adaptations, *The Client* and *A Time to Kill,* as well as two Batman features. But he later created controversy about the pornography industry in the movie *8 MM.*

DIALOGUE WITH THE GOSPEL

Focus: The crosses of life may sometimes seem too hard and heavy to bear and people despair, opting to lose their lives as Bill Foster ultimately did in Falling Down. *Martin Prendergast, by contrast, finds a way to bear his crosses.*

The short reading from the prophet Zechariah highlights a symbolic savior-figure who is pierced through and for whom people will mourn. The outpouring of the spirit will stir people to sorrow for their sins; all of society will take part in this act of repentance. In *Falling Down,* Bill Foster is a victim of what has gone wrong in society as well as a symbol of those who need God's salvation.

The Gospel is Luke's version of the confession of Peter. It is really the aftermath of Peter's declaration that is important when Jesus teaches his disciples about suffering, death —and resurrection. It is in this context that he challenges his disciples to renounce themselves and take up their cross daily to follow him and thus save their lives.

Falling Down reminds us that many people have no knowledge of this promise of Jesus and are so caught up in the crosses they have to bear that they lose life instead of gaining it. Both Bill and Martin desperately need today's Gospel message.

Bill Foster wants to save his life but instead experiences the crosses of family division, loss of wife and daughter, loss of job and security, loss of self-image and self-worth, loss of true self-respect. Trapped on the freeway, he breaks down. We then follow him on the last day of his life in a continual downward spiral of harassment, despair, and rejection. He finally sees no other way of coping with life than to opt out of it.

Martin, too, needs this gospel message. Prendergast has lost his daughter, experiences tension with his aging wife, and is patronized by his superiors. But he does his job, "takes up his cross," by compromising his principles and learning to survive. He thus chooses to live, but what kind of life will be his?

KEY SCENES AND THEMES

- The opening-credits sequence: the build-up of traffic, Bill Foster trapped on the freeway, the noise, the clashes, the heat, and finally snapping, abandoning his car because he just wants to go home; the violent confrontations, Bill's growing despair that brings out all his prejudices and aggression; collecting guns; the irony that he worked in the missile defense industry.

- Bill holding the family on the mansion grounds; their fear and his speech about being a family man, the loss of his job, being obsolete and not economically viable; Bill's wife, phoning her, confronting her on the pier; the comparisons with Prendergast and his wife; meeting with his wife and daughter, Bill's love for his daughter, his desperation.

- The final confrontation between the two men, their conversation, Prendergast telling Bill that everyone has been lied to and that that does not give him the right to behave as he did; Bill provoking the shootout and his death.

FOR REFLECTION AND CONVERSATION

1. French sociologist Emile Durkheim (1858–1917) could have scripted *Falling Down*. He believed that shared moral and religious values form the basis of a society and that when these bonds of social order are broken, anxiety, dissatisfaction, and depression will result. In fact, this is how he explained the causes of suicide. He called this social alienation "anomie." He

also believed that a sense of inferiority would lead to anti-social behavior. A diagnosis of psychosis for Bill would have meant he was out of touch with reality. But was he? What were the elements of moral and social "change" that he railed against? Why was Bill no longer able to cope, but Prendergast was? Is it fair to compare people? In the context of today's Scripture readings, what truly could have saved Bill? He is so surprised to find out that he is the bad guy. Why do you think this is so?

2. Prendergast had a desk job in the police department. Most people thought this was because he was afraid because he was once shot. But what do we find out about him and his "fears"? What bad habit that would have made him a "man" did he finally acquire at the end of the film? Does this kind of unimaginative use of language "make" a man (or a woman)? Or was Prendergast's learning to be ill-mannered and foul-mouthed mark the way he would now be socialized, and accepted, into the police department? Did he really learn to carry his burden, or did he learn to compromise his values so he could survive? Why or why not? What else did he compromise as he lived his life? What do you do to survive in the various social strata in which you live? What positive means can believers employ to help create a culture built on human dignity, truth, beauty, and goodness? Who defines the social bonds on which a society is built and exists?

3. Some of the visual motifs in *Falling Down* are the American flag, guns, masks, camouflage, white supremacy, and prejudice, economic value, race/multiculturalism, billboards and signs, lack of human worth, fast food, gangs, violence as a way to resolve issues,

the defense industry, marriage, relationships, and so forth. What do motifs like these mean for you? Did you blame Bill, sympathize with him, or have other opinions about him? Was death the only way out for him (given that this is a story that had to be told within two hours so as to respect the structure of the medium)? How did he get to that condition? How did the movie make you feel? Have you ever felt alienated? How did you handle it? Did you see *Falling Down* as a vigilante film or perhaps as a commentary on society? Why?

Prayer

Lord, you know so many people who are harassed and dejected, in danger of losing their lives. Give them strength to bear their crosses, to choose life, and to make a difference in society, no matter how small it may seem. Amen.

Julie Andrews and children from *The Sound of Music*.

The Sound of Music

U.S.A., 1965, 165 minutes
Cast: Julie Andrews, Christopher Plummer, Eleanor Parker,
Richard Haydn, Peggy Wood, Angela Cartwright
Writer: Ernest Lehman
Director: Robert Wise

The Sound of Music

Climb Every Mountain...

SYNOPSIS

Maria would prefer to be singing in the Alpine country-side outside of Salzburg rather than observing the rules and regulations of the convent she has entered to become a nun. The mother superior realizes that Maria is not suited to convent life, and when Captain Von Trapp asks her for a governess for his seven children, she sends Maria. Von Trapp is a widower and he disciplines his children as if they were in the military.

The children have driven away many governesses with mischievous tricks and they try some on Maria, but she eventually wins them over. Her fresh and charming manner and her delight in everything brightens the children's lives. She also wins over their father, who falls in love with her, despite expectations that he marry the baroness. He and Maria are married.

When Hitler invades Austria, Von Trapp finds himself in opposition to the prevailing politics and plans to escape with his family. The Nazis want him to head their navy. With the help of his friend, the entrepreneur Max, the family performs in one of the famous Salzburg concerts. They escape before it is over and elude Nazi surveillance and conscription for the captain. They hike over the Alps to freedom.

COMMENTARY

The Sound of Music is the one film that proves that some movies are critic proof, if for no other reason than for the overwhelmingly enthusiastic reception of audiences around the world. *The Sound of Music* proved so popular that it actually played in theaters in some cities for three or more years straight. It was nominated for ten Academy Awards in 1965 and won five, including one for Best Film. It still remains a film favorite for millions.

The Rogers and Hammerstein score is one of their most popular. Director Robert Wise, known for serious dramas, was able to skillfully combine music with the more dramatic elements of the plot. By the time he directed *The Sound of Music*, he had already won an Oscar for *West Side Story*.

But it was Julie Andrews who charmed the world. The year before making *The Sound of Music*, she had been snubbed by Jack L. Warner, who declined to have her reprise her acclaimed Broadway role of Eliza Doolittle in the movie version of *My Fair Lady* because she was unknown off Broadway. Walt Disney was more astute and cast her as the lead in *Mary Poppins* for which she won the 1964 Oscar for Best Actress and went on to a long and successful screen career.

The Sound of Music is loosely based on the 1949 autobiography *The Story of the Trapp Family Singers* by Maria Augusta Trapp. Several books about the family are in print, including a more true-to-life version of Maria's life, *Maria*, published in 1974.

DIALOGUE WITH THE GOSPEL

Focus: In today's Gospel, Jesus invites his disciples to follow him; when they offer their excuses, he enjoins them not to look back on what they have left behind. Maria thinks that God is calling her to religious life but then discovers her vocation lies in being a wife and mother. She does not look back.

Luke's Gospel tells of the beginning of Jesus' long and arduous journey to Jerusalem that will culminate in his death but then in his resurrection. With its stark injunctions that the disciples never look back once they have responded to their vocation, it is obviously a Gospel about following one's call in life—whatever it may be—with full commitment.

In the past, "vocation" was narrowly considered only in terms of the priesthood or religious life. Today, wherever and however it is lived out, faithfully responding to God's call is considered responding to one's vocation. The first part of the movie shows Maria trying her vocation in religious life. Paul's vigorous words to the Galatians remind us of how difficult the struggle can be to find one's true vocation. Maria is shown to be a free spirit and the convent restrictions of that day are too much for her—what can the sisters do with a "problem" like Maria! The mother superior's song, "Climb ev'ry mountain—ford ev'ry stream," can be seen as a musical variation on Jesus' words in the Gospel, which echo the story of the prophet Elijah's call to Elisha in the first reading.

Maria would eventually climb mountains to escape from Austria with her husband and his children in search of freedom. Paul today speaks of this freedom as an ideal: love for others. Maria Von Trapp demonstrated this love for others long after the events portrayed in *The Sound of Music*; during the 1950s, she and some of her family went to Papua New Guinea as lay missionaries.

One of the most appealing aspects of *The Sound of Music* is watching Maria follow her convictions as she confronts the severe Captain Von Trapp, faces the challenge of the mischievous children, commits herself to their singing, and is willing to endure the difficult journey to freedom. In following her vocation, once she "put her hand to the plow," Maria did not look back.

KEY SCENES AND THEMES

- The introduction to Maria as she sings "The Sound of Music," her exhilaration in life contrasting with her difficulties in following the discipline in the convent; the mother superior's wisdom in sending Maria to the Von Trapp home and her song, "Climb Ev'ry Mountain."

- Maria challenging Von Trapp over his stern discipline of his children; committing herself to the children and their welfare; her falling in love with the captain and discerning God's will in her life; her total loving loyalty to God, the captain, and the children.

- The Nazi invasion of Austria and the opposition of the Von Trapp family, the plan for the escape, the concert, their escape.

FOR REFLECTION AND CONVERSATION

1. The vocation, or call, to follow Jesus in the vowed life is one of three "ways" to live the Christian life: marriage, the single life, or the priesthood/religious life. To follow Christ in the religious life means to follow Jesus as a man or woman who takes the vows of poverty, chastity, and obedience in a religious community or institute, with a specific purpose, such as prayer for the world, education, health care, evangelization with the means of communication, and so forth. For centuries the Catholic Church has applied today's Gospel to those who are thinking about or have responded to Christ's call to live as a priest or a religious. But it can be applied to all who want to live a more focused Christian life. How does Maria discern her true vocation to follow God's will? What obstacles are in the way of her becoming a nun? Could she have made a "good" one? Why or why not? What characteristics make for a good "nun" or "priest" or dedicated layperson, married or single? How does this Gospel apply to those who choose marriage or the single life?

2. Several films have been made over the years about convents, nuns, and sisters, or women religious: *Heaven Knows Mr. Allison, Dead Man Walking, The Nun's Story, The Black Narcissus, The Song of Bernadette, The Singing Nun, The Trouble with Angels,* and so forth. Which of these represent best what it means to follow Christ more closely in religious life? How do the films show the challenges of such a life? Have you ever thought that Christ might be calling you? Which of these films seem to tell a real story instead of one that falls into stereotypes? Have any of these films inspired you? Why or why not?

3. Although some may think *The Sound of Music* is a fairy tale more than a real story, the fact is that the political reality of the times forced severe hardships on the Von Trapp family and posed a great question of conscience, especially for Captain Von Trapp. What are the religious, moral, and ethical dimensions of political life? How have politics challenged the religious dedication of people like Jean Donovan *(Choices of the Heart)*, Oscar Romero *(Romero)*, Dorothy Day *(Entertaining Angels)*, and others whose stories have been told via film? To what extent was "their inheritance" the Lord, as the responsorial psalm prays today? Have I yet "set my hand to the plow" by discerning and then following my vocation in life? What is the next best step for me as I seek to follow Christ more closely today and always?

Prayer

Lord, make known to us where you are calling us in life and give us the strength to make our commitment complete. Amen.

Pale Rider

U.S.A., 1985, 115 minutes
Cast: Clint Eastwood, Michael Moriarty, Carrie Snodgress,
Sydney Penny, Christopher Penn, Richard Dysart
Writers: Michael Butler, Dennis Shryack
Director: Clint Eastwood

 *Pale Rider*

Lambs and Wolves in the West

SYNOPSIS

The western town of Carbon Canyon is a frontier mining community. The owner of the local mining company, LaHood, exploits the people and he hires gunfighters to do his dirty work for him. They raid the settlement and kill some of the miners.

Sarah Wheeler and her daughter Megan live in Carbon Canyon. Hull Barret has supported them ever since Sarah's husband died. Fourteen year-old Megan is caught up in one of the raids and her dog is killed. She takes the body out into the woods to bury it. She prays the Good Shepherd psalm with hope, despair, and as a plea for deliverance. As she prays a lone rider comes down from the mountains into the town.

He confronts some of the gunfighters and rescues Megan from them. She gratefully brings him to the Wheeler house. When he washes, Hull, Sarah, and Megan see that bullet wounds scar his back. He then surprises them by putting on a clerical collar. He joins them for a meal and they explain the town's desperate situation to him. He wants to be called "Preacher."

LaHood then tries to buy out the miners' claims. At first they are tempted to sell, but then they decide to stand their ground. When his intitial plan fails, LaHood hires a professional "marshal" named Stockburn with his six henchmen to get rid of the settlers. The Preacher has a history with Stockburn. With the support of the people, the Preacher confronts Stockburn and his men. Shootouts erupt, culminating in the deaths of the villains. The town is once again at peace. Sarah, Hull, and Megan have been changed by the presence of the pale rider and there is hope for them as a family. The pale rider, the Preacher, rides off.

COMMENTARY

By the mid-1980s, Clint Eastwood had established himself as a serious and prolific director as well as an actor. In 1992, his movie *Unforgiven* won the Oscar for Best Film and he received one for Best Director. He has continued with a significant number of movies since, ranging from *The Bridges of Madison County* to *Absolute Power* to *Blood Work*.

One of his central interests has been the American West and the ambiguity of its values. In *High Plains Drifter* (1973), he created a figure that was a terrible avenging angel, cleansing a corrupt town, which he named "Hell." In *The Outlaw Josey Wales* (1976), his character was on a quest for revenge but became a savior of the marginalized. *Bronco Billy* (1980) explored the same issues but in a contemporary context. Then, in 1985, came *Pale Rider*, which took up the previous themes and provided another avenging angel/savior who rescues the oppressed in a Western mining town.

DIALOGUE WITH THE GOSPEL

Focus: As in Pale Rider, *Clint Eastwood has told many stories about oppressed and marginalized people in the Old West whom a hero saves. Jesus sends out disciples who are to serve and save the oppressed by preaching the kingdom of God.*

There is such a joyful tone in the first reading that initially it may seem too much at variance with *Pale Rider*'s plot. Jerusalem is to take heart after being liberated. Those who mourned for her should now rejoice. In the movie, however, the residents of Carbon Canyon are finally liberated after oppression and they, too, can finally rejoice.

On the other hand, the reading from Galatians takes a very different tone, highlighting suffering. The world is crucified to Paul and he bears the marks of the sufferings of Jesus. Clint Eastwood is a man of God and on his back are the marks of violence and suffering. The residents of Carbon Canyon also suffer because they work hard and live under the oppressive power of the mine owner.

Themes of both suffering and joy can be found in the Gospel. While there is a rich harvest for God's grace, Jesus knows that the world is an ambiguous place where lambs go out among wolves. The responsorial psalm is a song of liberation and thanksgiving.

This is the world of Carbon Canyon, where innocent residents are overpowered by the wolves of industry who stop at nothing to intimidate the people and increase their own wealth. Jesus urges the disciples he sends out to stay where they are welcomed but to shake the dust off their feet if they are not. The enigmatic clergyman saves the young daughter of the household, who prayed for his coming. He is literally welcomed into the house and to the table. But, in his confrontation with the villains, he does not shake dust from his feet. Instead he uses the traditions of the West for a shootout to free the people; once more, the avenging angel who supports the oppressed is an ambiguous mixture of grace and vengeance.

KEY SCENES AND THEMES

- The situation of Carbon Canyon, the people, the mines, the hard work, the exploitation by the owners and their henchmen; Megan going into the woods to bury the dog and praying the twenty-third psalm, her own words about her lack of faith and wanting life; the pale rider coming down from the mountains.

- The family and the young girl as symbolizing the people; the shooting and the death of the girl's dog; the pale rider being welcomed into the house after saving Megan; the meal and his being part of the household.

- The revelation of the rider being a minister, his wearing the collar of a clergyman as well as the marks of shooting and violence on his body; the final confrontation, the shootout, and the restoration of justice and peace to the town.

FOR REFLECTION
AND
CONVERSATION

1. Eastwood gives *Pale Rider* an explicit religious tone with its title from the book of Revelation and the reference to the Four Horsemen of the Apocalypse. A young girl prays Psalm 23 for help to come to her town—and down from the mountains comes the "pale rider," the "Preacher." What other religious references are there in *Pale Rider*? How would you explain the symbolism of the rock? What is the meaning of the "money" for Hull, the Wheelers, and the mining community?

2. Some of the recurring themes in Westerns (e.g., John Ford's and Eastwood's) are the family, the role of religion in settling the West, the strength of the community against the forces of nature or human oppression as the United States was settled. Hull talks about schools, churches, and a better life than his parents had as the American dream. Do you agree? How would you describe the ideology or worldview of this film? Is it fair and just for all? Toward the end of the film, someone asks: "How much is it worth to have a conscience?" and "If we sell out now what price do we put

on our dignity the next time? More, or less, or the best offer?" Is *Pale Rider* a morality tale?

3. In one of the final scenes of the film, the Preacher talks about loving and we can only see half of his face because the other half is in the shadows. How does this shot express the ambiguity of the morality of the film's premise? Does the Preacher act in completely moral ways, or is he a mythical character (that reflects the mythic nature of U.S. westward expansion and the "West" of which Westerns are made)? Is he justified in doing what he did, or is he the "creation" of people desperate for hope? What are some other Westerns you have seen? How are they similar to or different from *Pale Rider*?

Prayer

Lord, remember your people who are oppressed. Send them courageous men and women who will champion their cause and bring them true justice. Amen.

FIFTEENTH SUNDAY OF THE YEAR

Deuteronomy 30:10–14;
Colossians 1:15–20;
Luke 10:25–37

Amistad

U.S.A., 1997, 152 minutes
Cast: Morgan Freeman, Matthew McConaughey,
Jeremy Northam, Nigel Hawthorne, Anthony Hopkins,
Djimon Hounsou, David Paymer, Pete Postlethwaite,
Stellan Skarsgård, Anna Paquin
Writer: David Franzoni
Director: Steven Spielberg

Amistad

And Who Is My Neighbor?

SYNOPSIS

In 1839, a cargo of slaves, led by Cinque, overpowers the crew of *La Amistad* and takes over the ship. Two surviving crewmembers promise to guide them back home to Africa. Instead, the crewmen, helped by the tides and winds, drive to the Long Island shore where the slaves are arrested and taken to a New Haven prison.

Martin Van Buren is president. He is pressured into adopting political positions to condemn the slaves but wants to please slave-owning Southerners at the same time. The debate in the courts concerns the ownership of the slaves. The contenders include the Spanish government, the English shipowners, and the two crewmembers. The legal status, and therefore the outcome of the case, depends on whether the slaves are found to be born of slaves (and therefore would be guilty of murder because their slavery was a preexisting status) or captured and enslaved in Africa (and therefore would have the right to defend themselves and escape since slave trading had by then been outlawed in the United States).

While they are in prison someone gives a Bible to the slaves, who see their plight parallelled by that of Jesus. Meanwhile, two abolitionists, former slave Theodore Joadson and an immigrant, Lewis Tappan, come to their aid. A young real-estate lawyer, Roger Baldwin, is appointed to defend them, but he is inexperienced and argues, at first, from the point of view that the slaves are "property." Protesters stand guard, praying. Judge Coglin, a closet Catholic, goes to a church to pray and does what is both morally right *and* legal: he decides in favor of the slaves.

But there are more court proceedings. Finally, former president John Quincy Adams defends the slaves with a rousing speech based on the U.S. Constitution.

COMMENTARY

Amistad is a dramatic lesson in historical ethics, because it is based on a story not found in history books. The film is based on events in 1839 when slaves from Sierra Leone, having made port in Cuba and in the process of sailing to another part of Cuba, overcame the crew of the ship, *La Amistad*, and massacred them.

Amistad is Steven Spielberg's clear and heartfelt plea for black Americans just as *Schindler's List* was his witness for Holocaust victims. The movie relies on courtroom drama, especially on the moving speech by Anthony Hopkins, who is excellent as the elderly John Quincy Adams. *Amistad* is a worthy film and dramatizes the experience of this particular group of African slaves to reveal a history that must continually be acknowledged so that a just future can be built on the past.

DIALOGUE WITH THE GOSPEL

Focus: One of the most important gospel questions addressed to Jesus was the one posed by the lawyer, "And who is my neighbor?" Jesus' response is the parable of the Good Samaritan. Amistad *is one of many visual stories illustrating love of neighbor.*

The parable of the Good Samaritan can be applied to many cross-cultural situations of prejudice, oppression, and brutality. *Amistad* shows the African slaves as victims of slave trading, the institution of slavery, and the involvement of such publicly "respectable" countries such as Britain, Spain, and the United States.

As the slaves lie in prison, victims of the American legal system and the humiliating question of who owns them, the officials, from the president down, condemn them and "passed by on the opposite side." The equivalent of the Good Samaritans in this movie are the abolitionists, the young, inexperienced lawyer, the judge who prays before making his politically incorrect decision and, finally, the retired and aging John Quincy Adams.

The role of the Good Samaritan has come to mean "to have compassion." The key message of the parable is directed at the lawyer who wanted to disconcert Jesus by his interrogation. The lawyer repeats "the law" but does not seem to grasp the spirit of the law expressed in the first reading from Deuteronomy. It is one of the finest statements in the entire Bible regarding where we will find the law of God: in our hearts and in our mouths; we have only to carry it out.

The lawyer then asked Jesus the eternal question, "And who is my neighbor?" After telling his story, Jesus makes the lawyer answer his own question regarding the true neighbor. The clinching statement of the Gospel is not Jesus' reply, "You are correct," but "Go and do likewise."

The reading from Paul's Letter to the Colossians blends well with the images of the crucifix in the film and with Jesus' suffering, which the slaves reflected on in their captivity. They understood that Jesus came "to reconcile all things [for the father], making peace by the blood of his cross through him."

KEY SCENES AND THEMES

- The inhuman conditions in the slave fortress, the brutal treatment by the slaves' captors; life on the ship, the slaves chained, humiliated, and tortured.

- The violence of the revolt and the revelation of the power of the human spirit to rise up against oppression; the slaves' dream of sailing the ship back to their home in Africa; the interment of the slaves in New Haven, the conditions in the prison, the affront to human dignity with the question of the "ownership" of the slaves, and the testimony of the various claimants in the courts.

• The slaves in prison, looking at the Bible sketches, their conversation paralleling their plight with that of Jesus; the three masts of *La Amistad* looking like the three crosses of Calvary; the verdict of the judge, the speech of John Quincy Adams, and the relevance of the Constitution, for later generations, of slaves and their freedom.

FOR REFLECTION AND CONVERSATION

1. After nine years on the air, the very last episode of the popular "show about nothing," *Seinfeld*, had the characters end up in a small-town jail in Massachusetts because they stood by and did nothing to help when a bank was robbed and people hurt. The town had a "Good Samaritan law" that Jerry and his friends knew nothing about. They went to trial, were fined, and were sentenced to five years in jail (something many viewers think was fair given the poor writing of that last episode!). Is being a Good Samaritan an option for people of faith or people of good will, regardless of their faith? Explain your response. Which characters in *Amistad*, or aspects of them, remind you of the Good Samaritan as described by Jesus in today's Gospel?

2. John Quincy Adams says: "The natural state of mankind is instead—and I know this is a controversial idea—is freedom...is freedom. And the proof is the length to which a man, woman or child will go to re-

gain it once taken. He will break loose his chains. He will decimate his enemies. He will try and try and try, against all odds, against all prejudices, to get home." How many kinds of freedom are there (physical, intellectual, spiritual, political, economic, personal, etc.)? To what lengths are you willing to go to assure your own freedom? What happens when your freedoms collide with those of others? How are freedom and responsibility balanced between individuals and societies? How free was each of the people in the parable of the Good Samaritan? How free are you?

3. Slavery is using the enforced labor of another, depriving that person of his or her freedom on many levels. It is a social institution that has been part of human experience for thousands of years. It existed in biblical times, and even seemed condoned. For example, Paul told his listeners to be kind to slaves. But does this mean slavery is right, moral, just, or ethical? Why or why not? Slavery is still a profitable practice today, for example, in the Sudan. Groups in the United States of America and other countries have raised money to ransom slaves, yet powerful organizations and some governments say that ransoming slaves only makes the slave trade more profitable. What do you think? Talk about ways you can help put a stop to slavery and its causes in the world today. How can you show compassion and be a Good Samaritan to those who are in bondage, no matter the cause?

Prayer

Jesus, one of your greatest gifts to us is compassion. Teach us how to show this compassion and to be sensitive to the needs of all our neighbors. Amen.

SIXTEENTH SUNDAY OF THE YEAR

Genesis 18:1–10a;
Colossians 1:24–28;
Luke 10:38–42

Babette's Feast

Denmark, 1988, 103 minutes
Cast: Stéphane Audran, Birgitte Federspiel, Bodil Kjer,
Jarl Kulle, Jean-Philippe Lafont, Gudmar Wivesson
Writer: Gabriel Axel
Director: Gabriel Axel

Babette's Feast

A Taste of Love and Life

Two sisters, Martina and Philippa, live in a remote Jutland village during the latter half of the nineteenth century. Their father had founded a pietistic and puritanical Lutheran sect and had ruled over it with some severity. Now that he has died, the sisters maintain the sect. There is a small group of followers who were initially devout but, over the years, began to fall out with one another.

When they were young, both sisters wished to marry. Martina was in love with a cavalry officer, Lorens Lowenheilm. Philippa, who had a beautiful voice, loved Achille Papin, an opera singer. But the sisters stayed at home to care for their father, who disapproved of their suitors, and they never married.

Madame Babette Hersant, the chef from the Café Anglais in Paris, comes to live with the sisters because Papin has recommended Babette to them. Babette is a refugee from the French political turmoil of 1871. She serves the sisters faithfully and they come to depend on her.

When she wins a lottery in France, Babette offers to make the sisters and the congregation a dinner, a banquet to commemorate the one-hundredth anniversary of their father's birth. They and the congregation are reluctant but, in order not to offend Babette, they agree to attend but decide that although they will eat, they will not take pleasure from any of the food or drink. Lorens Lowenheilm and his mother are also invited.

Babette's feast is magnificent. She imports the food from far away. The guests assemble and their resistance is slowly overcome. They enjoy the feast very much, so much so that they confess how they have offended and cheated one another over the years. They go outdoors and dance in a circle of life.

The sisters are amazed that Babette has spent all her money for them but Babette replies that she is an artist and this kind of cooking and hospitality has been her life.

COMMENTARY

Babette's Feast is based on a short story by Isak Dinesen (the pen name of Karen Blixen, whom Meryl Streep portrayed in *Out of Africa*). Originally set in Norway, it was transferred by writer-director Gabriel Axel back to Blixen's Denmark, to a remote village on the Jutland coast where the Lutheran tradition is strict and severe. This brings back memories of the renowned Danish director Carl Theodor Dreyer and his movies, *Day of Wrath* and *Ordet*.

Stéphane Audran, star of many French movies, especially those of Claude Chabrol, brings beauty and conviction to the role of the exiled cook, Babette. The rest of the cast, especially the two sisters, bring the religious community to life. They show its strengths and weaknesses and take the audience into a different cultural and religious milieu and ultimately into a transforming and transcendent experience.

Babette's Feast won the Oscar for Best Foreign Language Film

DIALOGUE WITH THE GOSPEL

Focus: Babette is a Martha-figure who gives unstintingly in preparing her feast. The two sisters have been like Mary, listen-

ing to God. Now they share the feast and learn what both human and divine joy is like.

Luke does not list any menu items from the meal Martha prepared for Jesus and his disciples. The reading from Genesis, however, does describe the feast that Sarah made for the strangers at Abraham's behest, as well as some of the details of the cooking. The point, of course, is not so much the menu but the heartfelt hospitality.

In the movie, the two sisters hospitably take Babette into their home. Although she is a servant in the household, she is a respected member, even a confidante, of the sisters. She is foreign, has different customs, and does not share the sisters' puritanical attitude about life or food, but she is still welcome. The final song and the sisters' words to Babette about angels rejoicing because of her artistry highlight the beauty of the friendship.

Martha and Mary are hospitable and welcome Jesus and his disciples into their home. Martha has a touch of the work ethic about her and views others accordingly. Mary, on the other hand, knows the value of listening and contemplation.

While in this story Martha frets, is preoccupied, and does not hesitate to complain to Jesus and nag Mary, Babette has another perspective on how a meal is to be provided. Babette is the complete giver who delights in cooking, serving, and in the joy that the diners experience. She gives her time, her skills, her artistry—and all her money—to make the beautiful feast.

The result of such a generous feast for the diners is that they mellow. The shared food binds them together and they listen to one another. The grace of the feast is that they can listen to God and contemplate divine love rather than retain their image of a fierce God. They confess and ask pardon of each other. In the Gospel, contemplation is the good quality that Mary possesses and that Jesus advises Martha to nurture;

when experienced alongside a wonderful meal, both body and spirit are nourished.

- The sisters' father and his control of his congregation; his harsh Christianity, moral rectitude, and puritanical approach to pleasure and joy; the sisters' devotion to their father, their singing, their hospitality to the congregation. Philippa and her delight in singing with Achille Papin, Martina and her love for the cavalry officer, Lorens; the influence of their father and their decision not to marry.

- Babette's arrival and their kind hospitality; her place in the household, her work, the shopping, the response of the people in the village; Babette winning the lottery, her decision to make the feast, buying the ingredients, their preparation; the menu, the cooking, the serving-boy, each course, and Babette's attention to detail; the achievement of the feast and her satisfaction in giving all that she had to live on.

- The congregation and their unwillingness to enjoy the feast, their transformation, sharing with one another, confessing, pardoning; Lorens and Martina, the reconciliation and the congregation's dancing the circle of life.

1. In 1995, to commemorate the one-hundredth anniversary of the cinema, the Vatican's Pontifical Council for Social Communication issued a list of forty-five "Important Films" in the areas of religion, values, and art (www.usccb.org/fb/vaticanfilms.htm). *Babette's Feast* rightly appears on the list under religion, and has become a staple for classes and groups who appreciate the interface of religion and film. What most

impressed you about the film? In addition to hospitality, what other scriptural themes and human values come to mind when viewing *Babette's Feast?* What other religious symbols beside food are in the film?

2. To compare Babette to the active Martha and Martina and Philippa to the contemplative Mary makes for insightful conversation. Babette was forced into exile, and the two sisters chose to live in exile from the normal adult life of their neighbors. What were they missing that Babette possessed? What was the community missing that Babette's generosity provided? What could the sisters and Babette learn from one another about the image of God that influenced their lives? What is the image of God that motivates your spirituality and life choices?

3. People who appreciate religion and film often consider Babette a Christ-figure, that is, a character whose life mirrors that of Christ in many ways. (This is in contrast to a film with a Jesus-figure where the person of Jesus is actually portrayed such as *King of Kings* or Pasolini's *The Gospel according to Matthew.*) The last hour of the film starts with Babette's decision to prepare a meal for the community's special feast. Think of all the ways that Babette imitated Christ in this part of the film. In addition to the story of Martha and Mary, how does the film present the Eucharist as food for body and soul, and Babette as the one who sacrifices everything for the sake of others? Think of other movies from the "food" genre, such as *Big Night,* where Primo says, "Food is like God." What does this

mean in the context of the meal that Babette prepares? How is Babette's food "like God"?

Prayer

Jesus, you loved life and appreciated the kindness of friends. Give us the grace of joy in both serving and being served. Amen.

SEVENTEENTH SUNDAY OF THE YEAR

Genesis 18:20–32;
Colossians 2:12–14;
Luke 11:1–13

Groundhog Day

U.S.A., 1993, 103 minutes
Cast: Bill Murray, Andie MacDowell, Chris Elliot,
Stephen Tobowsky
Writers: Danny Rubin, Harold Ramis
Director: Harold Ramis

 *Groundhog Day*

Bargaining with God

SYNOPSIS

Pittsburgh TV weatherman Phil Connors has been assigned to cover "Groundhog Day" in Punxsutawney, Pennsylvania—again. February 2 is the day, according to a rural American tradition, that the groundhog, "Punxsutawney Phil," emerges from hibernation to check on the length of winter. If he sees his shadow, it means there will be six more weeks of winter. Connors is a cynic and a grump. He has covered the day several times in the past and thinks this assignment is beneath him. His producer, Rita, is more enthusiastic, and the cameraman Larry dutifully tags along. A snowstorm hits and they are stranded in Punxsutawney.

When Connors wakes the next day, he finds that it is February 2 again and that he is going through exactly the same scenario of the day before. He is the only one for whom the day is repeating itself. And the next day. And the next. And... Though he seeks psychiatric help, he soon realizes that he can use his information about the people in the town to exploit them, to have his way with women, to rob a bank. Even his suicide attempt fails and he wakes up the next day to the same routines.

After talking to Rita and realizing that he loves her, he changes and begins to use his knowledge of what will happen for people's good. Eventually, he is hailed as a local hero. The next day he wakes up and it is February 3.

COMMENTARY

Groundhog Day charmed audiences on its release because it was a comedy that really pleased everyone. Co-writer and director Harold Ramis comes from a tradition of broad humor *(Stripes* and *Caddyshack)* and he also co-wrote *Ghostbusters I* and *II* and starred in them with *Groundhog Day* star Bill Murray.

This comedy is far more restrained than Ramis's earlier work but just as funny. Bill Murray is effective as the world-weary, grouchy weatherman who has to relive February 2 until he is redeemed. Murray would go on to do more serious comedy in such movies as *Ed Wood, Cradle Will Rock, The Royal Tenenbaums.* Andie MacDowell, another Ramis alumnus *(Multiplicity),* is attractive as the producer. Ramis had a big success in 1999 with his parody of gangster movies with *Analyze This* with Robert De Niro and Billy Crystal and with the more modestly successful 2002 sequel, *Analyze That.*

DIALOGUE WITH THE GOSPEL

Focus: Just as the story of Abraham "haggling" with God gives us an example of persistent prayer, Jesus illustrates his profound teaching on prayer with down-to-earth stories about perseverance in asking for our needs. He might have used Groundhog Day *to illustrate with a light touch how to keep interceding with God and how to repent of our transgressions.*

Today's readings focus on prayer, using haggling and bargaining to make their point. "Bargaining" here is not to be understood as placing conditions on God, "you give me this and I will do that...." Rather, in the Eastern tradition from which our scriptures come, bargainers repeat the same thing again and again, modifying the offer a little every time until the buyer and the seller have reached the desired price—which they may even have intended originally. There is even an element of fun in this ritual.

This is very clear in the Genesis reading. Abraham and God go through the motions in a classical way, with God allowing Abraham to whittle him down to the minimum price: ten just men in Sodom. It is as if God and Abraham are going though the bargaining procedure; one making requests from the person with the power to grant the requests.

Christian tradition does not refer very much to Jesus' humor. This seems a pity, because, since Jesus was human in every way, he had a capacity for laughter and jokes. Commentators refer to today's Gospel as one of those times when Jesus preached in a light-hearted way to make a serious point. Some have used the image of the routines of the stand-up comic, who engages listeners in the humorous interplay of his jokes and his message. While the setting is serious—that of profound prayer in the Our Father—the subsequent preaching is humorous: the comic questioning about what good fathers give their children to eat, and the old routine of pestering repetition that also marked the widow's complaining to the unjust judge (Luke 18).

The conclusion, however, is serious. If cranky fathers can be lavish toward their sons, how much more will God be in giving the Spirit to those who ask.

In a sense, *Groundhog Day* follows these routines. With the repetition of the day, Phil has the chance to look at his life. Since he is a cynic, all he sees is cynicism. His first haggling steps with himself focus only on his nasty characteristics, even to his contemplating suicide. When he finally exhausts this approach and it is still Groundhog Day for him, he is able to move toward the goodness within him. He does some haggling with Rita, who responds positively, and he begins to be savior-figure rather than a devil-figure.

It is as if God is offering Phil more chances to repent than he knows what to do with, as if God is haggling with him, wanting him to change his heart and find redemption. It is God who is persevering, hoping that his desire for Phil's change of heart will be heard. Once Phil has surrendered, he actually receives the gift of a new spirit of happiness in his life and he can begin again.

- Phil as cynical and cantankerous, not wanting to go to the annual event, making it hard on everyone else; the routine of Phil's first Groundhog Day, the citizens and the ceremony, the people encountered, the places, the bar, the hospital, his hotel; Phil waking to the same day, the clock, the music, the messages, the food, the meetings, the ceremony, the party and its effect on him; his inability to cope.

- His malevolent use of the repetition: greed, robbery, swindling, and exploiting sex; his failure and his attempted suicide.

- The effect Rita has on Phil by her listening; his introspection and seeing his good side; his kindness and heroism; how the repetition changes him, how he makes peace with himself and surrenders his self-centeredness to find love and redemption.

KEY SCENES AND THEMES

1. To repeat a day over and over again is a popular device of science fiction or of psychological enlightenment. American baseball legend Yogi Berra said it perfectly: "It's *déjà vu* all over again" and it's a little scary. Here, the device is used to create a comic moral fable about repentance and redemption. Why do you think its easy and popular presentation attracts a wide audience? Did you like the film? Why or why not? How

FOR REFLECTION AND CONVERSATION

did it make you feel? Some people think Phil's experience is what purgatory might be like because it's like being in a time warp that you cannot get out of until you are ready. What do you think?

2. Comedy is so often culturally defined that it is often difficult to understand across cultures. When it comes to the scriptures, we are taught from an early age to approach them with great seriousness. Therefore, until we engage in some "serious" Scripture study so as to understand the language and context of the Word, it may be difficult to think of comedy or humor in the Bible. Yet, it most surely exists, for no culture can exist without laughter and humorous stories. How does *Groundhog Day* teach a profound human lesson? Do you think it parallels the lesson taught by today's readings? Why or why not? It is said that the brain releases endorphins, pain relievers, when we laugh. How is laughter a gift of the Spirit? Do you think God wants us to laugh? If so, how do you integrate this with your image of God? Talk about your response.

3. By the end of the film, Phil says: "When Chekhov saw the long winter, he saw a winter bleak and dark and bereft of hope. Yet we know that winter is just another step in the cycle of life. But standing here among the people of Punxsutawney and basking in the warmth of their hearths and hearts, I couldn't imagine a better fate than a long and lustrous winter." How well would you be able to handle reliving a bad or undesirable day over and over again until you got it right? How is Phil's experience one of a spiritual winter?

Have you ever lived through a transforming experience? What was it like?

Prayer

Lord, you taught us to pray the Our Father. You also urged us to pester the Father with our petitions. Teach us the many ways to pray and to enjoy humor in our lives. Amen.

Brad Pitt and Anthony Hopkins in *Meet Joe Black*.

Meet Joe Black

U.S.A., 1998, 181 minutes
Cast: Anthony Hopkins, Brad Pitt, Claire Forlani,
Marcia Gay Harden, Jeffrey Tambor
Writers: Ron Osborn, Jeff Reno, Kevin Wade, Bo Goldman
Director: Martin Brest

Meet Joe Black

Encountering Death

The Parrish family's lavish estate is on the Hudson River in Poughkeepsie, New York. In Manhattan one day, medical resident Susan Parrish meets a young man in a coffee shop. They part ways after a chat and he is almost immediately knocked down and killed by a car. Her father, Bill Parrish, hears voices warning him about death. He also experiences severe chest pains but conceals it from his family because he is too busy at work, planning mergers.

Death comes to visit in the form of the young man who was killed. He arrives during a family dinner at Bill's Manhattan mansion and Bill "senses" his presence at the door, though he does not know who the young man is. Bill realizes that Death has come to him and the "young man" moves into the Parrish house. Death allows Parrish some extra time to live. Because Death is "interested" in Susan as well, they make a pact that as long as Bill does not tell anyone who the visitor is, only Bill, and not Susan, will die at the appointed time. The young man is introduced to the family and to the members of Parrish's company's board as Joe Black. Joe accompanies Bill everywhere and shows an ingenuous curiosity about how humans live.

SYNOPSIS

Drew, the man Susan seems destined to marry, is Bill's number-one man at the company and organizes a coup. Parrish is forced to retire and Drew arranges for the company to merge with a larger corporation and thus dissolve itself. Susan begins to fall in love with Joe.

The climax comes on Bill's sixty-fifth birthday at a lavish party organized by his older daughter, Allison. Drew's treachery is revealed. Death/Joe has now fallen in love with Susan and wants to take her with him when it is really Bill's time to die. However, Joe finally agrees to allow Susan to live. Bill and his daughters tell of their love for one another. Death and William leave the party together.

Susan sees the young man from the coffee shop at the party. Death has permitted him to come back to life for Susan.

COMMENTARY

Meet Joe Black is a long movie. Hollywood and world audiences seemed preoccupied with angels and the afterlife during the 1990s with such films as *City of Angels, Michael,* and *The Preacher's Wife.* Anthony Hopkins plays a mild-mannered media mogul who realizes that wheeling and dealing is a very worldly and temporary activity and that life is fleeting. Brad Pitt is filmed with a kind of glow about him. He plays a nice and breezy young man whose body Death appropriates for his journey to find out what life is all about. Claire Forlani is Hopkins's younger daughter and the main reason why Death chooses this particular household to visit.

Under the gloss and the desire to explore life and death, some of the plot lines, especially Death's passion for peanut butter, are more than a touch corny. The dialogue is heavily loaded with clichés. It is a remake of the original play by Alberto Casella, the 1934 movie *Death Takes a Holiday* starring Fredric March, and the made-for-television movie made in 1971 with Melvyn Douglas.

Focus: Meet Joe Black *illustrates the parable of the rich man who is busy building bigger and bigger enterprises but who is about to die. Wealthy businessman William Parrish is given the opportunity to re-examine his life before death comes for him.*

DIALOGUE WITH THE GOSPEL

The first reading is from Ecclesiastes, which opens with Qoheleth's famous warning "Vanity of vanities! All things are vanity!" *Meet Joe Black* is a good example of a man who heeds the "vanity of vanities" admonition, takes notice of Death, and tries to put his life in order before he dies.

Luke's Gospel tells of a man in the crowd who asks Jesus to arbitrate a dispute about his inheritance. Jesus responds with the dramatic parable of the rich man who builds more barns just as he is about to die. Jesus takes the "vanity of vanities" theme and warns against avarice in this direct example about storing up things for no purpose when compared with eternity. Owning things is not the main object in life. As St. Paul tells the Colossians, "Think of what is above, not of what is on earth."

William Parrish is given a chance to review his life and prepare for death rather than dying suddenly. He takes advantage of it. William has the opportunity to meet Death and to discuss the meaning of life, to profess his love for his daughters, to recover his corporate integrity, and to grow as a better human being. He is finally ready to go with Death, having rediscovered what is important in life.

KEY SCENES AND THEMES

- The charming young man and Susan, his death and reappearance as Death; Death's choice to come to the Parrish family and Death/Joe wanting a few days to experience what human life—and love—are like; the deal between Bill and Joe.

- Bill Parrish as the self-made mogul, his lavish home, his staff and board members; the prospect of lucrative mergers to create media empires; Bill's relationships with his daughters; Parrish hearing the voices, the warnings about death, and the grim sequence of the heart attack; the dying woman at the hospital and her conversations with Joe.

- Parrish accepting death, the conversations, the reflection on the meaning of his life and its coming to an end; his readiness; Death wanting to take Susan with him, the clashes with Bill, and Bill's determination that Death keep his end of the deal; Death finally agreeing; Bill and Death walking into eternity; the return of the young man.

FOR REFLECTION AND CONVERSATION

1. The theme of the readings today reminds us not to invest too heavily in the things of this world. Greed is the strong desire for more. Our political economy in the West is constructed on what Drew testifies to in the film: to exist, a corporation must expand, regardless of the consequences. Talk about some recent corporate scandals that have cost innocent people their jobs, life savings and retirement funds. At the end of the day, who really profits from greed and acts of avarice? Will humanity ever learn the lessons of the scriptures, of plays like *You Can't Take It with You* (Moss Hart and George S. Kaufman, 1938) or films such as *Meet Joe Black*? Identify the explicit or implicit expression of the seven principles of Catholic social teaching in *Meet Joe Black* (human dignity, the common good, universal distribution of goods, collegiality, subsidiarity, the integrity of creation, the preferential option for the poor) and talk about practical ways you or your group can implement them in your daily lives.

2. How is the character of the dying woman from Jamaica like an oracle, or source of wisdom (compare with *The Matrix* and *The Stand*)? How is her attitude toward death different from that of Bill? Bill wants to make sure everything is in order before he dies, yet the woman wants memories. What do you think is the main theme of this film, death or love or something else entirely? Why?

3. There are many symbols in the film that have biblical significance. For example, the models and paintings of ships in Bill's study signify power (commerce and ordering human activities without God), safety (Noah's ark), human vulnerability (shipwreck), communication (ways to spread the Word), salvation (those who weather the storms because of faith and good works). Light is always contrasted with darkness in the film, the interiors of the rooms are appointed in black, and often the characters wear black. There are also many references to the senses. Recall the scenes where touch (in the opening sequence, Susan is constantly touching her father's arm), smell, taste, hearing, sight and even intuition are integrated into the story as ways to contrast life and death. What other symbols did you notice, such as the music? What did the film mean for you? How will it influence your life? Will it?

Prayer

Lord, we pray that we may be ready for death, our lives in order and our hearts with you. Amen.

Wisdom 18:6–9;
Hebrews 11:1–2, 8–19;
Luke 12:32–48

Mrs. Brown
U.K., 1997, 103 minutes
Cast: Judi Dench, Billy Connolly, Geoffrey Palmer,
Antony Sher, Richard Pasco
Writer: Jeremy Brock
Director: John Madden

 *Mrs. Brown*

Alert and Faithful Servants

SYNOPSIS

Queen Victoria has been on the throne of England since 1837. She and her devoted husband, Prince Albert, had nine children together. He has died after twenty-one years of marriage, and three years later, the queen remains inconsolable. She has withdrawn to the Isle of Wight and no one can persuade her to go back to London and resume her duties of state.

John Brown, a Scotsman who was master of Prince Albert's horses at Balmoral Estate in Scotland, is sent for and given the task of getting the Queen outdoors to go riding. She refuses to do so. He waits patiently outdoors with the horses, rain or shine, until she eventually approaches him out of curiosity and he persuades her to go out. The queen and her family go to Balmoral, where Brown takes her riding and they visit local people. The queen's spirit revives but she is still unwilling to take up affairs of state.

Her physician cares for her but there is a steady stream of politicians, family, and friends who entreat, even demand, that she return to London. Prime Minister Benjamin Disraeli uses all his diplomatic skills to no avail.

People gossip about the queen and John Brown and give her the nickname Mrs. Brown.

The queen is finally persuaded by her ministers and by political circumstances to return to London with a renewed sense of duty. John Brown, whose presence and authority in the palace has grown because of his friendship with the queen, is now out of favor. Politicians hope for his final fall from grace and contrive situations to show him as disloyal. While the queen goes on to rule her empire, Brown, only a shell of the man he once was, dies.

COMMENTARY

The striking cast for this movie includes Judi Dench who received an Oscar nomination for her performance as Queen Victoria. She was to win an Oscar in 1999 for her performance as Queen Elizabeth I in *Shakespeare in Love.* Comedian Billy Connolly is surprisingly effective in the dramatic role of Brown. Antony Sher is Disraeli.

Queen Victoria has been a very popular subject for British movies over the years, with Anna Neagle playing her in *Victoria the Great* (1937) and in *Sixty Glorious Years* (1938). George Arliss won a Best Actor Oscar for his portrayal of the prime minister in *Disraeli* (1931). Movie buffs will remember *The Mudlark* (1950), with Irene Dunne as the queen, Finlay Currie as Brown, and Alec Guinness as Disraeli.

The re-creation of the decor and costumes of the period will delight those who enjoy historical dramas. Several companies were involved in the making of *Mrs. Brown*, including Mobile Masterpiece Theater and Boston's Public Broadcasting Station, WGBH, both known for their support of superb period dramas.

DIALOGUE WITH THE GOSPEL

Focus: Servants such as John Brown are no longer fashionable in our days of social equality. Jesus uses the example of servants and masters but turns the image on its head by showing a master who waits on faithful and alert servants. John Brown is a model of this faithful servant.

Jesus often shatters his audience's (and our) expectations of what he had to say. Here he begins speaking of the characteristics of good servants and their duties. But then, he surprises us by telling a story about faithful and alert servants, ready for the master's arrival, whom the master does not permit to wait on him; instead, he waits on the servants! The readings from Wisdom and Hebrews remind us of the generous nature of God's covenanted relationship with us. God does not love us because we first offer our love and service; rather, God loves us unconditionally.

At the opening of today's Gospel, Jesus speaks of simplicity. Queen Victoria, in her grief, wanted to retire from the trappings of the public arena and lead a "simple life" (in the Victorian royal sense) with her family.

However, most of the Gospel concerns stewards and servants and so John Brown's characterization is relevant for reflection. Brown fulfils many of the injunctions that Jesus suggests are characteristic of a faithful servant. The image of Brown, holding his horse, waiting patiently day after day for the queen, is a symbol of the attentive servant. As the queen grew to trust him, Brown was able to minister to her needs and to help her emerge from her staid life of imposed mourning for her deceased husband.

Brown also takes her visiting where she helps to set the table, shares a meal, and drinks with ordinary people. In an ideal world, not only would the servant become a better servant (as Brown does), but the person in charge would learn to serve the servant, as Jesus urges. Although Queen Victoria mellows in Brown's company and offers him deep friendship, she does not follow the Gospel invitation to its conclusion, perhaps prevented by the expectations and protocols of the Victorian era.

Courtiers and politicians, envious of Brown's place in the queen's household, are jealous of him and accuse him of the kind of irresponsible and self-serving attitudes that Jesus condemns. Brown certainly does become high-handed, keeping the queen apart from people, even preventing her from attending her son, the Prince of Wales, when he becomes ill. When Brown oversteps his bounds, he is condemned and his stewardship comes to an end. The final sentence of the Gospel sums up both Brown's loyalty to the queen as well as his demise: "Much will be required of the person entrusted with much, and still more will be demanded of the person entrusted with more."

KEY SCENES AND THEMES

- Queen Victoria, her age and experience, marriage, the death of Prince Albert; her grief and her long mourning through the 1860s; the waning of her popularity because she is out of public life; her refusal to participate in government; the court on the Isle of Wight and at Balmoral, the formality and the queen's control.

- John Brown's coming from Scotland, his friendship with the now-deceased prince and his loyalty to his memory; his gruff Scots manner and character; John's plain talking with the queen and her angry reaction; his standing and waiting beside her pony, his discussion about orders; the queen rebuking him and his refusal to give up on her; going for the swim with all the formalities—the box, the costumes, and the hats; her decision to visit the Scots family and enjoying it, setting the table, coming back late, drinking whisky; his encouragement that the queen write her memoirs.

- The queen's platonic love for Brown, their friendship; treating Brown better than the other servants, taking orders from him, his control of her life instead of being controlled by Sir Henry; the change in Brown: his growing formality, his loyalty to the queen, respect, the sense of duty, his love and his inability to express it; being with the servants, their disdain, taking the head of the table, becoming more autocratic; his demise, his drinking, the later years, being mocked, and his final loyalty.

FOR REFLECTION AND CONVERSATION

1. Jesus used examples his listeners could understand, and even we understand the analogy of servants and masters. "Honest to God, woman, I never thought to see you in such a state. You must miss him dreadfully," John Brown tells Queen Victoria when he sees her two years after Prince Albert's death. This is not a statement defined by the rules of class distinction, but by friendship based on a strong sense of self. How does the servant John Brown serve Queen Victoria by being a friend rather than by accepting the role of a second-class citizen? How many servant relationships are there in *Mrs. Brown* (the servants downstairs, the prime minister to the nation, queen to her people, secretary to the queen, queen to her children, etc.), and which ones are examples of service, selflessness, virtue, duty, loyalty, and friendship?

2. Some say that the British people are obsessed with "class" and "class distinctions" because the class system was hereditary and institutionalized but Americans, for example, don't care about social class. Is this really true? The United States was founded on the idea that all "men" are created equal and that all human beings share certain inalienable rights, yet prejudices, race, and economics continue to divide us. How

are race, social class, and economics connected in our real world? How can we put the Gospel image of Jesus' serving others without distinction into practice today?

3. An interesting dimension of *Mrs. Brown* is the role of the tabloid press in the nation's life. How is the tabloid press both annoying and subversive at the same time, that is, how does it critique the political status quo while managing to spread untruths through innuendo? How did the tabloids help form public opinion in that time, and how do they do it now? On the other hand, Queen Victoria's memoirs were very popular and also played a part in forming public opinion in favor of the monarchy. Talk about the role of the press or the news media. How can the press be at the service of truth and responsible and free at the same time?

Prayer

Lord, you ask us to serve you and to be alert. You also told us that when we love you, we are no longer your servants but your friends. Give us your loving friendship. Amen.

TWENTIETH SUNDAY OF THE YEAR

Jeremiah 38:4–6, 8–10;
Hebrews 12:1–4;
Luke 12:49–53

The Straight Story

U.S.A., 1999, 111 minutes
Cast: Richard Farnsworth, Sissy Spacek, Harry Dean Stanton
Writers: John Roach, Mary Sweeney
Director: David Lynch

The Straight Story

Family Discord and Reconciliation

SYNOPSIS

Alvin Straight is getting to be an old man. He can no longer drive because his vision is not very good. He also needs a hip replacement. He lives with his mentally slow daughter, Rose, who has lost custody of her children after an accident. Alvin receives news that his brother, Lyle, to whom he has not spoken for ten years, has had a stroke.

Alvin decides to go to visit Lyle so he can reconcile with him. He remembers how close they were as boys on a poor farm and how well they knew each other as brothers. He starts out for a three hundred-mile drive on his old lawnmower. It breaks down before he barely gets out of town and he buys a used one.

On the road he encounters a cross section of people. He listens, reminisces, and offers words of wisdom. The people include a pregnant girl, cyclists, a woman who keeps running down deer with her car, a welcoming family, an old veteran who shares terrible war stories with him, bickering twin mechanics, and a friendly priest.

He finally arrives at Lyle's and they sit down on the porch to look at the stars as they used to when they were boys.

The Straight Story is one of the best screen stories about old age and the wisdom that comes with a lifetime of experience. It is based on an article that appeared in the *New York Times* in 1994 that caught the attention and imagination of screenwriter Mary Sweeney.

As played by veteran character actor/stunt man Richard Farnsworth in an Oscar-nominated performance, Alvin is a genial soul who lives quietly with his daughter, Rose, played by Sissy Spacek, and with the company of friends.

David Lynch is best known for his surreal pictures of the dark side of American society *(Blue Velvet, Wild at Heart, Twin Peaks, Mulholland Drive)* but he also made deeply human films such as *The Elephant Man* and *Dune.* Instead of his previous less-than-successful film, *Lost Highway,* Lynch has now found an American road and drives, with Alvin, straight down it to our souls.

COMMENTARY

Focus: While Jesus says that belief in him will cause violence and division in families, we know that faith in Jesus means that we are called to heal divisions and foster reconciliation. This is what Alvin Straight believed and achieved.

DIALOGUE WITH THE GOSPEL

The reading from Jeremiah sets a hostile tone and focuses on the antagonism of the religious leaders who want to put the prophet Jeremiah to death, throwing him down a muddy well because his teaching irritates them. The Jesus in Luke is best known for his compassion. In this Gospel passage, however, he speaks in an impassioned, dramatic, and absolute manner, saying that he will bring violence and division and turn members of families against one another. This is because believing in Jesus and accepting his baptism is so different from the status quo.

Given that the entire Gospel message is about good news and reconciliation, *The Straight Story* offers a reflection on the consequences of division and hatreds. Faced with these, followers of Jesus will seek reconciliation.

At the end of the reading from Jeremiah, the prophet is rescued and continues his ministry. The reading from the Letter to the Hebrews shows that Jesus is ultimately triumphant, leading us in faith and bringing that faith to perfection. The reading encourages us "to rid ourselves of every burden and sin, to run the race...for the sake of joy...."

Alvin Straight is a man who has had division in his life, not over following Christ, but because he was angry and drunk. He can now talk plainly about the war and his falling-out with his brother. He speaks to the pregnant girl and to the bickering twins about family ties and the bonds between brothers, highlighting his will to achieve reconciliation. Alvin's arrival at his brother's place and their time on the porch together is a moving scene of what might be achieved once stubbornness and bitterness are gone.

Alvin's various encounters on the road demonstrate the wisdom of age and experience and offer those he meets a heritage of understanding, peace, and harmony, where divisions are healed and reconciliation celebrated.

KEY SCENES AND THEMES

- Alvin collapsed on his floor; his independence and lack of fuss; Rose's care for him; the advice of the doctor; the news of Lyle's stroke; Alvin's determination and motives for going to him; Alvin's world: Iowa landscapes, the highway, its beauty and its weather; Alvin's stoically enduring the elements on his journey.

- The people Alvin meets and his giving them something of himself: the pregnant girl and the bundle of sticks story, the cyclists, the woman who hit the deer, the veteran and their sharing confidences, the moment of healing for each; the kind husband and wife; the bickering brothers and the occasion for Alvin to reflect on how well brothers know each other and how fighting is bitter and a waste.

- The encounter with the priest, the talk about the cemetery and the explorers buried there; the priest's having met Lyle at the hospital; the mower's breaking down again near Lyle's place; help to restart and arriving; sitting on the porch with Lyle.

FOR REFLECTION AND CONVERSATION

1. Alvin is on a three hundred-mile journey on a lawn-mower from Laurens, Iowa, to Mt. Zion, Wisconsin. He didn't exactly "run" the race, but he persevered and went as fast as he could go. It took him more than five weeks to reach his brother's house. Along the way he met many people and experienced the kindness of strangers. How were these people like "a crowd of witnesses" for Alvin? How did they and Alvin unburden themselves? How did the music and the symbolism in the film help create meaning for you on an emotional level?

2. Talk about each of the people or groups of people that Alvin meets along the way, for example, the pregnant girl. How did her journey change through her encounter with Alvin? How were the cyclists a metaphor for modern, global life as compared to rural, small-town life? What did the incident with the deer mean to you? Why do you think Alvin mounted the antlers on his trailer? Strangers were kind to Alvin and welcomed him—how was he with them? Was he a kind of prophet, do you think? Talk about the kind of person you would like to be at the end of your life. How did Alvin begin preparing for his journey even before he left?

3. Division and healing have been part of Alvin's life for a long time. His regret and pain because of the war and his estrangement from his brother show his inner reality. Now, his physical infirmities threaten his independence. His soul and his body need healing, especially from his traumatic war experience. And all the people he meets need healing in one way or another. Looking at people from the outside, it is often hard to see what they are suffering. Does Alvin ever judge the people he meets? How does his style of relating to people provide the opportunity for him to communicate what he believes and lives? What do Alvin and all the people he meets learn from this journey to reconciliation? What did you learn? Discuss the ways this is might be a paradigm for a film about life and family.

Prayer

Lord, while you urge us to choose you above all others, bless the families we love and all those with whom we come in contact on our journey through life. Amen.

Tim Robbins and Morgan Freeman in *The Shawshank Redemption*.

Twenty-First Sunday of the Year
Isaiah 66:18–21;
Hebrews 12:5–7, 11–13;
Luke 13:22–30

The Shawshank Redemption
U.S.A., 1994, 142 minutes
Cast: Tim Robbins, Morgan Freeman, James Whitmore,
Bob Gunton, William Sadler, Clancy Brown, Gil Bellows
Writer: Frank Darabont
Director: Frank Darabont

The Shawshank Redemption

The Last First and the First Last

SYNOPSIS

It is 1947 and bank accountant Andy Dufresne's wife is having an affair with a golf pro. Andy is desperately jealous. When she and her lover are found murdered, Dufresne is arrested. Although he protests his innocence, he is convicted and given a life sentence at Maine's Shawshank prison. Life in Shawshank is brutal yet he is able to keep an inner calm. Eventually, he wins the respect of his fellow prisoners. He and Red, who is in prison for a murder he committed as a young man, become close friends. Red has been refused parole many times. He is an authority figure among the men and runs an undercover operation to obtain contraband items for those willing to pay. Through Red, Andy obtains a little rock hammer. Over almost twenty years, Andy talks to Red about his dreams and his hopes.

Using his wits, Andy ingratiates himself with the guards by offering to help with inheritance issues, accounts, and tax returns. The sanctimonious and cruel warden also uses him to manage and cover up shady financial deals. To cover the paper trail created by the scheming warden, Andy creates a fictitious personality for the funds he manages. Andy makes friends with Brooks, who runs the prison library. Later, Andy

301

writes letters to politicians asking for library funding for books and they respond by giving him an annual budget. A new prisoner arrives who knows the truth about who murdered Andy's wife. When Andy asks the warden for help to reopen his case, the warden refuses and has the other prisoner killed.

All along, Andy has been using the rock hammer to secretly burrow a tunnel behind large wall posters—first of movie star Rita Hayworth, then Marilyn Monroe, and finally Raquel Welch—to the sewers. He escapes, uses the I.D. he created to obtain funds, sends evidence of the warden's crimes to the press, and takes off for Mexico. The Bible-thumping warden kills himself.

Red is finally granted parole. He follows clues that Andy has left him, finding money and a letter that leads him to his friend Andy in Mexico.

COMMENTARY

The Shawshank Redemption was one of the top movies of the 1990s. It received seven Oscar nominations, including one for best film of 1994.

There is a cinematic tradition in Hollywood that uses prison as an image of the human condition. Films from this genre dramatize aspects of human dignity and heroism that transcend their prison setting, such as the *Birdman of Alcatraz, Cool Hand Luke, Papillon, The Count of Monte Cristo,* and *The Green Mile.*

Tim Robbins plays with perfection the young financial adviser found guilty of murder and sentenced to Shawshank. Morgan Freeman gives another fine performance as a man who retains great dignity in the face of prejudice. His voice-over commentary contributes to the powerful impact of the movie. Character actor Bob Gunton is the sinister, Bible-quoting warden.

The movie is a satisfying mix of the expected and the surprising, an intelligent adult drama that relies on a thoughtful response rather than on sensationalism. It is based on a

Stephen King short story, "Rita Hayworth and the Shawshank Redemption." Frank Darabont wrote the screenplay and directed the film. His subsequent movies were *The Green Mile*, also based on a Stephen King story, and *The Majestic* with Jim Carrey.

> *Focus: God's criteria for who will be saved are different from society's standards for success and public righteousness. The hypocritical warden of Shawshank prison was first but will now be last; Andy Dufresne, the falsely accused prisoner, was last and is first.*

DIALOGUE WITH THE GOSPEL

Today's readings all offer ways to interpret the *The Shawshank Redemption* meaningfully. The reading from the book of Isaiah speaks of fugitives being sent to distant coastlands. Andy Dufresne's escape from Shawshank means that he is a fugitive, an innocent survivor who has been able to use the defects of the system for his own salvation. The reading from Hebrews can be read in connection with Andy Dufresne's twenty years of unjust imprisonment. There is a kind of cruel irony here for the arbitrary "bad luck" that befalls Andy: "…whom the Lord loves, he disciplines; he scourges every son he acknowledges." There is hope as well, because Andy is a man who has suffered wrongly, and he makes the best of the situation. Indeed, "discipline…brings the peaceful fruit of righteousness to those who are trained by it."

The Gospel opens with a question asking if only a few will be saved. Jesus answers with an image: the gate to salvation is narrow. In the movie, the people who seem worthy on the outside, like the warden, are hypocrites who contrive to avoid the narrow door while urging others through it in the name of the Bible. As Jesus warns, they will try to enter the gate but it is closed to them because they have ignored the Word.

The warden fulfills the epitome of the evildoers that Jesus describes. He has presumed his closeness to God and fears he will be sent away to the sound of "wailing and grinding of teeth" as the police come to arrest him. Who, then, will be saved? Those who were last, like Andy Dufresne, like Red, like Brooks, who is unable to survive in the outside world, and like Tommy, who is killed for the sake of truth. They will find redemption and be first. Jesus' words and the characters from this movie enhance our understanding of God's call to redemption.

KEY SCENES AND THEMES

- Red's voice-over, his perspective, and his judgments on the situations in prison and on Andy Dufresne; Andy, self-contained, going to prison, chained in the line, the prisoners' speculations, the delousing, the cell, his not crying out; his adapting to prison life, loneliness, routines, laundry work, the homosexual group and their provocation, the shower, the fight, the rapes, the effect on him; his endurance while being "the wrong man."

- The initial encounter with Brooks in the dining room with the bug and the bird; Brooks and the library; his parole, the rented room, the supermarket work, his loneliness, despair and suicide; his need for redemption; the warden, his speech, fundamentalist religion, the Bible, anti-swearing yet his sexual tone, corruption, unfair management of the prison, power, spot-searching; Andy notifying the newspapers, the arrests, the warden deciding to shoot himself.

- Andy at his desk, his office, respect, the letters for the library, keeping the books, the money deals, laundering the money, the documentation in the safe; Andy creating a fictitious person and documents, the untraceable money; the irony of his sculptures and the tunnel behind the poster, going through the walls and then the sewer of the prison to escape, coming into the light and sharing freedom with Red.

1. As recently as 2001, the two most popular films for college students taking the course "Film and Theology" at the University of Dayton were about prisoners: *The Spitfire Grill* and *The Shawshank Redemption*. When asked which aspects of *The Shawshank Redemption* impressed them the most, the students replied that it was the enduring friendship between Andy and Red and the theme of hope. How did the film make you feel? What impressed you the most about it?

2. Talk about some of the themes in the film, such as life (Brooks and the bird), music, books, religion, education. Discuss the importance of a person's name. A man dies in the beginning of the film and Andy wants to know his name, "He must have a name." All the way through, names are carved on the prison walls and Brooks and Red leave their names carved in the rafters of the boarding-house room. What is the link between a person's name, and his or her dignity, identity, and destiny? How did Andy even get the idea to escape?

3. The hypocrisy of the warden in *The Shawshank Redemption* is terrible. He preaches the Bible to keep the prisoners in control but by his actions contradicts everything the Word of God is meant to be. Every person ever born has had to endure trials, as the reading from Hebrews reminds us. But how are we as Christians and seekers and promoters of justice meant to "endure"? Do the readings today indicate a passive or active response on our part to the trials of life? What does a Christian philosophy of the person indicate

regarding our personal response to human suffering? How did each of the characters in the film respond to what they had to endure? Make a list of the Gospel values and virtues you can identify in the film and talk about them. If you were in a similar situation, how would you cope and respond?

Prayer

Lord, open the door for us and invite us into your kingdom. Amen.

Twenty-Second Sunday of the Year

Sirach 3:17–18, 20, 28–29;
Hebrews 12:18–19, 22–24a;
Luke 14:1, 7–14

Evita

U.S.A., 1996, 120 minutes
Cast: Madonna, Antonio Banderas,
Jonathan Pryce, Jimmy Nail
Writers: Oliver Stone, Alan Parker
Director: Alan Parker

 Evita

Rise and Fall

SYNOPSIS

Born into poverty in the Argentinean countryside in 1919, the illegitimate Eva survives through natural cunning and street-wise ways and makes her way, eventually to the capital, Buenos Aires. She begins to sing in the city cafés, uses her sex appeal to earn money as a model, and eventually becomes a star of a radio soap opera.

Eva catches the attention of rising politician Juan Peron. He courts her and marries her in 1946. With Argentina struggling economically and in need of social reform, Peron comes to power. His popularity is increased because of his wife. The people, especially the poor, revere and admire her as a glamorous celebrity, calling her "Evita." She has attained the status of the country's first lady as well as of its leading lady, cultivating a reputation for works of charity and public concern.

Eva overreaches herself, as does Peron, in their unscrupulous quest for wealth and power. This does not seem to matter to the populace. When Eva Peron dies from cancer while still young, they venerate her as a saint.

COMMENTARY

Evita was shot in Argentina, Hungary (primarily for the funeral sequence), and England. The wide-screen photography is quite magnificent and has an epic sweep.

Antonio Banderas acts and sings as a number of characters as he takes on his role of Che, who is the "Everyman" chorus. He appears at every stage of Eva Peron's life as the personification of Argentina, explaining how the nation is affected by Evita's life. He is also her constant critic. Audiences understand events in the film through Che.

Jonathan Pryce appears as a complacent, sometimes weak Peron, who takes a back seat to Evita for purposes of the story. In real life, Juan Peron was quite able to continue once Eva had died.

The dialogue is almost completely sung and Tim Rice's lyrics for Andrew Lloyd Webber's score contribute strongly to character development. Director Alan Parker, who directed a variety of screen musicals such as *Bugsy Malone* and *The Commitments* (and would go on to direct *Angela's Ashes* in 1998 and *The Life of David Gale* in 2003), devised ways of combining the visual and aural elements of the movie through a variety of montages to create a more profound impact on the audience and to move the narrative forward. One of the great strengths of the film is its ability to develop the audience's awareness of the social history of the times through image and song.

DIALOGUE WITH THE GOSPEL

Focus: Eva Peron serves as a striking twentieth-century example of someone who claimed the highest status but was forced to lower places. As the Gospel parable attests, she had to give up her seat and take the lowest place.

The reading from Sirach tells us to "humble yourself more, the greater you are." The life and career of Eva Peron was a strange mixture of humble origins and material and political success. Her life was one of double standards, both in appearances and in reality.

Today's Gospel shows us Jesus as the victim of religious authorities who should have behaved humbly, given their role in the religious community. They watched Jesus closely at the dinner, and he watched them right back. When he noticed that as the guests arrived they picked the places of honor at the table, he offered a parable about choosing the lowest seat so that the host may invite you to go higher, should he or she desire to do so.

Poverty drove Evita to strive for the best places in Argentina and in the world. The movie is a parable illustrating how someone's drive to overcome their humble origins pushes them to claim the best of everything. Evita gave the appearance of helping those in need and giving to others while not expecting others to give to her in return. She was admired for this. Some saw it as holiness, and indeed some of it was influenced by her religious background. But mostly, she thirsted for this admiration and her ambitions drove her toward the best places, no matter the consequences.

With her illness, the time came for Evita to "move down," and she was humiliated by this diminishment. Her ambiguous reputation, colored by this film and by other movies about her, have contributed to the continuing reassessment of the private morals versus the public virtuous facade of a number of twentieth-century political figures.

Although we can understand Eva Peron's need to overcome her background, the Gospel message is for everyone, rich and poor: choose the lowest place and you may be asked to move higher; if you have a banquet, don't just invite those who will reciprocate. Invite the poor, and you will be "repaid at the resurrection of the righteous."

- Argentina 1952, the people watching the movie, the interruption, the news, their weeping; the transition to the funeral; Che's narrative and critique of Evita; her poor, working-class beginnings, her disdain of the

KEY SCENES AND THEMES

aristocrats; her move into the world of fashion, radio, and film; meeting Peron, and her political efforts for him as the way she won his heart; Peron and his presence; the continual political upheaval.

- The world's response to Evita's tour; the adulation in Spain and France, spurning in Italy, her visit to Pius XII and only receiving a rosary; the popularity of Peron and the election; the seven years of her achievement; her wealth, glamour, fashion, clothes; her response to the people; "Don't Cry for Me, Argentina" before and after she becomes ill; running for vice president and not being allowed to do so; the purpose of her Rainbow Trip, establishing charitable foundations, her generosity toward the people, literally throwing money away.

- Che as "Everyman": representing the people of Argentina; his appearances in the cinema, on the streets, in the cafés, in the restaurants, in the city, as a worker; his comments, questions, judgments; his response to Evita; kissing her casket at the end; the huge funeral processions; Evita lying in state and people touching her coffin; the singing of "Santa Evita"; the people who hated her, her star quality and ambition; her lasting influence on Argentina.

FOR REFLECTION AND CONVERSATION

1. Evita is certainly an enigmatic figure for the subject of a musical and a major motion picture. But the mystery of her personality and her bold campaign to become rich and happy are documented by history. We know she became wealthy, but do you think she was truly happy? The lyrics of one of the songs have her singing about Nicolo Machiavelli (1469–1527), author of *The Prince* and amoral architect of "the ends justify

the means" philosophy of modern living. From what you know about Evita from history and from the film, was she amoral? What role do you think her faith really played in her life?

2. Despite the fact that many people must have known that she was skimming from the money given to her charitable foundation, the populace seemed to forgive Eva. Her beauty and rise to wealth and fame caught their imagination and offered them a vicarious way to escape, perhaps, their own poverty and dreary lives. Why is a celebrity so powerful? How does being a celebrity bring a responsibility with it? Are our motivations ever completely pure? Che tells Evita that she has let the people down: she was supposed to live forever. Is this what a celebrity is about? Why are audiences attracted to the rich and famous? Whether rich, poor, or in between, how are all called to live today's Gospel?

3. One of Andrew Lloyd Weber and Tim Rice's approaches to musicals is repetition—of melodies, songs, and words. Over and over again Evita or someone sings: "Where am I going to?" And the answer comes, "Don't ask." At the end, Peron tells Evita she is dying and she asks again, "Where am I going to?" He responds, "Don't ask anymore." Blessed James Alberione (1884–1971), founder of the Daughters of St. Paul and other congregations and institutes of the Pauline Family, used to ask his spiritual sons and daughters: "How many times do you ask yourself the great question: where is humanity going, how is it moving, toward what goal is it aiming as it continually renews itself on the face of the earth? Humanity is like a great river flowing into eternity." Why did God make us?

What is the purpose of our lives? When you ask yourself, "Where am I going?" what is your answer?

Prayer

Lord, give us a true and realistic understanding of ourselves so that we may be honest and humble, so that we may discover the meaning of our lives and live them in justice. Amen.

Gallipoli

Australia, 1981, 114 minutes
Cast: Mel Gibson, Mark Lee, Bill Hunter, Bill Kerr
Writers: David Williamson, Peter Weir
Director: Peter Weir

Gallipoli

War and Peace

In 1915, while World War I rages in Europe, Archie Hamilton works on the family farm in the outback in Western Australia. He is very athletic. At a weekend competition, Archie races against Frank and wins. Afterwards, both young men try to enlist in the army to support England, but they are too young. Excited by the prospect of action overseas, they travel across the desert to Perth to try to enlist because no one there knows they are underage. They are accepted into different brigades and go their separate ways.

Later, Archie and Frank meet again at a war-training exercise outside Cairo, Egypt, and Frank transfers to Archie's outfit as they set sail for Turkey. There, the troops await the British forces so they can advance together against the Turks, who are allies of the Germans. Finally, the Australian and New Zealand soldiers are deployed as decoys to engage the Turkish army so the British can land safely on another beach.

The general asks Archie to be a runner between officers in the field, but Archie, who has wanted to fight all along, suggests that Frank be the runner instead. In the chaos, orders are confused and information is contradictory. British officers decide that the Australians and New Zealanders must

SYNOPSIS

advance even though the Turks, who have machine guns, are massacring them. Frank's friends are killed. When the order to attack is countermanded, Frank runs through the trenches to stop the slaughter, but he arrives just as the general gives the signal for battle. It is too late. Archie is killed almost immediately.

COMMENTARY

Gallipoli is a purposeful war movie because it shows the reality of battle and, at the same time, highlights the futility of war and the loss of life. It is the story of the Australian landing on the Turkish coast at Gallipoli, an event that quickly became the "myth" of the heroes of the Dardanelles, the ANZACS (Australian and New Zealand Army Corps). It is an epic tale of self-sacrifice and defeat that defined Australian and New Zealand history and how it would be characterized in terms of glory and honor. Anzac Day, April 25, is a public holiday in Australia.

Gallipoli is one of Peter Weir's greatest films. It won eight Australian Film Institute Awards, with Mel Gibson and Bill Hunter winning for acting, and Peter Weir for directing.

Weir's movie is a re-creation of war and a powerful and emotional criticism of it. *Gallipoli* is Weir's tribute to the men who died with valor because of the stupidity of generals.

DIALOGUE WITH THE GOSPEL

Focus: The strategy that Jesus speaks of in his parable about kings planning for battle and deciding to negotiate instead evokes the memory of Gallapoli and the ANZACS in World War I, and the tragedy that resulted through lack of prudence and patience.

The reading from the book of Wisdom highlights the limitations of the human reasoning and planning needed for our earthly pathways to "be made straight." This highlights the tragedy caused by the British strategy for the landing at Gallipoli. The sad consequence of such unsure reasoning and unstable intentions was that lives were unnecessarily put at risk and destroyed. The Spirit is indeed needed for wise leadership—a spirit of discernment when faced with uncertainty.

The Gospel begins with Jesus urging a spirit of detachment for his disciples, even from their families, in order to follow him. Jesus uses the image of taking up the cross and being prepared to lose one's life. He teaches us to renounce, to surrender, everything we hold precious to follow him because this is true self-sacrifice, true discipleship. On a patriotic level, the soldiers who followed orders at Gallipoli gave their lives for what they believed was a noble cause. Archie Hamilton exemplified the idealistic and generous "laying down of one's life" for a cause greater than himself. At the same time, the generals exemplified a lack of planning that would have saved their men. They were not like the king who would rather negotiate for peace than fight a battle he knows he will lose.

This passage from Luke is the only time Jesus uses the imagery of war in the Gospels. Jesus makes basic, even common-sense observations about strategy and the deployment of armies, but he uses this example to highlight how difficult following him can be. We must make no mistake in understanding that following the way of discipleship requires careful calculation before setting out. *Gallipoli* illustrates the results of such mistaken calculation, using Jesus' example of war. Instead of prudently discerning the outcome, *Gallipoli's* generals implicitly follow the "principle" of collateral damage, putting their own glory and reputation above the safety of their men. Ultimately, they lose not only the battle, but the lives of their men. *Gallipoli* examines the morality of war and the meaning of self-sacrifice, and in light of today's readings, asks us to discern our own behavior with honesty and prudence.

KEY SCENES AND THEMES

- Archie training to run, his uncle and the images from *The Jungle Book*; his desire to join the army; Frank and his friends talking about joining up; Archie and Frank meeting at the race; becoming friends; their hopes and dreams; the atmosphere in Australia in 1915; the old camel driver who hears about the Germans wanting to take over Australia ("They're welcome to it"); patriotism and the desire for adventure.

• The Australian and New Zealand soldiers causing mischief in Cairo and not realizing what war really would be like; mocking the English, playing football, training; Frank and Archie meeting again; their arrival at Gallipoli, meeting Frank's friends, their easygoing manner and the swimming; the chaotic camp, the growing tension; the trenches, the officers, the men, their morale, and prayer.

• The British officers and their strategies and the role of the ANZACs; the protection of the British and the expendability of the ANZACs; the arguments between the officers and the intransigence of the British generals; the prospect of massacre; Archie giving up the security of being a runner for Frank; Frank's desperate race to countermand the attack; the commanding officer's sacrificing himself and his men; Archie repeating what his uncle used to say when they trained; going over the top of the cliff and the final freeze-frame.

FOR REFLECTION AND CONVERSATION

1. Screenwriter David Williamson has developed the script in three precise acts that contrast geography and men: the introduction of Archie and Frank against the isolation of the outback of Western Australia; large numbers of troops training in Egypt against the backdrop of the crowded marketplace, the desert, and the pyramids; the troops landing at Gallipoli and the massacre set amid the barren

trenches and cliffs of Turkey. What other elements do the filmmakers use to contrast the concepts of war and peace (e.g., the friendship and discord among the friends), good and evil, strategy and errors in judgment, innocence and guilt? Recall how often water is used in the film. What purpose does it serve to tell the story and drive the plot? How would you articulate the plot of *Gallipoli?* How does the use of both classic and contemporary music work with the images to evoke an emotional response to the film?

2. The U.S. abolitionist, writer, and orator Frederick Douglass (d. 1895) said in a speech in 1852, "He who will, intelligently, lay down his life for his country, is a man whom it is not in human nature to despise." And the Italian nationalist leader, Giuseppe Garibaldi (1807–1882), said soon before his death, "Anyone who wants to carry on the war against the outsiders, come with me. I can't offer you either honors or wages; I offer you hunger, thirst, forced marches, battles, and death. Anyone who loves his country, follow me." Talk about these two statements and what they mean when examined under the lens of patriotism and today's film. What is patriotism? Why do you think Jesus used the analogy of war in today's reading? What is the connection between the Gospel, love for one's country, and what is true and just for all people? Is there a legitimate parallel to be made between sacrificing self to be a disciple of Jesus and/or to do so for one's country? Who makes the real sacrifices in *Gallipoli?* Why? Who benefited from the decisions made during the siege and battle of Gallipoli?

3. The *Catechism of the Catholic Church* says, "The fifth commandment forbids the intentional destruction of hu-

man life. Because of the evils and injustices that accompany all war, the Church insistently urges everyone to prayer and to action so that the divine Goodness may free us from the ancient bondage of war" (n. 2307) and "All citizens and governments are obliged to work for the avoidance of war" (n. 2308). Read and study the entire section of the *Catechism* that deals with war, as well as those sections that teach about peace, justice, solidarity, and human dignity. How were these themes present in *Gallipoli*? Do you think *Gallipoli* is a story with a moral, or one that bears witness to an ideal, history, and memory? Why?

Prayer

Lord, give us the grace and strength as your disciples to pray and work for peace. Amen.

Exodus 32:7–11, 13–14;
1 Timothy 1:12–17;
Luke 15:1–32

Restoration

U.S.A., 1994, 118 minutes
Cast: Robert Downey Jr., David Thewlis, Sam Neill,
Meg Ryan, Polly Walker, Ian McKellen, Hugh Grant
Writer: Rupert Walters
Director: Michael Hoffman

Restoration

Degraded and Restored

SYNOPSIS

The setting is London 1663 during the reign of Charles II. Robert Merivel is a talented doctor. However, he dissipates his earnings and his life in licentious living. His father and a fellow doctor, Jack Pearce, criticize him. When he saves the king's dog, Lulu, Merivel is appointed the royal canine physician. He takes his place in the king's entourage and succumbs to the ease and luxury of life at court.

The king uses Merivel, then forces him to marry one of his mistresses who has become tiresome. Merivel is knighted and sent off to a country estate with lavish ceremony, but the king calls him a fool and forbids Merivel and his wife, Celia, to ever be intimate. Merivel accepts his fate but falls in love with his wife. Thus, the king ousts him from his position and Merivel sinks to the depths of poverty.

His old friend Pearce, who is a member of a Quaker community, takes him in. The religious experience within the community helps him to regain his life and recommence his career. Merivel adapts to Quaker ways and introduces new treatment for mentally ill patients. One of the patients, an Irish girl named Katharine, responds to his treatment. He falls in love with her and they have a child, but Katharine dies while giving birth.

During the plague in London and the Great Fire that follows, Merivel makes many sacrifices and uses his medical skills to help the suffering. He saves the life of the king's mistress. Ironically, he finds himself back at the home the king gave him at the time of his marriage. But he is now a changed man.

COMMENTARY

The period from 1660, under Charles II, was called "The Restoration" because it marked the return of the monarchy after the austere parliamentarian rule of Oliver Cromwell. While it was a period of development in science and human understanding, it was also a period of licentiousness and excess both for the royalty and the upper class. *Restoration* was capably directed by Michael Hoffman (*One Fine Day, Soapdish, A Midsummer Night's Dream, The Emperor's Club*).

Rose Tremain's novel (1989) was adapted by Rupert Walters for the screen. *Restoration* won Oscars for Best Costume Design and Best Art Direction and is a visual treat.

The hero of the film's moral journey is Dr. Robert Merivel, played with extraordinary skill as well as with a perfect British accent by Robert Downey Jr. (as he did in *Chaplin*). We follow him through his period of dissipation and royal preferment to his downfall and his coming to his senses, with the help of a Quaker community and an Irish woman, played by accent-perfect Meg Ryan.

With worthy performances from Sam Neill as the king and David Thewlis as the Quaker doctor, this is a film that is of interest for its representation of history as well as for its hope that each person will discover their life's vocation and in so doing, will find themselves.

DIALOGUE WITH THE GOSPEL

Focus: The parable of the Prodigal Son is one of the greatest of Jesus' stories because it is a story of the Father's compassion.

*Robert Merivel experiences the degradation and the restoration
of a prodigal son.*

The reading from the book of Exodus speaks of God's forgiving his apostate people in the desert. The excess of the incident of the golden calf reminds us of the overindulgence of the age of the English Restoration. Paul speaks of himself in terms of a prodigal son in First Timothy. He testifies to the mercy of God who forgave him and welcomed him back to his love.

There is a parallel between the stories of Robert Merivel and the prodigal son that facilitates the dialogue between the film and today's Gospel. Merivel's father is disappointed in his dissipated son, who is a talented young doctor who squanders his gifts in a life devoted to womanizing and drink. To find favor at court, Merivel gives up his medical practice and, therefore, numerous opportunities to exercise compassion. The king takes advantage of him and then reduces him to nothing. Merivel collapses, disillusioned, impoverished, and without hope. Like the prodigal son, it is in the depths of despair that he comes to his senses.

His friend John Pearce and the Quaker community save him. With their simple lifestyle and hospitable ways with no questions asked, he is able to reconstruct his life. He is a doctor once again and ministers to the most afflicted of patients. When the plague breaks out, he is prepared to sacrifice himself completely for the sick. He also discovers genuine love and is blessed with a child.

At the end he rejoices because he recovers the king's favor, but even more because he has been restored to his humanity when he gives of himself to others. He has become a redeemed man.

- Robert Merivel at work with John Pearce, his skills as a doctor and treatment of his patients; Merivel squan-

**KEY SCENES
AND THEMES**

dering his inheritance in a life of licentiousness; his treatment of the King's spaniel; the worldly rewards and giving himself over completely to them.

- Merivel's humiliation by the king followed by his desperation and poverty; his coming to his senses and taking refuge with the Quakers; his sharing their life, lifestyle, poverty, prayer, and dedication; the treatment of the mental patients; dance and movement, a holistic approach to healing; his love for Katharine, the birth of their child, and her death.

- Merivel's dedication during the plague, the fire and his search for his child; his changed approach to life; his restoration to the king's favor but as a reformed and redeemed doctor, not as a frivolous wastrel.

FOR REFLECTION AND CONVERSATION

1. Samuel Pepys was a civil servant in England in the seventeenth century who kept a very personal and detailed diary of his life and times over a nine-year period. His eyewitness accounts of the plague (1664–1666), when seventy thousand people died in London over an eighteen-month period, and the Great Fire of London (September 2–7, 1666), make for fascinating reading. *Restoration* incarnates Pepys's version of that history for us today through film. These devastating events called for the "restoration" of society on the basic human levels of health, food, water, and shelter. What kinds of social restoration are called for in the various strata of society today, whether domestic, local, national, or global? Recall the seven principles of Catholic social teaching (see page 286, *Meet Joe Black*). Talk about which of these principles apply to both the readings and the film and how they can be applied today.

2. All of today's readings talk about forgiveness and the value of the human person. The parables in the Gospel all show that people have value whether seen through the metaphor of a lost sheep, lost coins, or a lost son. How are people valued in *Restoration* by the king, by Merivel and the Quakers? How important is the dignity of the human person in today's world and how can we enhance this value?

3. Talk about how the film contrasts the lavish life of the court with the life of the "common people." How did the situation lure Dr. Merivel into giving up his life's work of healing the sick? Do you think he became a better man because of his experiences resulting from poor choices than he would have been had he never strayed? Why? Which characters change and grow in *Restoration*? In what ways? How do Merivel's father, the father in the parable, and God the Father compare? How might Merivel's story of restoration speak to you personally?

Prayer

Lord, you revealed your Father's love in your stories of compassion. Give the grace of repentance and new hope to all your prodigal children. Amen.

Michael Douglas in *Wall Street*.

TWENTY-FIFTH SUNDAY OF THE YEAR

Amos 8:4–7;
1 Timothy 2:1–8;
Luke 16:1–13

U.S.A., 1987, 126 minutes
Cast: Michael Douglas, Charlie Sheen, Martin Sheen,
Hal Holbrook, Daryl Hannah, Terence Stamp,
James Spader, Sean Young, Richard Dysart
Writers: Stanley Weiser, Oliver Stone
Director: Oliver Stone

Wall Street

You Cannot Serve Both God and Mammon

Gordon Gekko is one of Wall Street's most celebrated traders. He retains his edge through "insider trading." He risks being caught and prosecuted but continues to "play" dangerously and profitably. He lives a life of luxury that includes possessions, house, wife, and a mistress.

SYNOPSIS

Bud Fox is an ambitious young stockbroker from a working-class family. His father is a union leader in an aviation company who unwittingly shares some inside information about the company with his son. Bud wants to get inside Gekko's circle, so for thirty-nine days straight, he tries to get an appointment. Bud then leaks the information about the aviation company to Gekko. Gekko recognizes Bud's capacities and ambitions when the information proves profitable. Gekko becomes Bud's patron and mentor; he gets Bud to engage in espionage and to negotiate secret deals.

Gekko gives a speech to the stockholders of his company and proclaims: "Greed, for want of a better word, is good."

Bud wants "the good life" but has to deal with his conscience, especially when he tries to get his father to come in on the deal about the aviation company. Their relationship becomes strained. In the middle of negotiations, his father suffers a heart attack. The authorities are on to Bud and, realizing that he will be convicted for his part in Gekko's illegal activities, Bud reflects on his father's integrity and listens to his own conscience. He agrees to cooperate with the law by wearing a wire when he talks to Gekko in return for a lesser sentence. Gekko incriminates himself when he rejects Bud, but not before boasting about himself and his achievements. Gekko is arrested and Bud begins to serve his time.

COMMENTARY

Wall Street was one of the major box-office successes of 1987. Not only did the critics like it, it won many awards as well, including a Best Actor Oscar for Michael Douglas as Gordon Gekko. His speech on greed is now considered a classic movie scene.

Oliver Stone, whose father worked on Wall Street, wrote the screenplay at a time when some financial tycoons were being prosecuted for insider trading, not unlike events that unfolded in 2002 with Enron, ImClone, and other major companies. The filmmakers did not expect the Black Monday collapse of the stock market in October 1987. *Wall Street*, released at the time, proved prophetic.

Charlie Sheen's Bud has the right blend of naïvete and ambition that makes his interactions with Gekko believable. *Wall Street* brought Charlie Sheen and his father, Martin Sheen, together for the first time in a major motion picture. Although Oliver Stone can create strong roles for men, he is much less successful with women characters. Daryl Hannah and Sean Young, for example, have much more sketchily written roles than the men in *Wall Street.*

Wall Street is a movie that symbolizes the "economic rationalism" of the 1980s. A 1990s counterpart is *Rogue Trader* (1999) with Ewan McGregor in the lead role. The year 2003 has already given us the television movie *The Crooked E: The Unshredded Truth about Enron*, starring Mike Farrell.

Focus: Jesus' parable shows a steward who was wise according to the world where greed is good. Wall Street *shows us that no one can serve both God and money.*

The steward in Jesus' parable would have been at home as a character in *Wall Street* but he would not have taken kindly to the admonitions of the prophet Amos. Amos's prophesies in the first reading passionately denounce the unscrupulous and powerful rich because they tread on the heads of ordinary people.

If deals are "business as usual" in *Wall Street,* they are also normal for the steward whose "insider trading" with his master's clients unmasks who he really is. In the 1980s and today, just as in Gospel times, these "children of this world" are often acclaimed for their astuteness. In the 1980s they were hugely successful. But then came arrests and an increasing awareness among the public that this kind of worship of money is "tainted" and impossible for persons of integrity.

Gordon Gekko, especially in his "greed is good" speech, is the apostle of money worship. He wants to make Bud Fox his acolyte once he realizes how willing the young man is. Bud, challenged by his father and his own conscience, has to choose between the extravagantly good life that money can bring him or some measure of personal integrity. He cannot serve both God (conscience) and money.

- Gordon Gekko at work in his office, with his staff, the frenzy, the data coming in, the phone calls, yet his calm approach to the excitement (taking phone calls on the lonely beach).

- Bud Fox, his ambitions, chasing Gekko, subservience to him, imitating, dealing, and going against his conscience for him; Bud's relationship with his father and the company, the union; leaking the information to

Gekko, the pressure from Gekko about selling the company, Bud's interventions; his father's illness and questions of integrity.

- Gekko's "greed is good" speech, its contents, motivation, and perceptions about American society, business, success, ruthlessness; the acclaim with which it was received; the final confrontation in the park, Bud wearing the wire, sparring with Gekko; Gekko's manifesto, his despising Bud and hitting him; his arrest and Bud accepting the consequences for his own actions.

FOR REFLECTION AND CONVERSATION

1. Carl Fox tells Bud, "Stop going for the easy buck and start producing something with your life. Create, instead of living off the buying and selling of others." Talk about some recent incidents and financial scandals that make the movie *Wall Street* look like a precursor to many other morality tales to come. Why is it so hard for us to learn that "greed, for want of a better word, is *not* good"? What makes riches seem so attainable and desirable? How do the names and the characteristics of a "gecko" and a "fox" add to the meaning of the story? (For example, a gecko or "gekko" is a lizard and some species have unpleasant temperaments and a severe bite; they like the darkness. A fox is a member of the dog family; it is small and solitary and runs fast.)

2. Charles Dickens began writing about the consequences of the industrial revolution and the rise of "speculation" and risk in his novels, particularly in *Nicholas Nickleby* (published in serial form from 1837–1839; its most recent incarnation in film was released in 2003). How far back in the Bible do greed and

ambition go? Is money the root of all evil? Capitalism is the economic system of the United States and of the globalized village. Is it good or bad? What is our responsibility in regard to capitalism, the human person, and principles of Christian social teaching (compare *Meet Joe Black,* page 286)? How can we give capitalism a conscience in a consumer society? How do the values of the different film characters represent those of God and money? How is conscience the "place" where these values collide?

3. In one of her books on religious life, Joan Chittister, OSB, writes about the virtue of poverty and explains it in terms of "enoughness." How can "enoughness" be a standard, criterion, or measure for the practice of evangelical poverty in our own lives? A woman was overheard saying, "I have to go to the mall; I have to find out what I need." What's wrong with this statement? How can we balance real needs, money, and "enoughness" so that we can share with those who do not have access to what they need to survive? What does today's Gospel really say to us?

Prayer

Lord, in our busy and greedy world, help us to learn how to be satisfied with what we have and generous in giving to those in need. Amen.

TWENTY-SIXTH SUNDAY OF THE YEAR
Amos 6:1a, 4–7;
1 Timothy 6:11–16;
Luke 16:19–31

What Dreams May Come
U.S.A., 1998, 113 minutes
Cast: Robin Williams, Annabella Sciorra, Cuba Gooding Jr.,
Max Von Sydow, Rosalind Chao
Writer: Ron Bass
Director: Vincent Ward

What Dreams May Come

Heaven and Hell

SYNOPSIS

Chris, or Christy, and Annie meet on a mountain lake on the Swiss border and soon marry. Their early years of marriage are happy, but when their two children are killed in a car accident, Annie becomes depressed, is hospitalized, and attempts suicide. While trying to assist a victim in a multiple-car accident, Chris, who is a pediatrician, is also killed. Bereft and increasingly depressed, Annie continues with her painting and then takes her own life.

Chris goes to heaven, where he discovers that heaven is the creation of our own imagination. He finds himself in the middle of some of Annie's paintings and he sinks down into the actual paint of the beautiful countryside. The guide who takes him on a tour of heaven and who teaches him about life after death is actually his son in disguise. Another guide, also disguised, is his daughter.

When Chris learns that Annie has committed suicide and is now in some kind of hell, he seeks a guide who will take him there to see her because he intends to rescue her. She is trapped in her own grim imagination and does not recognize him. He is prepared to stay in hell for love of her. This

330

act of true love awakens her to Chris's identity and they are able to begin over again.

In the 1990s there was a renewed interest in things of the spirit, a blend of pop spirituality, Eastern religions, and Christianity. Angels and devils became more popular on screens. *What Dreams May Come* is a film about death, heaven, and hell, loosely resembling the myth of Orpheus in the underworld.

Writer Ron Bass *(Rain Man)* based the script on a novel by Richard Matheson and the film "dreams" and "imagines" the afterlife. From a Christian perspective, it seems more an imagining of a purgatorial experience than of heaven or hell. The reincarnation theme mirrors the human desire to live forever and to "do it better" the next time. Robin Williams is sympathetic in one of his non-comedic performances. A range of classic artists has designed the visually arresting sets. They include hell as a "sea of faces."

This is a disturbing fantasy film that takes itself seriously and reflects on the themes of love and hope, death and suicide. There are two main difficulties with the film. The first is what what one critic has called the "squishiness" of the screenplay. The other is its theology, which of course provides the opportunity for further reflection and dialogue. While not a theologically accurate portrayal of Christianity's vision of the afterlife, the film uses fantasy and imagination to point to the depths of true Christian love.

Focus: In the parable about the rich man and Lazarus, Jesus says that we ourselves determine our future—heaven or hell—by how we live our lives on earth. What Dreams May Come *reminds us that it is not too late to change our lives so that we can avoid hell and enjoy heaven with those we love.*

DIALOGUE WITH THE GOSPEL

Jesus' parable from Luke about the banqueting rich man and Lazarus at his gate is prefigured in the first reading from

Amos: "Woe to the complacent in Zion...stretched comfortably on their couches.... They shall be the first to go into exile and their wanton revelry done away with." Today's Gospel is about the wanton carelessness of the rich, the blessedness of the poor, and the escatalogical reality of heaven and hell.

Lazarus has been a good man who makes the best of his fate as a beggar at a rich man's gate. The rich man has been self-absorbed, living solely for pleasure. For Lazarus, earth has been a hell, "Dogs even used to come and lick his sores." For the rich man who "dined sumptuously every day," his too-late awareness of the consequences for his hedonism make him ask Abraham to tell others what awaits them if they do not change their ways.

Chris and Annie suffered the loss of their children. After Chris's death, Annie's depression turns into despair. When she takes her own life, she finds herself in a part of hell that does not let her recognize her past or the possibilities for a future: a memory-less and hopeless eternity.

In today's parable Jesus wants to make the point that the rich man's brothers should not need Lazarus to come back from the dead (as he himself will actually do) to know what God's commandments are. They already have Moses and the prophets, whose memory and teaching point toward the hope that living justly brings.

The film further takes up the theme of self-sacrificing love as the power that can celebrate memory and restore hope, overcoming even the power of hell. Chris experiences a kind of heaven for himself, but it feels incomplete without his wife. His recognition of his own failings in their relationship and his love and perseverance bring her back from the place she had gone. She is imaginatively offered a "second chance," and we are reminded that, in view of eternity, our one life is brief indeed.

KEY SCENES
AND THEMES

- The initial lake sequence, Chris and Annie falling in love; their lives together, the children, their deaths; Chris and the experience of death; his after-death experience, watching his funeral, trying to help Annie; Chris creating his own heaven, his pain and remembrance; the beauty of his heaven, flight, and transcending ordinary experience.

- Annie's depression, her suicide, going to hell, the visuals of hell; Annie not able to recognize Chris; the experience of the damned.

- The "tracker" going to the inferno, the sea of faces, the experience of the damned, the power of Chris's love; drawing Annie from hell; the transition to a heaven for both of them, the possibility of starting their romance and love over again.

FOR REFLECTION
AND
CONVERSATION

1. In literature, fantasy is fiction that creates imaginary worlds with magical or even supernatural events taking place in them. The "laws" of nature and reality are suspended for the purpose of telling stories that entertain, teach, or both. *What Dreams May Come* is one of the most intense fantasy films to come our way in a long time. How did the film make you feel? Did it "work" for you on an emotional level? Why or why not? Did its rather eclectic eschatology (theology concerning the "final times," whether personal or universal) obscure the underlying theme of the relationship between Chris, Anne, and their two children for you? Do the facts of theology "matter" when it comes to fantasy? If so, how?

2. One of the most poignant moments in the film is when "Leona" tells Chris that her father always praised the

intelligence, beauty, and talents of Asian women, so that's why she looks Asian in heaven. What does this say about the relationships between parents and children and parental expectations? Why did Chris and his son, Ian, have such a hard time communicating? What was the best time that Marie remembers with her father? If it can be said that *What Dreams May Come* is about never giving up and the eternity of love, talk about the journey Chris makes so that when he crosses to the "other side," his outlook on life and family is transformed. How many times does he cross over from one place to the next, to one state of being to another? As the film and today's Gospel seem to encourage, how can we see *now* the reality of our behavior in relation to others so that we can reach heaven after we die?

3. It would be impossible to look at this film and not talk about suicide. "Suicide" means the deliberate taking of one's life. "Deliberate" means intentional and premeditated. The teaching of the *Catechism of the Catholic Church* roundly condemns suicide (nn. 2280–2282). At the same time, the Church teaches, "Grave psychological disturbances, anguish, or grave fear of hardship, suffering, or torture can diminish the responsibility of the one committing suicide. We should not despair of the eternal salvation of persons who have taken their own lives. By ways known to God alone, God can provide for the opportunity for salutary repentance. The Church prays for persons who have taken their own lives" (nn. 2282–2283). How can Annie's story (and others) be understood within the embrace of God's love and understanding? Do you think that *What Dreams May Come* is just a fantasy, a

metaphor for life, or even a morality tale? Talk about your answer in the light of hope and other themes, such as constancy, love, forgiveness, repentance, conversion, self-sacrifice, families, and perseverance.

Prayer

Lord, life after death remains a mystery for so many people. Help us to have faith in your promise of eternal life with you. Amen.

Steve Martin in *Leap of Faith*.

Habakkuk 1:2–3, 2:2–4;
2 Timothy 1:6–8, 13–14;
Luke 17:5–10

Leap of Faith
U.S.A., 1992, 107 minutes
Cast: Steve Martin, Debra Winger, Liam Neeson,
Lolita Davidovitch, Lukas Haas, Meat Loaf,
Philip Seymour Hoffman
Writer: Janus Cercone
Director: Richard Pearce

Leap of Faith

Help My Unbelief

SYNOPSIS

Jonas Nightingale is an itinerant preacher, a successful hi-tech con-artist healer with a large entourage that helps him put on a huge "show." On their way across country, one of the trucks breaks down and they are stuck in a small, drought-ridden Kansas town while they wait for a spare part. Jonas decides to make the best of the situation. He announces a revival that attracts crowds. His staff handles the seating arrangements using computer data about the town and its people. A microphone links Jonas to Jane, his partner, so that she can feed him additional information that the crew has gleaned by talking to the people. Jonas "heals" based on this information; he also gives advice on personal problems and the drought.

Will, the local sheriff, suspects a scam and wants Jonas out of the town, but he is legally forced to grant the necessary licenses so Jonas can put on a healing "show." At the same time, Jane attracts his attention. Jonas tries to woo Marva, a local waitress. She has a younger brother named Boyd who is disabled because of a car accident. Marva is unimpressed by Jonas but Boyd shows great faith and wants to go to the revival to be healed.

The opening night "service" is spectacular. Jonas impresses the townspeople with his "supernatural" knowledge. To further impress the crowd, he paints the eyes open on a statue of Christ during the night and claims it is a miracle. Will does his own background research on Jonas and denounces him as a fake, a petty criminal.

Jonas acknowledges to himself that he is a con-man. He spends some time reflecting on his "career" and on the power he exerts over people by taking advantage of their good faith. However, his show-biz histrionic approach always overcomes his conscience. When Boyd actually is healed and walks, it affects Jonas so much that he abandons his troupe and hitches a ride to some unknown destination, perhaps a changed man. It starts to rain.

COMMENTARY

Director Richard Pearce has made some moving though little known pictures about small town America, such as *Northern Lights, Country,* and *The Long Walk Home.* Here Pearce has brought to life a cross-section of this population and has authentically created the atmosphere of a town in a rural region that is strapped economically and suffering from drought.

Steve Martin steps out of his usual comedic persona to play Jonas, a master at exploitation and deception. Debra Winger is Jane, Jonas's assistant. She is more than capable as the realistic half of what she considers a business partnership, though she has her doubts. Liam Neeson is the wary and sensible sheriff. Lukas Haas, who captured audiences with his acting abilities in another film focused on religion, *Witness,* plays a sensitive young man who seeks healing.

Jonas dances and cavorts in a "leap of faith," but it is Boyd's faith that bears fruit. His cure is a powerful sequence that brings on a crisis in Jonas's understanding of what he does and what he believes. *Leap of Faith* takes its place somewhere between such movies as *Elmer Gantry*, with its religion-salesman main character, and the ultimate sincerity of Sonny in *The Apostle*.

Focus: Jesus reminds us that faith is a privileged, humble service. Jonas is a superficial showman who experiences God's miraculous power despite himself, and in the end, makes a leap of faith when he recognizes God's work in the world.

The final words of the first reading from the prophet Habakkuk evoke some of the themes of *Leap of Faith*: "The rash one has no integrity; but the just one, because of his faith shall live." The integrity of the film's Gospel troupe is continually scrutinized by the characters in the film and by us, the viewers. Faith is rewarded and sometimes discovered in relationships and in the miracles of life.

The reading from Second Timothy refers to the laying on of hands and the gifts of the spirit. Paul exhorts his disciples to "Take as your norm the sound words you heard from me.... Guard this rich trust with the help of the Holy Spirit that dwells within us." Jonas, the imposter, places healing hands on the people in their time of hardship. The people are sincere and they believe despite the fraudulent messenger while the sheriff tries to guard them from further disaster.

The Gospel focuses on faith and on the disciples' prayer for an increase of faith. The passage says that to be a true son of God means to do one's duty in faith, and that this service is a privilege. Jonas and his ministry must be judged by these criteria. Does he preach and heal because of the obligation of his faith? Is he really a believer? He is a phony who is at odds with God but who has moments when his conscience speaks up. It seems that Jonas has little faith and cannot face the truth, so he reverts to his on-stage persona.

Jane and the sheriff challenge Jonas but he always has an answer to justify himself. His world collapses when he suddenly and unexpectedly experiences actual faith and witnesses Boyd's cure. Jonas flees when he realizes he cannot continue as he is. It is a challenge to live according to faith and to be a true servant. The responsorial psalm seems especially appropriate for Jonas: "If today you hear his voice, harden not your hearts."

KEY SCENES AND THEMES

- Jonas, his troupe, his disdain for the townspeople and the opportunity to exploit them; the elaborate process to prepare the tent meeting; Jonas's welcoming the people, how he finds out about their problems; Jane's role and how she lets Jonas know where they are sitting; the elderly woman given the chair, her "cure" and dancing.

- Jonas standing before the crucifix; the place of the crucifix in the tent, during the prayer meetings and during the healing.

- The boy at the diner and his sister; how he listens to Jonas and believes in him; the sequence of the healing; Boyd's approaching the stage, his cure so he can walk; Jonas's reaction and that of the crowd; Jonas and the aftermath of the healing; his decision to run away and the reason for it; the challenge to his faith and to his way of life.

FOR REFLECTION AND CONVERSATION

1. Itinerant preachers have been an integral part of U.S. religious culture and history. Their lives have been documented in films such as *Elmer Gantry* and *The Apostle*. The electronic church is a phenomenon of our age, reaching its high point with the televangelists of the 1980's. In *Leap of Faith*, the latest technology and traveling evangelists come together, along with a "con" element. Did the seeming lack of holiness of

the messenger make any difference to the faith of the people or the "truth" of the message? Why or why not?

2. Do you think *Leap of Faith* is a comedy, a satire, or just entertainment? Why? Could it be another genre such as a road movie? Talk about your response. What other Gospel passage, besides the one in today's liturgy, does this film remind you of, as healing and drought relief occur despite the fake "show"? What visual symbols does the film use to draw our attention to faith and to the miraculous? What point, if any, do you think the filmmaker was trying to make with his use of natural and man-made symbols (e.g., the butterflies, the final sequence)?

3. Jonas runs his scam with the help of Jane, but her relationship with Jonas is not clear. What are the characteristics of Jonas's relationships with her and with the other characters? What does his pursuit of Marva mean? How did Jonas's early life and relationships color his choice of a "profession"? Is he changed at the end? Does he have faith like a mustard seed? How does faith color my life and how do I nourish this gift in my life?

Prayer

Lord, you remind us that faith is not merely an external display but a deep commitment of mind and heart. Increase our faith. Amen.

TWENTY-EIGHTH SUNDAY OF THE YEAR

2 Kings 5:14–17;
2 Timothy 2:8–13;
Luke 17:11–19

Philadelphia

U.S.A., 1993, 126 minutes
Cast: Tom Hanks, Denzel Washington, Jason Robards Jr.,
Antonio Banderas, Mary Steenburgen, Joanne Woodward
Writer: Ron Nyswaner
Director: Jonathan Demme

 *Philadelphia*

"Have Pity on Us"

SYNOPSIS

Andy Beckett works in a prestigious law firm in Philadelphia. He has not revealed to the partners that he is sick and that he makes routine visits to an AIDS clinic. He is always able to brush off comments about his health and the lesions on his face.

After a collapse, he shaves his head and refuses to use any cosmetic make-up to conceal his condition. All of a sudden, the senior partner, Charles Wheeler, removes him from an important case and then fires Andy from the firm. Andy asks an African-American colleague, Joe Miller, a contingency lawyer, to represent him against the firm for illegal dismissal. Joe is reluctant and comes to realize that he is homophobic. But he takes the case.

The case becomes a civil-rights event with protests and appeals to the U.S. Constitution in its founding city, Philadelphia—the City of Brotherly Love.

Joe calls Andy's boss, who denies any discrimination on the part of the firm. As Andy gets weaker, he begins to plan his funeral, helped by his partner, Miguel. His family, especially his mother, support him. He throws a party and then meets with Joe to discuss strategies for the trial. Andy puts on

342

one of his favorite arias, "La Mamma Morta," from the opera "Andrea Chénier," and translates the piece for Joe with great emotion. The tragedy of the character Maddalena seems to parallel his own life.

Issues of sexuality, discrimination, and illness emerge during the trial. Andy dies and Joe attends the funeral gathering.

Jonathan Demme's *(Silence of the Lambs, Beloved) Philadelphia* became something of a landmark movie in the early 1990s because it was the first studio movie to deal directly with AIDS, though a number of independent movies like *Parting Glances, Longtime Companion,* and telemovies like *Early Frost* had already been produced.

Philadelphia also documents social justice issues for history, as so many Hollywood movies have done over the decades.

Denzel Washington represents and gives voice to the viewpoint of the mainstream public and the audience about AIDS and the conscious or unconscious homophobia that exists in the culture. With a popular actor like Tom Hanks playing the man with AIDS, *Philadelphia* was able to break through audience suspicion and put a face on the human reality and tragedy of AIDS. Tom Hanks is the first actor to win back-to-back Oscars since Spencer Tracy won for *Captains Courageous* (1937) and *Boys Town* (1938). Hanks won an Oscar for *Forrest Gump* (1994) the year after *Philadelphia*.

Focus: Lepers were outcasts in both Old Testament times and in the time of Jesus, as today's readings attest. Philadelphia *made twentieth-century society face the HIV and AIDS epidemic and test its attitudes toward those who became ill because of a disapproved of lifestyle.*

The readings focus on health and illness. There is a sense of pain throughout. "Leprosy," a name used to cover all kinds of "unclean" skin and body diseases in biblical times, gave rise to the use of the word "leper" for outcasts. The last decades of the twentieth century saw many avoided and labeled as outcasts. The HIV-AIDS epidemic spread throughout sophisticated first-world countries and through huge portions of developing countries in Africa in various ways that involved the exchange of body fluids between one infected person and another: sexual contact, blood transfusions, shared drug needles, and even breast-feeding.

The Syrian general, Naaman, is a leper who is healed in the reading from 2 Kings. The ten lepers are outcasts who stay a long way off, begging Jesus to heal them, and he does.

Andy Beckett is a contemporary leper because he is ill with a disease that society not only dreads and wants out of the way, but also because society fears gay people. Andy knows he will not be physically healed but he wants social healing, that is, some vindication as a human being. Discrimination, regardless of the reason for it, is contrary to human dignity and always wrong, legally, ethically, and morally. The court sequences and the dialogue dramatize this in explicit and powerful terms.

The film also focuses on Joe Miller, the person whom Andy Beckett asks to help obtain this social healing. Joe, as a limited human being, has to question himself deeply about his own beliefs and views so that he can defend Andy to the best of his ability.

Jesus is who he is, human and divine. He is the one who can heal both body and soul and he appreciates the exquisite faith shown by a foreigner (considered a second-class citizen by the Israelites), rather than by the nine compatriots, because the foreigner was the only one who returned to give thanks. Though he had lost the stigma of illness, the man was still an outsider. Jesus was not afraid when, once healed, the man fell at his feet to thank him.

- Andy's illness, covering the lesions with make-up, laughing off the sickness, hearing homophobic remarks in the clubs, keeping silent; Miguel's care; Andy's collapse.

- Approaching Joe Miller and Joe's hesitation to shake hands, Joe's checking with the doctor; Joe's views, his wife's criticism; the encounter in the video store, banter in the bar; Charles Wheeler as the voice of discrimination, how he finds alternatives to the truth and covers up the facts; the attitude of the librarian toward Andy so he can be more comfortable.

- The family standing by Andy; his relationship with Miguel, the party and the dance; sharing with Joe the Maria Callas aria, translating the lyrics about love; Andy's revealing so much about himself, Joe's inability to cope; the winning of the case financially, but Andy concerned more about his death and funeral; his readiness to die; Joe and his wife attending the funeral gathering.

1. There are many telling scenes in *Philadelphia*, such as the one with the uncomfortable librarian, Joe's encounter in the video store, Andy's illness, and the famous scene where he and Joe listen to Maria Callas singing the aria from "Andrea Chénier." What do you think Andy was feeling at that moment about God, life, love, and people? How did you feel as you watched and listened to this scene? Did you feel any empathy for this dying man, or did you, like many others, think he deserved what he got? Did you identify more with Joe or with Andy? Talk about your reaction to *Philadelphia*, and the now famous Oscar-winning Springsteen song, "Streets of Philadelphia."

KEY SCENES AND THEMES

FOR REFLECTION AND CONVERSATION

2. How much do you really know about HIV and AIDS? Did you know that they are not the same thing? HIV or Human Immunodeficiency Virus is an infectious agent that causes acquired immunodeficiency syndrome (AIDS). The body of an HIV patient no longer has the ability to fight infections because the virus has invaded the white blood cells and compromised the person's immune system. AIDS is a disease that leaves a person vulnerable to life-threatening infections such as pneumonia. Some people may not develop full-blown AIDS for several years. AIDS is the final, life-threatening stages of an HIV infection. While there are at least three antiviral drugs that can slow down the effects of HIV, the disease remains incurable. Why do you think it is important to have proper information about HIV-AIDS and other illnesses or conditions that carry a social or moral stigma with them? Did Jesus ever judge the sick or ask the source of their illness? How did Jesus treat the sick and those who came to him for healing? What can we do to help the hundreds of thousands of people who suffer and die every year of AIDS both at home and in places like Africa?

3. The *Catechism of the Catholic Church* (nn. 2357–2359) officially teaches that homosexual activity is objectively wrong. At the same time, the *Catechism* says, "They [persons who have deep-seated homosexual tendencies] must be accepted with respect, compassion, and sensitivity. Every sign of unjust discrimination in their regard should be avoided." Is this pastoral teaching difficult for you? Why or why not? Talk about the array of responses to Andy's homosexuality and illness. What did you think about the family gathering with

Andy? Was it an effort to model appropriate behavior for the audience or did it seem genuine to you? If you were a parent with an active homosexual child, what would your response be? How is it possible to reject a person's lifestyle yet love that person, show compassion, and avoid discrimination at all costs?

Prayer

Lord, you were attentive to those on the outskirts of society and healed them. Help us to be compassionate toward those who feel themselves on the margins today. Amen.

TWENTY-NINTH SUNDAY OF THE YEAR

Exodus 17:8–13;
2 Timothy 3:14—4:2;
Luke 18:1–8

The Winslow Boy

U.S.A., 1998, 104 minutes
Cast: Nigel Hawthorne, Jeremy Northam, Rebecca Pidgeon,
Gemma Jones, Guy Edwards, Matthew Pidgeon
Writer: David Mamet
Director: David Mamet

The Winslow Boy

Let Right Be Done!

SYNOPSIS

The Winslows are a very respectable London family living in London in 1912. Arthur Winslow is a banker and his wife Grace oversees the household. They have a son, Dickie, who is a student at Oxford. Their daughter, Catherine, who has just become engaged to an officer, is a suffragette. The youngest son, thirteen-year-old Ronnie, attends the naval academy. One Sunday he comes home because he was expelled from school after having been found guilty of stealing a money order. Arthur Winslow interrogates his son and believes that he is innocent.

The family immediately makes arrangements for Ronnie's defense but an independent inquiry results in another guilty verdict. Arthur insists on pursuing the case and Ronnie's cause gains national notoriety, mostly because the parents were not informed or present at the inquiries carried out by the government school. There are severe repercussions for the family because of the pressure and the legal costs. Arthur's health breaks down, he asks Dickie to leave Oxford at the end of the term, and he withdraws Catherine's dowry.

Arthur then asks a member of Parliament, Sir Robert Morton, to represent Ronnie. Morton seems aloof and caught up in his career. Catherine is particularly antagonistic toward him. After Sir Robert conducts a provocative interview with Ronnie, he pronounces him innocent and decides to accept Ronnie's case. To get the case reinstated, he sends a message to Parliament stating: "Let right be done." Catherine's fiancé breaks off his engagement to her because her future father-in-law is embarrassed by the Winslow's challenge to the government. When the case is almost thrown out of court again, Morton makes a speech in the House about the case, pleading that it is not right for the members of Parliament to side with the strong over the powerless. He ends by quoting the Gospel passage: "What you have done to these, the least of my brothers, you do to me."

His pursuit of justice for Ronnie has been at some cost to his career. When he comes to the Winslow house after Ronnie is found innocent, Catherine apologizes for misjudging him.

It is surprising to find that American playwright David Mamet, best known for his hard-hitting and hard-language plays like *American Buffalo, Speed the Plow, Glengarry Glen Ross* and movies such as *The Verdict, Wag the Dog, The Untouchables,* and *The Postman Always Rings Twice,* has a great admiration for the dramatic skills and English manners of British playwright Terence Rattigan *(Separate Tables, Sleeping Prince, The Browning Version).* Mamet has adapted Rattigan's play with enormous respect and has directed an elegant movie.

COMMENTARY

Mamet recreates Edwardian England in great detail, emphasizing its prim, pre-World War I social order. His screenplay stays closer to Rattigan's text (which is set solely in the Winslow house) than Anthony Asquith's 1947 classic version, which had a masterly performance by Robert Donat as Sir Robert with Cedric Hardwicke as Winslow and Margaret Leighton as Catherine.

All the actors in this 1999 version of *The Winslow Boy* play their roles with precision and credibility. *The Winslow Boy* is an intelligent movie that respects drama as an art form.

DIALOGUE WITH THE GOSPEL

Focus: Just as the widow confronts the unjust judge to demand her rights and receives justice, so Ronnie Winslow and his family are vindicated by the appeals of Sir Robert Morton that "right be done."

The Exodus narrative shows us Moses, who holds his arms upward in supplication until the battle is won. It is a story of perseverance in hope against all odds. Arthur Winslow's persistent fight for his son's honor parallels the determination of Moses. When things seemed to only get worse, Arthur Winslow meditated on another story that concerned Moses and held on.

The second reading from Paul's Second Letter to Timothy reiterates this picture of persistence and urges us to turn to the scriptures as a source for our integrity "whether convenient or inconvenient..." As the family's situation changed and they became poor, Arthur Winslow's integrity in the face of injustice shone forth.

Jesus' parable of the unjust judge and the spirituality of perseverance and persistence, embodied in the widow who does not give up in her pleas for redress, highlights the plight and efforts of Arthur Winslow and his family. The widow was a person on the fringes of society. The child, Ronnie Winslow, was of no concern to the Admiralty. The government authorities, caught up with their own importance, had no time or taste for the Winslow boy.

Like the widow, Arthur and his daughter, especially, did not give up, though they were tempted.

At the end of today's Gospel, Jesus says, "Will not God then secure the rights of his chosen who call out to him day and night? ... He will see to it that justice is done...." Through the dedication and skill of Sir Robert Morton, the day was won. The Gospel refers to the widow's "just" rights. The Winslow case was certainly about "just" rights and is epitomized in Sir Robert's conviction: "Let right be done."

**KEY SCENES
AND THEMES**

- The Winslow family in 1912, their relationship to one another, their social status, their daily life; Catherine's engagement.

- Ronnie hiding in the rain in the garden; his brother and sister supporting him, the protection of his mother; his father discovering what has happened; Arthur asking his son for the truth and Ronnie telling him he is innocent; Arthur's decision to devote all the family's energies to clearing his son's name; the independent inquiry and the frustrations with bureaucracy and the legal system.

- Sir Robert's psychological manner when he interrogates Ronnie; Arthur's interruptions; how Morton lays the "trap" and "escape" for Ronnie; Ronnie's truthfulness; Sir Robert's aloof manner and Catherine's haughty wariness; his political career and the sacrifice he makes; his note stating "Let right be done," his speech that members of Parliament are not allowed ethically to choose the side of power over the powerless, his quoting Jesus' words; the joy of the verdict and the result of self-sacrifice by the family.

**FOR REFLECTION
AND
CONVERSATION**

1. The legal case at the center of this story is a small one that concerns a boy who is accused of stealing a money order, cashing it, and is then expelled from a prestigious school. It is, however, a case that is symbolic of the need for truth and the rights of the individual in society. Recall the conversation between the mother

and father after the family's situation has suffered. Would you have let the whole thing go, since Ronnie was doing well and he seemed to have forgotten the case, or would you have persevered in clearing the boy's name? What do you think about the motivations of both parents? What would you have done in their place?

2. Sir Robert's note and the discussion about "Let right be done" is pivotal to the plot. At first it seems that Robert's use of this imperative is just doing his job. He does not seem interested in justice, but only in advancing his career, not unlike the unjust judge. The obvious observation is that his attraction to Catherine makes him want to win. What elements of his speech in the House of Commons show that it was the law and the Gospel that spurred him on and made him persevere? Do you have a favorite story or quote from Scripture that encourages you to persevere when things are difficult or unjust? What is it? What were the circumstances in which the story or phrase made a difference in your life and in the lives of those with whom you share faith? Why do you think Arthur kept reading the Scripture passage about the starving cattle (Gen 41:4)?

3. The main themes of the film are justice and right, but for whom? First there is Ronnie, then the family, and then the social dimensions of the society portrayed in *The Winslow Boy*. What are they (women's suffrage, equality among social classes, the responsibility of government for justice that protects the voiceless and the marginalized)? Were or are these "hopeless" causes? How do our personal beliefs about

justice and right influence society's perceptions and principles about justice and right? Sir Robert makes a distinction between justice and right. Do you agree? Why or why not? There are many obvious circular symbols present in the film (the knocker, windows, stairs, etc.) as well as a book on the rights of the individual and society. What do all these mean in the context of the film?

Prayer

You invite us to persist in prayer, Lord. Give us the courage to persevere in faith as we continually make our petitions to our Father. Amen.

A Few Good Men

U.S.A., 1992, 130 minutes
Cast: Tom Cruise, Demi Moore, Jack Nicholson,
Kevin Bacon, Keifer Sutherland, Kevin Pollak,
Cuba Gooding Jr., J. T. Walsh, Noah Wyle
Writer: Aaron Sorkin
Director: Rob Reiner

A Few Good Men

Humbled and Exalted

SYNOPSIS

Private Santiago has died at the U.S Marine Corps base at Guantanomo Bay, Cuba. Colonel Jessup, the embodiment of discipline and order who has an exemplary reputation, runs a first-class American military facility. His subordinate, Lieutenant Colonel Markinson, assists him unquestioningly, as does Sergeant Kendrick, only more carefully.

Washington officials send three JAG lawyers to Cuba for an initial investigation. The well-connected but inexperienced Daniel Kaffee is to defend the accused. Colonel Jessup treats the lawyers with ill-concealed contempt. Captain Jo Galloway is suspicious that Jessup issued an illegal "code red" hazing order to discipline the weak marine, an act that cost the man his life. The lawyers determine that Private Santiago did not die of natural causes but was murdered.

Kaffee collaborates well with third lawyer Lieutenant Sam Weinberg, although he clashes with the ambitious Jo. They resolve their difficulties and prepare to defend the two marines at their court martial.

The team uncovers disturbing evidence and build a case proving that the officials are lying about the code red. They find discrepancies about times and plane schedules regarding when Private Santiago was to have left Guantanamo, since he had requested a transfer. When Jessup is finally called to the stand, he lectures Kaffee on military law, tradition, and discipline. But taunted by Kaffee, he bursts out intemperately, admitting in his anger the truth of what has happened and his responsibility in Private Santiago's death.

A Few Good Men was nominated for an Oscar for Best Film of 1992 and Jack Nicholson received a Best Supporting Actor nomination for his role as Colonel Jessup. The movie was directed by Rob Reiner, who began his career as a comedian in television's *All in the Family*.

The film is based on a successful Broadway play by writer Aaron Sorkin and has been adapted well for the screen. Sorkin went on to write *The American President* and was the creator of television's *The West Wing*.

Tom Cruise is the very preppie-like defense counsel. Demi Moore is his ambitious and capable co-counsel; Kevin Pollak is the reluctant attorney on the team. A strong supporting cast includes Kevin Bacon as prosecutor, Kiefer Sutherland as an intense lieutenant, and J. T. Walsh as a former CIA man who cannot live with dishonor.

The film is stylishly made and relies on strong dialogue, forceful courtroom scenes, and the intensity of the characters, especially that played by Jack Nicholson, to reach its audience.

Focus: The parable of the Pharisee and the tax collector is one that everyone can identify with because we are all tempted to live a double standard: to be self-righteousness and look down at "sinners," all the while knowing we are sinners like everyone else. In A Few Good Men, *Colonel Jessup is like the Pharisee who accused others of being sinners.*

The first reading from Sirach opens with the theme of judges and trials. The Lord is a just judge, no respecter of personages, especially if the poor are the victims. In the second reading Paul refers to his trial before the Roman tribunal, claiming he has no witnesses to support him in his defense. In the Gospel, God is the judge of both the righteous man and the hypocrite.

Colonel Jessup can be seen as similar to the Pharisee in the parable. Jessup is definitely in charge and lays down the law as he sees fit. He overrides rules and regulations for the sake of maintaining order so that his outfit looks impeccable while carrying out its duties. When summoned to testify in court against two of his men accused of killing a fellow soldier, he does not hesitate to lie to the court. He thinks he is righteous even though he has broken the law.

The two accused marines have been set up to take the fall for their commander, but they think they did nothing wrong because they were obeying orders. That they do not even realize their position and that a young and inexperienced lawyer is defending them makes them the equivalent of the tax collector. They are ostracized by their own and their case seems hopeless.

However, when the young lawyer sees Jessop's double standards and his arrogance in the witness box, he turns on him and demands the truth. The Pharisee in the parable does not hesitate to trumpet his virtues. Colonel Jessup, when taunted, erupts, and yells the facts as a putdown to the lawyer. Rather than returning home justified, he is condemned.

KEY SCENES AND THEMES

- The atmosphere of Guantanamo marine base in Cuba; Private Santiago and the attack on him in his room, the two privates, the violence, his death; flashbacks to what happened as the attorneys discover the truth; the Washington officials, the plan for the court-martial, the authorities, their prejudgment; the decision to choose Daniel Kaffee and his reputation for pleading out his cases instead of going to trial, his deceased father's expectations; Jo Galloway's wanting to be part of the trial, her ambitions.

- The visit to the base, basic information, Kendrick and his style, honor, God, and religion; Lieutenant Colonel Markinson's role; the interview with Colonel Jessup, his command, his smooth way of talking, his expectations of himself, his self-promotion; attitudes toward the Cubans and women; his idea of honor, his men and their loyalty.

- The courtroom sequences, lawyers' skills, Kaffee's ambivalence, the clashes with Jo, Weinberg and his support, research, interpretation, Kaffee's change of strategy; the confrontation with Jessup, the cross-examination, his self-assurance, his arrogance; Kaffee's determination; Jessup's angry and self-defeating speech, his bewilderment at being arrested; his disgrace; the two accused men and their situation, victims of authority and the courts; their guilt and responsibility; the final judgment—one accepting it, one resenting it;

FOR REFLECTION AND CONVERSATION

1. Many films deal with the issue of personal integrity and ethics, such as *The Emperor's Club, On the Waterfront, Quiz Show, Changing Lanes, Wall Street, The Insider, The Hurricane, A Man for All Seasons*, and so forth. What is the definition of ethics? How do ethics and morality differ? Create your own list of such films that you have seen and identify the ethical dilemma. How does the main character in each deal with it? What choices does he or she make? What are the consequences? Do the characters grow and learn from their mistakes? Talk about what you would have done in their place.

2. It is interesting that most of the films dealing with serious topics such as ethics and the struggle between good and evil in society take place in a man's world, and with few exceptions, a white man's world. Why do you think Hollywood offers the male perspective as the norm for the universal human condition? Can you think of any equally powerful films that feature women's stories with female protagonists to add to your list of films about ethical choices? If you were a filmmaker, what kinds of stories would you tell? Why?

3. The Pharisee could only see his good points, as if to feel good about himself he had to put others down. The tax collector recognized his sinfulness without involving others. Which of the men in the film was honest and authentic? Why? Was suicide the only way out for Lieutenant Colonel Markinson? What are some strategies that we can develop for own emotional and spiritual well-being so as to become more authentic followers of Jesus in our work? What does Daniel say at the end to Harold about honor and what does it mean to you?

Prayer

Lord, be merciful to us sinners. Amen.

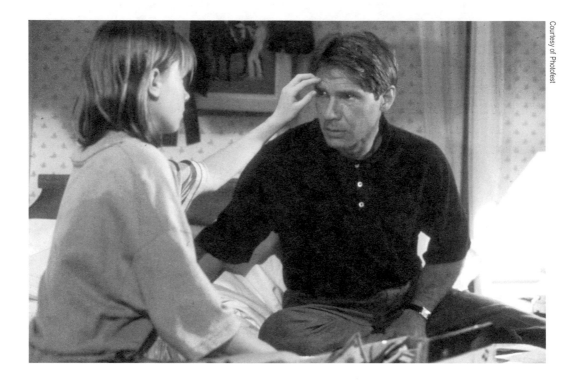

Mikki Allen and Harrison Ford in *Regarding Henry.*

Wisdom 11:22—12:2;
2 Thessalonians 1:11—2:2;
Luke 19:1–10

Regarding Henry

U.S.A., 1991, 102 minutes
Cast: Harrison Ford, Annette Bening, Bill Nunn, Mikki Allen,
Donald Moffat, John Leguizamo, Nancy Marchand
Writer: Jeffrey Abrams
Director: Mike Nichols

Regarding Henry

Salvation Has Come to This House

Henry Turner is a successful lawyer with a reputation for taking no prisoners. He owns a fine apartment and has an attractive wife, Sarah, and daughter, Rachel. He has everything he wants and is arrogant and unfeeling.

Late one evening, Henry goes to a corner store to buy some cigarettes. He walks in on a robbery in progress and is shot twice, in the clavicle and in the forehead. When he finally regains consciousness, he cannot remember anything, nor can he move. He transfers from the hospital to a rehab center and makes friends with his physical therapist, Bradley. He has sessions to help him regain his memory and rediscover who he is. It is a bewildering experience for him. The accident has made him similar to a child, and after several months, he reluctantly comes home.

What emerges is that his life before the shooting was one of external success hiding a great deal of inner chaos. He has been unfaithful to his wife, authoritarian with his daughter, and dishonest in his practice of the law. Day by day, he learns basic skills that jog his memory. He and his wife, who also had an affair, fall in love anew. Henry and Rachel develop a loving relationship when she teaches him to tie his

SYNOPSIS

shoes and how to read. He even brings home a puppy, something Rachel has always wanted that Henry would never before permit.

As time and therapy progress, Henry regains his memory, especially about a man he cheated out of a just reward in court just before he was shot. He realizes what it means to be a human being as he learns how to care about others. It is awkward when Henry returns to work and is confronted by and rejects the woman with whom he was having the affair. He finds he cannot return to his law practice because to be successful he will have to betray the man he has become. Henry quits his job and together with Sarah goes to bring Rachel home from the posh boarding school she has been attending. They are a family at last.

COMMENTARY

Regarding Henry was one of a series of movies in the early 1990s where a ruthless professional man is involved in a crisis that is not of his own making but where he becomes a victim. The challenge for him is to consciously choose to remake his life. Similar movies from this period include *The Doctor* starring William Hurt, and *The Fisher King* with Jeff Bridges.

Harrison Ford had become one the most successful stars of the 1980s, most especially because of the *Star Wars* and the *Indiana Jones* trilogies. He also appeared in science fiction classics like *Blade Runner* and moral tales such as *Witness*. That he is an actor of great ability was proven through his roles in *Mosquito Coast, Frantic*, and *Presumed Innocent*. He also worked with *Regarding Henry*'s director, Mike Nichols, in *Working Girl*. His success continued into the 1990s with *The Fugitive* and the two Tom Clancy action flicks, *Patriot Games* and *Clear and Present Danger*. Ford is one of the major American male screen icons. However, *Regarding Henry* was not so successful at the box office because the public preferred to watch Ford in action movies rather than in serious dramas. Annette Bening's career spanned the 1990s with films such as *Postcards from the Edge, Bugsy, The American President,* and *American Beauty.*

Focus: Just as Zacchaeus unexpectedly discovered Jesus and experienced conversion, Henry Turner is unexpectedly shot and his life is put on hold so that he can discover his true self and change his life.

DIALOGUE WITH THE GOSPEL

Regarding Henry may be seen as a conversion story, a kind of parallel to the experience of Zacchaeus in the sycamore tree.

The reading from the book of Wisdom is a fine meditation about God's perspective on humanity. God permits human sinfulness but does not will it. In fact, the reading highlights God's mercy rather than justice. God overlooks our sins, because God rebukes offenders little by little "and reminds them of the sins they are committing."

Zacchaeus was a tax collector and only marginally considered a son of Abraham by the Pharisees. In fact, on the day Jesus came to Jericho he chose to eat at Zacchaeus's and the Pharisees grumbled and called him a sinner. But at his encounter with Jesus, Zacchaeus professed his sincerity and committed himself to doing good, even beyond what was required of him. Zaccheus took the initiative that day. He wanted to gain a glimpse of Jesus, so he literally went out on a limb. Jesus showed Zacchaeus—and the Pharisees who were watching him closely—what God's mercy is truly like. Zacchaeus's conversion or change of heart was a complete renewal because he admitted his wrongdoing, atoned for it, and in so doing, renewed his whole life.

Henry is not seeking a conversion. Rather, he is "brought down" with the twentieth-century American weapon of choice, the handgun. Gradually, Henry comes to experience his weakness and to understand the ruthless ambitions of his past life. He discovers family love and chooses this love over his former life of neglect, criticism, and betrayal. When he comes fully to his new self, he acts like Zacchaeus did in terms of his profession. Henry sets his life to rights in the legal world by atoning for and arranging compensation for what he had done wrong in his past.

"Today salvation has come to this house," says Jesus to Zacchaeus. Salvation has come to Henry's house and what was lost has been saved.

KEY SCENES AND THEMES

- High-powered Henry in action in court, at the office, at home; his conduct regarding the case, the way he used people, how he was interested in winning at all costs rather than in achieving justice; his legal team and the firm, their admiration and support of him; the portrait of the successful American lawyer.

- Henry at home, the decision to go to the store after the party, the robbery, his intervention, his being shot and the aftermath, his injuries; in the hospital, the concern of his colleagues, Sarah's vigil, Rachel; Henry's physical problems, his lack of memory, the extent of brain damage; Bradley, his philosophy of life and his approach to physical therapy; Henry's gradual recovery: physical, emotional, mental.

- Going home, learning to read, returning to work, trying to do his job, sitting in his office, unable to do his work; the dinner and the speech in his honor, the party and overhearing the references to his being an imbecile; studying past case files, becoming curious, the change in his work for justice; making restitution to the Matthews; discovery of his own infidelity as well as Sarah's, their reconciliation; becoming a family; rediscovering Henry.

1. Henry's life is filled with concern over winning, appearances, and non-essentials. What things are more important to Henry than his own wife and daughter? Make a list of what makes up Henry's scale of values before the shooting. How does all this change because of the incident? By the end of the movie, what are Henry's values? Compare the lists. Have you ever had a spiritual conversion experience? What was it like? Like Zacchaeus, talk about (or describe in writing) what was important to you before the conversion experience and what is important to you now. What did Henry and Sarah learn through the experience? What insights have you gained through the film? What have you learned through your own conversion experience?

2. The audience seldom knows more than Henry at any given moment in the film. We are discovering his world as he does: the blue stationery in the little drawers, the meaning of "Ritz," the significance of all the symbols of masculine dominance and power such as the continued reference to balls and the images of skyscrapers outside his office and home windows. How does the power dynamic change in the film? Do the feminine and masculine balance in the end? Compare the symbols of corporate power vis-à-vis the power of love in action in the film. What scenes or scenarios impressed you the most? Why?

3. The story of Zaccheus suggests that he learned to empathize with others, so much so that even by the time he met Jesus, he had already made some changes in his life. The *Encarta* dictionary (2002) says that empathy is "the ability to identify with and understand an-

other person's feelings or difficulties." When and how does Henry learn empathy? Who teaches him? How important is empathy in your relationships at home, work, church, in the community, and for strangers?

Prayer

Lord, so often we are trapped in the wreckage of our lives. Give us the opportunity to acknowledge our sinfulness and rediscover our true selves. Amen.

Truly Madly Deeply

U.K., 1991, 106 minutes
Cast: Juliet Stevenson, Alan Rickman, Michael Maloney
Writer: Anthony Minghella
Director: Anthony Minghella

Truly Madly Deeply

A Life after Death

SYNOPSIS

Nina's lover, a musician named Jamie, dies from a simple sore throat. Nina goes to a therapist to cope with her grief. She often senses Jamie's presence and hears his music. He speaks to her in poorly accented Spanish. At home, she has let herself go while living in a flat that is falling apart and infested with rats. She receives some support from friends at the translation agency/language school where she works as well as from her pregnant sister. The maintenance man in her building is attracted to her.

Then she begins to "see" Jamie and starts a whole new relationship with him as a man-ghost. She is completely happy, although somewhat unsure of the reality of what is happening. After some time, Jamie begins to bring his ghost friends to the flat. They especially like to watch their favorite videos, like *Brief Encounter*, and speak the dialogue along with the cast.

When one of her students, Maura, and Maura's boyfriend become involved in an argument in a café, it is stopped by a young magician named Mark. Nina encounters him later in the street and learns that he is an art therapist who works with a group of young adults with Down's syndrome. They like Nina and invite her to join them. Nina and Mark start to date. This enables Nina finally to confront Jamie and ask him to leave (and to take the ghosts with him). She tells him she must let him go and live her life. As she goes off with Mark, the ghosts watch from her window and Jamie sheds a tear.

COMMENTARY

Truly Madly Deeply struck a chord with audiences, not only in its country of origin, Great Britain, but also in the United States and around the world. It was nominated for many awards and won several, including the Australian Film Institute's 1991 award for Best Foreign Film. Its romanticism, presented in a cool "British" way, held a universal appeal. *Truly Madly Deeply* was released soon after *Ghost* and some of the advertising capitalized on the "supernatural" connection between the two.

The screenplay and direction are by British playwright, screenwriter, and director Anthony Minghella. His reputation as a writer/director was made with his screenplay for *The English Patient* and his very successful adaptation of Patricia Highsmith's *The Talented Mr. Ripley* followed.

Juliet Stevenson is best known for her British stage performances and for television appearances. She complements her ability to play a woman in love with a ghost in other roles, such as the comedic Mrs. Squeers in *Nicholas Nickleby*. Alan Rickman is a classically trained, versatile actor who began his film career as the villain Hans Gruber in *Die Hard* and recently appeared as Professor Snape in the first two Harry Potter films.

Truly Madly Deeply is gentle, funny, and sad. Its underlying themes of bereavement and letting go are explored as a love story that can no longer be.

DIALOGUE WITH THE GOSPEL

Focus: The Sadducees concocted an exaggerated case study about the resurrection to mock Jesus. Jesus today might have shown them Truly Madly Deeply *to get them to reflect on the experiences of love and death and afterlife.*

The reading from the second book of Maccabees introduces the theme of death in a graphic way. It also introduces a theme that was comparatively new at this stage of Jewish history: a full life after death, a resurrection for all.

However, all Jews did not accept this new doctrine, even at the time of Jesus. The Pharisees and scribes were believers in the resurrection of the dead and the Sadducees, who were part of the wealthy ruling class, were among those who did not.

The confrontation between those who believed in the resurrection and those who did not is the setting for today's Gospel. It is a pseudo-search for Jesus' stance on the issue of resurrection on the part of some of the Sadducees. They proposed an exaggerated scenario of the widow who married seven brothers, all of whom died. She eventually finished up in heaven as the wife of...whom? And Jesus says that those who "are deemed worthy to attain to the coming age and to the resurrection of the dead neither marry nor are given in marriage." The age to come will be completely transformed from the present by the living God.

Many people are skeptical about a life after death. The Sadducees invented a story about relationships and marriage according to Jewish law to try and prove that the idea of the resurrection is absurd. Contemporary storytellers often want us to imagine a life after death. And if they are romantic tales, there is usually an accent on the value of life in the present here on earth, while saying good-bye and moving on if one of the partners dies.

We all empathize with Nina's grief at Jamie's death. His separation from Nina seems so cruel and unnecessary that we are delighted when he reappears. This relationship, however, is unreal. Nina has to learn to let Jamie go and to live her own life. We can take Jesus' words at the end of the Gospel as salutary reminders that God is a God of the living and that we must live our lives here to the full. The afterlife is different from the here and now and we must let go of those who have died. As they go into their new and eternal life, we may continue our own journeys in hope.

KEY SCENES AND THEMES

- Nina's sadness, the regrets and the chaos in her flat, the rats; the invasion of the ghosts, their friendliness, their watching the videos; the sense of intrusion that Nina feels and her gradually realizing that the situation with Jamie and his friends cannot last.

- Nina's sessions with the bereavement counselor, knowing that she must let go but her feeling that Jamie was still around; Jamie's appearance and Nina's delight; their new relationship.

- Nina's talking to Jamie, letting him go, beginning a new life, and the tear in Jamie's eye.

FOR REFLECTION AND CONVERSATION

1. Many films in this volume of *Lights, Camera... Faith!* deal with both the natural and the supernatural aspects of dying, death, grief and the afterlife: *One True Thing, What Dreams May Come, Life as a House, Beyond Rangoon, Bringing Out the Dead, Fearless, Frequency, Meet Joe Black, Pale Rider, Saint of Fort Washington, Titanic,* and *Wit* (among others). Why do you think this is so in relation to Luke's Gospel? Talk about how *Truly Madly Deeply* made you feel and what the story means to you. What does death teach us?

2. The film asks several questions, such as: What happens to the capacity to love? What's it like to die? Where do you go? How does the film then answer

these questions? The whole plot turns on Jamie's return: Why did he come back? What did you think when Nina and Jamie recited the "poem" with the words "truly madly deeply" in it? How does love go on forever, yet change? How willing are you to make a commitment to love in your own life, to another person, to a family, or perhaps to a calling to ministry or religious vocation? How does love go on forever? How does it transform the lover and the loved?

3. *Truly Madly Deeply* is an art-house film that has been constructed very carefully. Nothing is without meaning. For example, the infestation of rats parallels with the infestation of ghosts—why? What is the symbolism of the flowers, of Nina's chaotic life; of the use of windows as a medium for "seeing"—what are Nina and the viewer meant to see, to understand? What is the meaning of the language of music, the cello, the use of Spanish—what does communication mean in the context of the film? Did you care about the characters? Why or why not? What are some other symbols that you noticed? How did you interpret them?

Prayer

Jesus, help us to understand what love means in our lives. Help us to understand the pain of separation in death and, finally, help us to believe in the happiness of a life after death. Amen.

Malachi 3:19–20a;
2 Thessalonians 3:7–12;
Luke 21:5–19

Far East

Australia, 1985, 102 minutes
Cast: Bryan Brown, Helen Morse, John Bell, Raina McKeon
Writer: John Duigan
Director: John Duigan

Far East

Perseverance

SYNOPSIS

Morgan Keefe is the Australian expatriate proprietor of the Koala Klub, one of the sleazy strip joints that exist in Manila during the 1970s, after the Vietnam War. It caters to the multinational business community. Easygoing, Morgan fits in well with the exploitative culture of the city.

Into his club, of all the clubs in the world, comes Jo, whom he had loved many years before. She is now the wife of Peter, a prominent Australian journalist who has come to Manila to report on social and political issues.

Peter makes contact with trade unions and a church social worker, Rosita, so that he can get full and accurate stories of life in the Marcos-era Philippines (1965–1986). Rosita and the journalist are kidnapped by government agents and tortured. Jo presumes on her past love for Morgan to use his influence to free her husband.

This requires Morgan to confront the criminal element in Manila and risk losing his club. The situation is dangerous and he succeeds in helping Jo and her husband leave Manila secretly at night by boat. Rosita, however, decides she must stay in her country to work for people in need. As she flees government agents across the rooftop with Morgan's partner, Morgan is shot and killed while trying to save them.

Two Australian movies released in 1982 were loosely based on aspects of the classic, *Casablanca*. Peter Weir's *The Year of Living Dangerously* was set in Indonesia in 1965, the year of the overthrow of President Sukarno. It featured a Casablanca-like finale at an airport. John Duigan's *Far East* was set in the Manila of the 1970s after the Vietnam War and during the Marcos era. Like Humphrey Bogart's Rick, Bryan Brown's Morgan owns a bar and into it walks Jo, his past love, with her husband.

What gives the film an interesting dimension is the prominent inclusion of a church worker in the cast. She is a courageous woman who is imprisoned and tortured for her faith and her work for justice.

John Duigan went to the Philippines to research his movie and said that he had been most impressed by nuns and church workers in their struggle against poverty and oppression. The impact of the humanity shown in *Far East* was what influenced Fr. Elwood Kieser to employ Duigan to direct *Romero* (1989).

Bryan Brown and Helen Morse had appeared together in a popular Australian miniseries version of Neville Shute's *A Town Like Alice*. Brown has had a successful international career, while Morse, who appeared with Dustin Hoffman and Vanessa Redgrave in *Agatha*, has concentrated on a stage career in Australia.

COMMENTARY

Focus: Images of persecutions, disasters, and troubles remind us that the final times will be about judgment and justice. Far East *offers a story of disaster and persecution, judgment and justice in recent times.*

DIALOGUE WITH THE GOSPEL

The thirty-third Sunday of the year takes up the apocalyptic themes that the conclusions of the Gospels speak of;

they will recur in a few weeks during Advent. Malachi sets the stage for the day of the Lord which he says will come "blazing like an oven," bringing God's justice and testing the people. There will be a complete conflagration except for those who remain faithful or listen to God's message.

The Gospel shows the people speaking about the beauty of the Temple and Jesus responds in Malachi's apocalyptic mind-set. He takes the occasion to say that the very Temple of which they speak will be destroyed. Further, he tells of wars, earthquakes, famine, plagues and signs of doom. Indeed, even the faithful will be betrayed, imprisoned, turned on by family and authorities alike. While the Spirit of God will inspire them in their defense, they must persevere. Their endurance will save them.

In retrospect, the Philippines during the Marcos regime was an example of a nation at war, beset by poverty, oppressed by social injustice, and marked by persecution, trials, and torture. The peaceful overthrow of the government by the people in 1986 reinforces the message that endurance will win out at the end.

Far East shows the slums, criminals, terrorists, police, and military of Manila and other cities like it as ugly, abusive, and exploitative. It is a city of violence and sexual abuse, of betrayal and imprisonment. It challenges the values of the three expatriate Australians, none of whom is without fault. The character of Rosita focuses the themes of the Gospel. She suffers and is then offered the opportunity to escape to Australia where it is said that she can do good work by exposing the injustice. She chooses to stay with her people and to give witness with her life.

KEY SCENES AND THEMES

- The sleazy aspects of life in Manila, the Koala Klub and its patrons, local corruption, expatriate customers; Morgan in the context of his club, genial but hardened, participating in the exploitation; the context of the Vietnam War and its effects on the American presence and on Manila.

- Jo and the memories of the past with Morgan; her marriage and her relationship with her husband; her moral choices.

- Rosita as a journalist, the role of the church in the Marcos regime; Rosita's work, her room, her faith, her devotion; the arrests and imprisonments, the viciousness of such regimes; Morgan and his involvement, "selling" the dancer for information, his personal self-sacrifice, saving Jo and her husband; Rosita and her decision to stay.

FOR REFLECTION AND CONVERSATION

1. *Far East* seems like a simple, low-budget movie made about life in the post-Vietnam era in the Philippines. However, many of us will never know the reality of life under a dictator, with its human exploitation and misery that the film manages to convey in a convincing manner. It is easy, however, to compare *Far East* to *Casablanca.* How do the social situations and the characters of Morgan and Rick, Jo and Ilsa, Peter and Victor, compare (and other characters as well)? Would you say that Morgan is amoral? Does he really change? What makes his conscience so limited? How do "the ends justify the means" for Morgan?

2. *Far East* is an interesting movie to look at through the lenses of the characters themselves. One by one, look at the personal, social, economic, political, religious, and cultural situation through the eyes of the characters, from Morgan, to the eyes of the children who see everything to the multinationals who create a market for women and profit. What do you see through their eyes? In the twenty or so years since the

film was released, what are the effects of globalization in various parts of the world? What is our personal response?

3. What can Rosita do to change the situation of her country, even if she escapes to the provinces where the authorities may not find her? Talk about the saying: "If a tree falls in the forest, but no one is there to hear it, does it make a sound?" What is the value of doing the right thing, of integrity and self-sacrifice even as a person's world is coming to an end? Why is freedom of the press so important for human justice in a world becoming smaller every day because of globalization?

Prayer

Lord, when we experience suffering that makes us think that the end of everything is near, increase our faith and strengthen us with a more committed hope and the joy of your love. Amen.

Paul Newman in *Cool Hand Luke.*

CHRIST THE KING

2 Samuel 5:1–3;
Colossians 1:12–20;
Luke 23:35–43

Cool Hand Luke

U.S.A., 1967, 126 minutes
Cast: Paul Newman, George Kennedy, J. D. Cannon,
Strother Martin, Jo Van Fleet, Ralph Waite,
Harry Dean Stanton, Dennis Hopper
Writers: Frank Pierson, Donn Pearce
Director: Stuart Rosenberg

Cool Hand Luke

A Good Thief

Luke is a happy-go-lucky ex-serviceman who, while drinking, knocks off the heads of parking meters. He is sentenced to prison for two years to work on the chain gang for destroying municipal property.

He seems to live something of a charmed life because he is always smiling. At first the other prisoners dislike him but his attitude eventually wins over his fellow convicts, especially when he wins an egg-eating competition. He is able to put up with the cruelty and vindictiveness of the bosses even when he gets solitary confinement.

Life is harsh in the prison and Luke enables the others to keep going because he refuses to bend to the arbitrary authority of the bosses. His mother, Arletta, visits him in prison but it is a sad experience for them both. He willingly takes on one of the prison bullies named Dragline in a fight. Battered, Luke refuses to stay down. Dragline becomes his champion.

Luke escapes twice and is captured. The bosses are crueler than ever and beat him into complete submission. Then, without any planning, he steals a truck and his friend and "disciple" joins him. They decide to split up. Luke goes to a

SYNOPSIS

church where he begins to pray and tries to bargain with God, "the old man" up there. His friend reappears telling him that the bosses have promised not to shoot him if he surrenders. But when he stands at a window repeating what the warden had once said, "What we have here is a failure to communicate," he is shot. Bleeding and seriously wounded, they take him to the prison infirmary where he will die because the bosses refuse to allow him to go to the nearest hospital.

Later, his friend regales the prisoners with stories of Luke who, with his smile and cunning, could never be beaten down.

COMMENTARY

Cool Hand Luke is remembered as one of the best and most popular Hollywood movies of the 1960s. It is reminiscent of the chain-gang prison movies of the 1930s with their cruel wardens and guards and the prisoners' desires to escape. Donn Pearce, who at one time spent two years in prison, wrote the novel on which the film is based.

Paul Newman was nominated for an Academy Award for his role as Luke. His line, "What we have here is a failure to communicate," is one of those that has entered into popular consciousness.

The 1960s was the era that saw the "death of God" movement highlighted on a cover of *Time* magazine (1966). The sequence in the church where Luke prays to God and confesses that he killed people in war and is a drunk and a destroyer of public property has become a symbol of the need for prayer even though the person praying doubts the existence of God.

The authorities kill Luke out of cruelty and jealousy but his spirit lives on in the stories and memories of the prisoners. George Kennedy, who plays Luke's friend "Dragline," won an Oscar for his performance. A young Dennis Hopper plays "Bobalugats."

*Focus: The Good Thief repents on the cross and Jesus promises
him paradise. Cool Hand Luke is a repentant petty criminal
whose suffering for others suggests parallels from the life of both
the Good Thief and Jesus' life and teaching.*

The first two readings exalt Jesus as king because he was
a descendant of David, the first king of Judea. However, the
Gospel presents a more lowly perspective of Jesus' kingship,
because he is "exalted" on a cross between two thieves. The
revelation of Christ the King is of someone who is humiliated, suffers, and shares the fate of common criminals. Jesus
generously and freely shows mercy and forgiveness when one
of the thieves mocks him. In today's Gospel Jesus promises
the repentant thief that they will share the same destiny: paradise.

The character of Luke can be seen as a Good Thief-character, as well as a Christ-figure. The movie tells us about Luke's
youthful irresponsibility and inability to settle down. He really does exist outside of society's limits and he does not try
to hide it. Going to prison does not seem to bother him, but
the injustices that he experiences and the brutal treatment
that is meted out to him there take their toll. Despite this, he
pulls all kinds of stunts to keep up the morale of the other
prisoners. After the egg-eating stunt, he stretches out on his
bed in the form of a cross, evoking an image of Jesus, as one
who gave himself for others. His second escape lasts for some
time and he sends the men a phony picture of himself in a
magazine that makes him look popular and successful, the
ideal of the other prisoners. For a while they are encouraged
by his audacious behavior. When they find out the picture is
a fake, they are disappointed in him. Luke's life culminates
in what seems to be his arbitrary death. It is the warden's
vengeful whim that allows him to bleed to death when he
could have been taken to the nearest hospital. Once again,
Luke can be seen as a Christ-figure because he suffers tor-

ment so that others may have life, even if only through encouragement to survive prison.

At the last moment, the Good Thief prays to Jesus on the cross. Alone in the church, Luke prays in his desperation, even though he does not see God.

Christian tradition loves the Good Thief and has invented a name for him, Dismas. Apocryphal stories about his life exist as well, including one about his saving the Holy Family during their flight into Egypt. Just as Luke's story was told and re-told by the prisoners, so the Good Thief's story has become part of Jesus' own story and has been told and re-told for two thousand years, giving courage to the fainthearted and strength to the weak.

KEY SCENES AND THEMES

- Luke and his carefree and irresponsible life, as a young man about town, drinking, and petty crime; Luke in prison; the harshness of the life, the barracks, the isolation box, the work on the chain gang.

- Luke's effect on his fellow prisoners, their warming to him, his charisma, the egg-eating contest, how he encourages them to be better and to survive in prison; the contrast between the bosses, their appearance, guns, brutality, and inhumanity; the "failures in communication." Luke and the fight, battered but not down, his determination to stand; the response of the prisoners and their respect.

- The final escape, Luke in the church, kneeling and praying, calling God an old man, his quizzical look to the empty ceiling as the answer to prayer; mocking the bosses by repeating the warden's words, the shooting and his wounded side; his memory and his spirit living on in the stories told.

1. To anyone who experienced the 1960s in the United States, *Cool Hand Luke* just about sums it all up. Luke represents a generation of young people who were fighting for their own identity in a rapidly changing world, struggling with social and cultural mores and questioning the arbitrariness of the authorities, from their parents to the state to religious faith. Many young people became harmless hippies and flower children; others rebelled so much that they broke laws and were sent to prison. How is Luke's experience a metaphor for a particular time in history? How does his individual experience stand for what society was going through at the time? Can you think of any contemporary films that function as a commentary on society or question society today in the same or similar ways (e.g., *Life as a House, Thelma and Louise*)? What do you think about these kinds of films that seem to have subtexts—more going on in them than what meets the eye?

2. The refrain for the responsorial psalm says, "Let us go rejoicing into the house of God," the reading from Colossians speaks of deliverance from darkness, and the Gospel testifies to eternal life to men dying on crosses. How does the idea of freedom, whether spiritual or physical, emerge from the readings? How do the camera angles and shots of feet, shoes, open roads, streams, lights, darkness, shackles, guards, fences, and bars communicate Luke's and the other prisoners' yearning for freedom? How did you feel as you watched the film? What function did the "man without eyes" fulfill in the movie? What did the reflection in his sunglasses mean and why were they crushed at the end?

FOR REFLECTION AND CONVERSATION

3. "What we have here is a failure to communicate" is one of cinema's most memorable lines, coming first from the prison warden and then repeated by Luke. What form of communication was the warden referring to? How many kinds of communication were really going on in the prison? How was Luke a "communicator"? Was anyone really "listening" in the prison? How are forms of power and communication linked? What about the conversation between Luke and his mother? What do we learn about the role Luke played in his family? How did his family members communicate among themselves? How was it similar to the role he was playing in prison? Do you think Luke was a good person? Why or why not? How did he communicate who he was and what he was searching for? Who was he, really?

Prayer

Today, Lord, we celebrate your kingship by remembering how you forgave the Good Thief. Forgive us our sins and help us to learn to forgive others. Amen.

Bless the Child
U.S.A., 2000, 104 minutes
Cast: Kim Basinger, Jimmy Smits, Rufus Sewell,
Holliston Coleman, Ian Holm, Christina Ricci
Writers: Tom Rickman, Cliff Green, Ellen Green
Director: Chuck Russell

1 John 1:5—2:2;
Matthew 2:13–18

Bless the Child

Attack on the Innocents

Drug addict Jenna visits her sister, Maggie, on Christmas Eve, bringing her newborn daughter, Cody, whom she then abandons. Six years pass while Maggie cares for the gifted but withdrawn child. Although Maggie was educated in Catholic schools and is no longer a believer, she entrusts Cody to the sisters for her education. Cody progresses well, though she seems autistic.

SYNOPSIS

A series of child murders disturbs FBI agent John Travis, who is an expert in cults and ritual murders. All the children who have been killed had the same birthday and it is also Cody's. The killers are a group of Satan-worshippers, led by Eric, a media celebrity and self-help guru. They are looking for a special child born on the day when the Star of Jacob (which had shone over Bethlehem) appeared again. They hope to absorb God's power from the child to strengthen the power of the devil.

Maggie asks John for help when a cult runaway, Cheri, contacts her. Eric has now married Jenna to get access to Cody and he has abducted her. John continues to investigate the children's murders and links them to Eric and his followers. Maggie snatches Cody during a visit to the dentist and flees the city. However, their car crashes and Cody is taken to a mansion where she is to participate in a satanic ritual.

One of the sisters takes Maggie to see Fr. Grissom, who explains what is at stake. Maggie and John go to rescue Cody. Cody refuses to cooperate with Eric, and Maggie is shot while trying to save her. Cody heals her. Eric and his followers are destroyed. Later one of the Satanists attempts to kill Cody, but her power for good turns him away.

COMMENTARY

For over thirty years, movies have dramatized "alternate" theological stories that have some kind of biblical foundation in the scriptures. Some critics consider them corny melodramas because they play off an uninformed mixture of religion and superstition on the part of both filmmakers and audience. However, as long as audiences do not take these kinds of movies literally—which a generation unfamiliar with the scriptures is in danger of doing—they can be seen as "religious thrillers." For those more in tune with the scriptures, these kinds of movies can form a bridge to the popular audience, perhaps guiding them to a deeper understanding of the biblical texts.

Kim Basinger plays Maggie, a woman unable to bear children and the aunt who wants to protect her foster daughter. From his days on *NYPD Blue*, Jimmy Smits is no stranger to his role as a policeman. British actor Rufus Sewell makes the guru a diabolical phony. Ian Holm has one scene as the priest who, unlike the vast majority of the clergy, has some inside knowledge regarding the arcane secrets of Satan worshippers. The director is Chuck Russell *(The Mask, Eraser, The Scorpion King)*. Screenwriters Cliff and Ellen Green were also responsible for writing a movie with a similar theme, *The Seventh Sign*.

Focus: Bless the Child *tries to imagine today's Gospel about the massacre of the Holy Innocents in a contemporary context with a modern Herod seeking power.*

The massacre of the Holy Innocents is one of the most dramatic of Gospel stories, with its cruel king, violent soldiers, and distraught mothers lamenting their murdered children as Jesus and his family escapes. Those familiar with Old Testament stories know it is a parallel with the story of Moses being saved from Pharaoh's similar violent murder of children. First Moses then Jesus, and today a movie about wonderfully gifted children who are the targets of evil and are saved amidst the dreadful suffering of other mothers and their children.

Bless the Child speculates that this is the first time that such a gifted child has appeared in 2000 years (which is not exactly flattering to the saints!). But the millennial world is different from that of Jesus, and this new story is told in terms of contemporary realities. No longer does a royal tyrant pretend to pay homage to the child he persecutes. Instead, there are modern false prophets and implacable cult leaders who want a child's supernatural power for themselves. In today's version of the story, the mother of the chosen child is a drug addict and the father unknown, yet God is present to every child, no matter his or her situation.

To dialogue with this Gospel requires that we do what the screenplay does: identify the similarities with the Gospel narrative, highlight the differences, and speculate on what this story might mean in our own times. Just as in Jesus' time, children were victims of physical abuse and cruelty, so today this Gospel challenges a culture where children are victims in their own homes, in institutions, at the hands of trusted Church ministers, and as the innocents of war.

In the movie, the agnostic Maggie is the foster parent committed to protecting the child. She must rely on civil authorities for the power to do what she cannot do. By believing in the child and by being prepared to die to save her, she reminds us of Mary and Joseph's committment to Jesus. And as the wonder-working child gifts Maggie with healing grace, so does Jesus gift us with the grace that makes us whole.

KEY SCENES AND THEMES

- Maggie on the bus with the woman prophesying a new child because of the appearance of the star; Jenna and her helplessness, abandoning Cody to Maggie; the child's growing up and her creative powers; Jenna and Eric taking her back.

- Eric and his role in the cult, his smooth-talking style with Maggie, keeping Jenna addicted, his henchman, the massacre of the children, his satanic ceremonies and his desire to possess God-like power.

- Maggie fleeing with Cody, the pursuit, Cody's being taken from her; the house and the rituals; Maggie's powerlessness and death; Cody's raising her to life.

FOR REFLECTION AND CONVERSATION

1. The Church of the Holy Innocents in New York City has a shrine of the Holy Innocents dedicated to children who have died unborn. Although today's film, *Bless the Child*, does not refer to today's holy innocents, it is easy to make the connection beyond the story's parallel with the Gospel account. Further, the sound of Rachel weeping for her children has seen a modern parallel with the foundation of Project Rachel, a post-abortion healing ministry of the Catholic Church. Project Rachel is for anyone who is struggling after an abortion loss, including women and men, parents, grandparents, siblings, friends, and others whose lives have been impacted by an abortion loss: www.

marquette.edu/rachels. Talk about the culture of life and the message of today's Gospel and feast, its meaning for today, and your personal efforts to promote life in a culture where power is the greatest value. Can any of us say that we are "without sin" when it comes to the responsibility for building a culture of life? What positive actions can we take that reflect the Gospel of life?

2. A cult is a system of religious or philosophical beliefs that the majority of people in a society consider unorthodox. Its leader is usually a charismatic person who claims to have supernatural powers or the ability to heal. The followers of a cult often idolize the leader and rarely if ever question his or her authority. Experts say that cults flourish in a time of instability, when values and social mores change and people are searching for meaning. Why do the people in the film follow Eric? What do they hope for? Why is Christianity not enough for either Maggie or Jenna and what might have changed this for them? How are Cody's and Maggie's souls snatched from the snare of the devil?

3. Satanism is an inversion of traditional Judeo-Christian and Islamic beliefs because it "worships" evil instead of good. Satanism is often considered a parody of Christian rituals. Because there is much confusion about satanism, witchcraft, and so forth, some tolerance groups define satanism as the worship of the Christian devil or view satanists as those who "accept Satan as a pre-Christian life-principle." Review the numerous references to "demon" in the *Catechism of the Catholic Church* including all references to Satan, exorcisms, and the origin of evil. Would you describe

the Christian life as a battle of good versus evil, or is it more complex than that? Does the film treat the problem of evil in a way that encourages faith and hope? Why or why not? What did the film, or what it symbolized, mean to you?

Prayer

Lord, we pray today for all children in danger, for children who suffer, for children who are victims of human greed and lust for power. Amen.

One True Thing
U.S.A., 1998, 122 minutes
Cast: Meryl Streep, Renée Zellweger, William Hurt,
Tom Everett Scott, Nicky Katt, Lauren Graham
Writer: Karen Croner
Director: Carl Franklin

One True Thing

A Mother's Care and Blessing

SYNOPSIS

The district attorney interviews Ellen Gulden about her mother's death from an overdose of morphine tablets. There seems to be some doubt as to whether or not Katherine Gulden, who was terminally ill from cancer, took her own life. Maybe she had help. As she talks, Ellen remembers her mother and how she cared for her and her brother, Brian, when they were children.

Ellen, an ambitious and successful journalist, recalls when she returned home for a surprise birthday party for her father, gleefully and perfectly organized by her mother. She learned then that her mother had cancer. Ellen practically worships her father, George, who is a successful professor. His approval means everything to her. Though Ellen has never felt close to her mother, her father asks Ellen to give up her job and stay at home to care for Katherine. Ellen agrees.

Through housework and the constant demands of her father, Ellen learns the hard way just how hard her uncomplaining mother has worked. Unwillingly, Ellen is drawn into the charity work of the "Minnies," her mother's friends. She discovers the care they offer to people in need. As the months pass, she realizes that her academic father is not the genius she thought him to be. Instead, he is self-centered and has been unfaithful to his wife. When she confronts her mother about her life, Ellen learns amazing lessons about fostering a marriage, sacrificing for the sake of a family, and forgiveness.

As Katherine's health deteriorates, she asks Ellen to end her pain and her life. Ellen is tempted, but cannot. When her mother dies, Ellen assumes her father gave her the pills. They discover, finally, that Katherine took them herself. Ellen and her father reconcile.

COMMENTARY

Meryl Streep won yet another of her many Oscar nominations for Best Actress for *One True Thing*. Here, Streep proves once again what a versatile actress she is.

The movie is a mother and daughter story, adapted from a novel by Anna Quindlen. Renée Zellweger is an ambitious young journalist who has absorbed her father's academic ethos of excellence and has neglected her mother. William Hurt plays the father who is unable to face up to his wife's illness. Lauren Graham, lately of the *Gilmore Girls* television series, plays Ellen's friend Jules.

The movie is a departure for director Carl Franklin whose crime thrillers, *One False Move* and *Devil in a Blue Dress*, marked him as a tough storyteller. Here he handles strong family emotions with great sensitivity.

DIALOGUE WITH THE GOSPEL

Focus: George Gulden says of his wife that she was the one true thing in his life. The life and death of Katherine Gulden also shows us a mother's unfailing love for her children. Katherine brings to mind Mary, Mother of God, who reflected on her loved ones and her life, keeping them in her heart.

Although no longer a holy day of obligation in many places, the Church's celebration at the start of the calendar year begins with the theme of blessing, associated with the motherhood of Mary. God's word of blessing in Numbers is about protection, graciousness, and peace. The shepherds experience this blessing at the stable when they find Mary and Joseph and the child lying in the manger. The shepherds cannot contain themselves and spread the news of God's blessing. Mary ponders all these things in her heart. Jesus is, of course, God's word of blessing. Eight days after his birth, his parents name him "Jesus," the name given to him by the angel at his conception.

In *One True Thing*, the blessing for this mother is her daughter. As so seldom happens in major Hollywood films, the father and son are in the background. Katherine Gulden dramatizes what a mother is and can be. In her house, she has tried always to be a giver of life and blessing, even when it is taken for granted, ignored, or considered menial, especially by her daughter, Ellen. Even the audience might think of Katherine as a drone as we see the initial flashbacks of the caring wife and mother, then see her dressed up as Dorothy for the birthday party, or watch her fussing and giggling with her hobbies and friends from the volunteer group.

When we look beneath the surface, we find that Katherine is a good, even heroic woman, who values her marriage and family, is sensitive to their needs, and is completely self-sacrificing. Her mother's cancer, and the way she deals with it, becomes an extraordinary blessing for Ellen, who learns to look closely at and to appreciate reality in the present. In a sense, her mother gives Ellen life—again. We could use St. Paul's words to say that this was the "fullness of time" for Ellen as she learned about the grace and dignity she inherited from her mother.

- • The portrait of Katherine as loving mother during Ellen's childhood, the birthday celebration, her support for Brian when he gives up study for a job, her charity work with the "Minnies"; forgiving her husband; sharing her illness with Ellen, the exasperation and the pain, speaking honestly and lovingly to her.

KEY SCENES AND THEMES

- Ellen as an ambitious daughter, neglectful of her mother; her father imposing on her to stay with her mother, discovering her father's self-absorption; learning the practical details of working at home and how unappreciated she is; joining the "Minnies"; the Christmas celebration in the town.

- The months of Katherine's illness; the growing closeness of mother and daughter; the pain and the dilemma of wanting to give the overdose of morphine, Ellen's not being able to do it; the utter pathos and tragedy of Katherine's death, yet its blessings.

FOR REFLECTION AND CONVERSATION

1. By the end of the film, Ellen has learned a great deal of wisdom as she goes back to work and sorts out her relationships and priorities. Talk about the scene in the car when Ellen accompanies her mother on the regular outing with the woman whose life has fallen apart. What do her mother's actions and words reveal to Ellen? Why has Ellen considered her mother's Martha Stewart-like world so "small"? Why is it that we never quite know or appreciate our parents and the sacrifices they make for us until a life-changing event or illness happens? Why do you think Ellen almost always wears black? How and why does Ellen learn from her mother a more grounded appreciation of the ordinary values of life? What do you think these values are? How would you apply them to your own life? How do you think grown children from a broken marriage would interpret a film like this that makes a family look so "normal"? Is it?

2. Ellen discovers her father's selfishness and her mother's loving selflessness. Talk about George's view on how men and women differ in their ways of deal-

ing with difficulty and grief. Do you agree? Should Ellen have lied about her father's whereabouts on the night of her mother's death? Why did she? What would you have done if you had been in a similar situation? How could more open communication have helped the Gulden family? Who was the best communicator in the family? How did this family show its love? Was it that love was not there, or that people could not see it? Why? How did the film make you feel? Why? What, if anything, will you reflect on in your heart after seeing this movie?

3. The film concludes with the dilemma about administering an overdose of morphine to relieve the agonizing pain of the cancer sufferer, suicide, and issues of mercy and responsibility. Why are these matters of such huge import in the world of ethics (consideration of human behavior that is ordered to the highest good and in full harmony with reason, virtue, and duty) and morality (the goodness or badness of human actions based on freedom and responsibility and grounded in one's faith tradition)? What was the attitude of the district attorney? Do you think he would have let Ellen or George go even if they admitted to giving Katherine the pills? Why do you think Katherine took her own life? Is there a purpose to human suffering? What does faith tell us about coping with pain, suffering, and death? Are we to just accept the inevitable in passive silence or is there something more? What is a human and Christian response to helping others who are suffering and dying? Why is it sometimes easier to help those we don't know rather than those with whom we live? Do children owe their parents anything? Should Ellen have stayed? What would

you have done? What is the "one true thing" that George speaks of?

Prayer

Lord, bless us this year with the gift of reflection, as you blessed Mary. May we discover grace and meaning in whatever suffering comes our way. Amen.

St. Joseph, Husband of Mary

2 Samuel 7:4–5a, 12–14a, 16;
Romans 4:13, 16–18, 22;
Luke 2:41–51a

Frequency

U.S.A., 2000, 118 minutes
Cast: Dennis Quaid, Jim Caviezel, Andre Braugher,
Elizabeth Mitchell
Writer: Toby Emmerich
Director: Gregory Hoblit

Frequency

Father and Son

Frank Sullivan is a skilled fireman, known for his daring rescues. He is also a loving husband and close to his six-year-old son, John. During a fire on October 12, 1969, Frank Sullivan is killed and a spectacular display of aurora borealis appears in the New York City sky.

SYNOPSIS

On October 12, 1999, the thirtieth anniversary of Frank's death, the aurora borealis is glowing once more. John Sullivan's life is a mess. Instead of following family tradition and becoming a firefighter, he became a cop. He is introspective and depressed. His girlfriend leaves him. He is living in the house he inherited from his father, and while digging around under the stairs, he finds his dad's old ham radio. As John tries to tune it, a voice comes through the speaker from thirty years before. It is Frank, his father. They begin to communicate through time. John notices that all of a sudden the photographs of his Dad on the wall show him with grey hair. The images have inexplicably aged.

Eventually, John is able to give his father advice that saves his life thirty years before. Automatically, the details and direction of John's life story are changed.

The police find the body of a victim of a serial killer back in 1969. John is now able to get his father to prevent the death. Again, history changes. When his mother is about to become the next victim, John enables his father to stop the murder, but his father then clashes with the killer, a man named Jack Shepard, and is arrested as a suspect. The final confrontation with the killer takes place both in 1969 as he attempts to kill John's mother and in 1999 when he tries to kill John. Because of the changes he and his son have made in their histories, his father is still alive and he saves John.

The family history has changed from despair to love.

COMMENTARY

Writer and music producer Toby Emmerich has imagined a time-communication story rather than the typical time-travel tale. Instead of people, information goes back and forth over thirty years. Emmerich and director Gregory Hoblit (award-winning director of television's *Hill Street Blues* and *NYPD Blue* and the movies *Primal Fear, Fallen,* and *Hart's War*) consulted with at least one academic scientist to ensure that the physics theories used in the plot are plausible, even if only for their entertainment value rather than as practical science.

The relationship between the Dennis Quaid *(The Rookie, Far from Heaven, Savior)* and James Cavaziel's *(Ed, Thin Red Line, Pay It Forward, Count of Monte Cristo,* and Mel Gibson's *Passion)* characters is strongly drawn.

Although difficult to follow at times, the movie works as an intriguing drama that plays with the mysteries of time and is effective as a police thriller and a mystery. It also works very well in terms of portraying loving family bonds and imagining the possibility of reshaping and healing one's past.

DIALOGUE WITH THE GOSPEL

Focus: One of the great themes for the celebration of St. Joseph is his place as an earthly role model for Jesus. There has been

much pious speculation about his relationship with Jesus. Frequency *is a highly imaginative reflection on the relationship
between a father and a son.*

Paul's praise of Abraham in the second reading can be
applied to Joseph because like Abraham, he too is a father in
faith. Joseph is also a wise and just man as described in the
responsorial psalm.

Luke's account of the finding of Jesus in the Temple is
the principal Joseph story in this Gospel. While it is Mary
who speaks to Jesus rather than Joseph, she refers to their
sense of loss and their worry as they went through Jerusalem
searching for him. Jesus' response to this outpouring of anguish is that he must do the work of God, his father.
Nevertheless, Jesus returns to Nazareth with his mother and
his foster father and the Gospel notes his growth, his matur-
ing, and his obedience to Mary and Joseph. We can imagine
the power of Joseph's ability as a father and as a role model
when we examine the personality of Jesus revealed during
his ministry, especially his love and care for others.

In *Frequency,* the focus is a strong father-son relationship.
There is love in the Sullivan household. John and his friend,
Gordo, observe the love between mother and father as they
dance to "Suspicious Minds." Frank helps his son ride a bike
and play baseball. When Frank is tempted to be severe, his
wife reminds him that his son is only a child and Frank
mellows.

More of the power of the father-son relationship is shown
in the communication via the radio frequency. Each lovingly
tells the other his story. The son advises his father about the
mistake made that fateful day so that he will not be killed.
The pair works together to save lives and, ultimately, to save
John's mother. The final images of the movie are of fathers
and sons and the next generation. In a movie culture that

does not imagine biblical stories and characters frequently or very well, *Frequency* offers images that can help us to imagine the loving relationship between Jesus and Joseph.

KEY SCENES AND THEMES

- The quality of love and care in the Sullivan family; each parent's relationship with John; John watching them dance; the bike lessons, playing ball; Frank as a loving role model of fatherhood for his son.

- The power of the communication between father and son on the radio, the love conveyed through their storytelling, the shared baseball experiences; John's advice that saves his father's life.

- Father and son working together to solve the crime; saving John's mother; Frank saving John's life in the present; the theme of "what if" we were able to go back in time and change our lives.

FOR REFLECTION AND CONVERSATION

1. At the core of the movie is the story of love between a father and a son and how we might change things if we had the chance to go back in time and make different choices. One of the practices of Christian spirituality is the daily examination of conscience in which we reflect, review our day, week, month, recognize our good actions as well as the bad, and pray for forgiveness. We also try to foresee occasions for sin and discern how to be prepared to choose the good rather than what is contrary to God's will and human dignity. If you are a parent, and specifically a father, since we are commemorating the life of St. Joseph today, how can you create a relationship with your children now in order to build a positive Christian future, filled with the memories of your best efforts at sound parenting, with as few regrets as possible? How can

you make a place in your daily spiritual life for discernment and the examination of conscience?

2. Science fiction, speculative fiction, science fantasy—all are genres in which *Frequency* would fit. Ever since 1895, when H. G. Wells published his now classic *The Time Machine*, and following subsequent discoveries in science, our imaginations have been entranced with the idea that we can suspend the laws of nature as we know them. Frank and his son John live in parallel universes rather than in one that is chronological. Instead of traveling through time, they communicate through time. Compare this film with others you may have seen about time travel *(Contact*, the *Back to the Future* trilogy, or even *It's a Wonderful Life)*. What elements of these films appeal to you, if any? Why? Make a list of any common themes that emerge and compare them with the Christian teaching that we find in the Beatitudes or other Scripture citations that come to mind.

3. How is communication at the heart of all these time-travel movies? The Gospels offer us no words directly from Joseph, yet we know he communicated with God and that God spoke to him. Joseph was a decisive man who took his role as foster-father of Jesus seriously. Joseph made great sacrifices to protect, provide for, and educate him and offered Jesus the best he could to assure his place in the world. Yet, nothing he ever actually said has come down to us. Is communication only verbal? Talk about the many forms of interpersonal communication that exist (spoken and written word, body language, etc.) and reflect on the power of nonverbal communication. How can discernment

help us respond to others and communicate in positive ways, even without using words? Do you think it might be a stretch to think of St. Joseph as the "silent communicator" who can be a role model for interpersonal relationships in families and in the community? What is Joseph's role for us today?

Prayer

St. Joseph, you lived with Jesus and loved and cared for him as a son. You showed him what it was like to be a father. Protect all families and especially guide fathers who struggle to care for their children. Amen.

ASCENSION

Acts 1:1–11;
Hebrews 9:24–28, 10:19–23;
Luke 24:46–53

Signs

U.S.A., 2002, 106 minutes
Cast: Mel Gibson, Joaquin Phoenix, Rory Culkin, Cherry Jones,
Abigail Breslin, M. Night Shyamalan
Writer: M. Night Shyamalan
Director: M. Night Shyamalan

Signs

"...To See"

Graham Hess is an Episcopal priest who has given up his ministry after his wife is killed in a road accident. He has lost his faith.

SYNOPSIS

One morning, he finds his children, Morgan and Bo, in the cornfields looking at mysterious circles in the middle of the crops. Caroline, the local police chief, is unable to solve the mystery of how the circles were made. Other signs of strange happenings appear. Dogs behave erratically. Graham and his brother, Merrill, glimpse a strange creature near their house.

The television news reveals that alien sightings have occurred around the world. Spacecraft appear in the skies over hundreds of cities. Helped by a book about extraterrestrial life, the Hess family tries to prepare for an invasion. Responding to a phone call from the man who caused his wife's death, Graham goes to the man's house where he wounds an alien. He dreams of the night of his wife's death and hears her tell him, "See."

It seems that an alien attack is immanent. The family votes to stay in their house and board it up. When the aliens assault the house, exuding some kind of gas, the family hides in the basement rather than flee. With the news that the aliens have departed, Graham, his brother, and the children come up into the house, only to discover the creature that Graham injured, who now attempts to poison and abduct Morgan. Because he is asthmatic, Morgan's lungs keep out the gas. Overjoyed that the family is saved, Graham begins to understand what his wife meant. He regains his faith.

COMMENTARY

Writer and director M. Night Shyamalan has proven himself a master of suspense with *The Sixth Sense* and *Unbreakable*. In his second film, *Wide Awake*, he dealt with issues of faith, death, the afterlife, and relationships. Here he brings suspense and faith together and wants his title to alert audiences to images and signs of Providence in our world.

Shyamalan has a gift for creating atmospheric fear, even terror. Mel Gibson is the solid center of the film and Joaquin Phoenix demonstrates his considerable screen presence and talent as Graham's younger brother. So far, Shyamalan's films all feature a young boy as central to the plot and his films concern father-son relationships, death, and grief, as well as discovering one's abilities and gifts. In *Signs* Rory Culkin plays Gibson's asthmatic son. This film truly is a supernatural thriller.

DIALOGUE WITH THE GOSPEL

Focus: When Jesus ascended to the Father he commissioned his disciples to live a life of faith and to be witnesses to his passion and death. In Signs, *Graham Hess shares the suffering experience of Jesus and begins to see signs of Providence that will help him recover his faith.*

While the feast of the Ascension celebrates the culmination of Jesus' mission on earth and his glorification with his Father, it is also a commemoration of Jesus' disappearance from earth. We now have to believe in what we do not see, based on the testimony of others and on the signs of Jesus' presence. In fact, the ending of St. Mark's Gospel refers quite explicitly to the signs and effects of Jesus' blessing. The ascension was a high point in the religious experience of the disciples. All of us can have strong experiences of God in our lives that are like this. But more often than not in the spiritual life, the "period after the ascension" can be one of doubt, and even loss of faith.

This is the situation of Graham Hess. He had been a devout and committed pastor, a man that the community respected. Then, like the disciples, he experienced the sudden loss of a loved one, a death that not only made no sense to him, but also led him to renounce his ministry, to forbid prayer in his house, and to hate God. His brother wants comfort from him in the face of the invading aliens. Graham can only explain that there are two types of people in the world. There are those who experience something "lucky" in their lives and connect it with other blessings. These events are miracles to them and they are filled with hope. Other people see "lucky" events as nothing more than arbitrary and, because they find no meaning, they are filled with fear.

The feast of the Ascension reminds us that we can be people of hope. Even if like Graham we are tempted to fear, we are invited to follow his wife's last words, "Tell Graham to see." As he defends his family against attack and deals with the threat to his son's life when he has the asthma attack, he begins to recognize the role of Providence in his life. The availability of the baseball bat; his wife's advice to Merrill "to swing"; then his son's collapsed lungs, which prevent him from inhaling the poison, help Graham see that the seeming coincidences have meaning. He is now able to define himself as a man of faith and to once again serve his people.

In the reading from the Acts of the Apostles, the second volume of St. Luke's contribution to the scriptures, he describes the angels telling the apostles, "This Jesus who has been taken up from you into heaven will return in the same way." The Letter to the Hebrews speaks of the sacrifice of

Jesus that once and for all takes away our sins and that has opened up a new way of living for us. Graham Hess shared in the passion of Jesus and in his sense of abandonment. After his ordeal, he is able to "hold unwaveringly to our confession that gives us hope."

KEY SCENES AND THEMES

- The family in the cornfields, bewildered by the circles, watching the television and seeing the lights of the alien craft in the sky, the glimpses of the creatures, the dogs barking; hiding in the basement from the harsh beating on the doors; the signs of the presence of an evil threat.

- Graham Hess not wanting to be called "Father," saying that he would not waste another minute in prayer, declaring that he hated God; the flashbacks to his wife's death and her final words; his explanation to Merrill about people of hope and people of fear.

- The signs that challenge Graham's recovery of faith: Ray's asking forgiveness for causing his wife's death; the family's surviving the night, the baseball bat, rescuing Morgan from the alien and realizing that his asthma had saved him; Graham resuming his ministry.

FOR REFLECTION AND CONVERSATION

1. Water is a frequent biblical symbol and a dominant theme in *Signs*. In Scripture, water has three basic meanings: a cosmic force that only God can control, purification, and a source of life. How is water represented in the film as a sign of God's action, of cleansing, and as a source of life? What other images and "signs" did you notice that functioned as cinematic

devices to narrate the story (such as patterns and their repetition, the television, etc.)? What do they mean?

2. Graham was a man of God who has lost his faith because of the seemingly arbitrary death of his wife in a road accident and now he does not want to talk about prayer. He feels disillusioned with God. When the crop circles appear, he has to deal with his fears for the sake of his son and daughter and for his brother, Merrill, who has come to live with the family. Talk about the conversation between Graham and Merrill about the two kinds of people. Do you identify or agree with Graham's observation? Why or why not? What is the difference between luck and divine Providence? If you were asked to describe your life of faith, what would you say?

3. What are signs and symbols, anyway? The *Encarta* (2002) encyclopedia says, "People have culture primarily because they can communicate with and understand symbols. Symbols allow people to develop complex thoughts and to exchange those thoughts with others. Language and other forms of symbolic communication, such as art, enable people to create, explain, and record new ideas and information." How does this definition fit with the various kinds of communication going on in the movie *Signs?* Are the aliens a "sign"? If so, of what? If not, why are they in the film? Do you think that a film about aliens and the environment could be a metaphor for how the peoples of one nation treat another, or how we all care for the earth's resources? Why or why not? Do you think

writer/director M. Night Shyamalan had a moral in mind when he wrote the screenplay? If so, how would you describe it and why?

Prayer

Lord, you said "You are witnesses to all these things." On this feast when we celebrate your glorification and your victory over sin, bless your people who often experience suffering and doubt. Send your comforting and strengthening Spirit upon us. Amen.

SACRED HEART OF JESUS

Ezekiel 34:11–16;
Romans 5:5b–11;
Luke 15:3–7

Life As a House

U.S.A., 2001, 125 minutes
Cast: Kevin Kline, Kristin Scott Thomas, Hayden Christensen,
Mary Steenburgen, Jena Malone, Jamey Sheridan,
Scott Bakula, John Pankow
Writer: Mark Andrus
Director: Irwin Winkler

Life As a House

Building a House

George Monroe lives in a shed on a cliff on the California coast. An architect for twenty years, he prefers building physical models rather than using computer programs for his work. He has been divorced from his wife, Robin, for ten years. She has remarried and, with her husband, Peter, has two sons. George's sixteen-year-old son, Sam, is a disturbed young man who takes drugs regularly and escapes reality by listening to loud, heavy-metal music. He barely speaks to his mother and is constantly rude to his stepfather.

SYNOPSIS

George is fired from his job because he refuses to upgrade to computers; he reacts angrily by destroying all his beautiful models. He has hated his job and when he leaves the building, he collapses. He is diagnosed with an advanced form of cancer, which he keeps secret. His one goal now is to finally build a new house to replace the shack that was left to him by his father. George enlists the help of the reluctant Sam for the summer.

Sam resists doing any work and complains about the primitive conditions. George practically has to force Sam to work so that George has a reason to pay him. Robin comes by with meals and, eventually, she and her boys help out with the demolition of the old building and the construction of the new. Sam is involved in drugs and sells his body for sex. Sam and George have a confrontation when George flushes the drugs Sam was holding for a friend down the toilet. He and Sam begin to talk, especially about George's love/hate for his own father. George also tells him about the accident that killed George's mother as well as the parents of a young girl who was permanently injured because George's father had been driving drunk. Sam gradually starts to cooperate with his father.

Despite complaints from the neighbors, especially about his dog's lack of training, George makes progress with the building.

As the pain begins to worsen, George collapses. Robin finds him and George tells her the truth about his health. Meanwhile, she has fallen in love with him again. Peter, feeling rejected and unable to express his feelings to his sons, walks out on her. As his illness progresses, George is hospitalized. Sam, along with friends and neighbors, finishes the house. George dies, leaving the house to Sam, who decides to honor his father by giving it as a gift to the girl paralyzed in the accident caused by his grandfather so many years before.

COMMENTARY

Kevin Kline plays George Monroe, a man who experiences a life-and-death crisis. It is familiar territory for the versatile Kline, who has already examined the depths of middle-age crisis, morality, and ethics in *Grand Canyon*, *The Ice Storm*, and more recently in *The Emperor's Club*. He excels in his role as George, the uninvolved father, who is ready to change before it is too late.

Life As a House will interest a wide spectrum of ages, from mature teens to young adults to parents. However, the picture of the sullen teenager, who is self-absorbed, drug addicted, willing to prostitute himself for drug money, angry, and unable to feel love, is very alarming. Hayden

Christensen is believable in this heartbreaking role. He next appeared as the young Anakin in *Star Wars: Episode 2—Attack of the Clones,* the young Jedi who eventually opts for the dark side and becomes Darth Varder. Irwin Winkler, who also has to his credit such films as *Guilty by Suspicion, Night and the City, The Net,* and *At First Sight,* directed the film.

Focus: The shepherd seeks out the sheep that was lost and rejoices in finding it. George Monroe has lost everything. By building his house before he dies, he seeks out his lost son and rejoices when he finds him.

DIALOGUE WITH THE GOSPEL

Luke 15 consists of short parables about losing something precious and finding it again. Today's Gospel is about a shepherd losing a sheep and finding it. The next story in Luke is about the lost coin and the woman who searched her house until she found it. These parables about God's love for the lost serve as a prelude to the greatest of all the parables, that of the prodigal son and of the father whose love is limitless.

Ezekiel offers the classic Old Testament text of the shepherd searching for the sheep. In that text, the shepherd is an image of God. George Monroe is himself a lost sheep at the beginning of the movie. A gift of Providence, in the form of his being fired from his job and the onset of a life-threatening illness, enable him to be found or, at least, to find himself. This frees him to seek for his lost and alienated son. The whole movie is the dramatization of a modern search for love in a family that has lost it. In that sense, Robin is like the woman who has lost the coin. Robin has lost her son in her own house. At the end she too can rejoice that she has found him. Her joy is complete when she accompanies Sam to visit the paralyzed girl. Robin sees Sam's transformation when he gives his father's house to the girl.

In Romans, Paul notes how hard it is to lay down one's life for someone worthy, harder still if for someone unworthy. George Monroe is willing to give the last months of his life so that his son can be loved and redeemed.

KEY SCENES AND THEMES

- George alone in his shack of a house; diligent at work; being fired and his angry reaction when he destroys the models; his collapse, waking up in the hospital, talking to the nurse about being touched; his dream of building his own house.

- Sam's chaotic way of life, his anger and resentment; resisting George's plan for work, making the deal, gradually changing, leaping from the cliff like his father, listening to his father's stories; giving the house to the accident victim.

- Robin's inability to deal with Sam; her demonstrative love toward Peter and the boys; visiting the site, working with George and the boys, falling in love again; coping with George's illness and death; finding Sam again.

FOR REFLECTION AND CONVERSATION

1. Jesus spoke to his audience about their own experiences. For the men, he told the parable of the shepherd searching for the lost sheep. For the women, he told the parable of the lost money. A feminist commentator noted how easy it is to speak of God as the shepherd but we are not accustomed to speak of God as the woman of the house, which is a valid scriptural perspective. It is interesting that Rembrandt's famous masterpiece, *Return of the Prodigal Son* (1669), interprets the parable with the father having both masculine and feminine attributes (observe the hands). Talk about your image of God. Is it of a shepherd, of the woman of the house, or does it reflect another rep-

resentation of which Jesus speaks? How do you relate to your image of God?

2. St. Paul's Letter to the Romans says that Christ gave his life at the appointed time for the "ungodly." Sam, George, and his father before him were "ungodly," but were they unredeemable? How does *Life As a House* show that each person is loved, even when they do terrible things, and that forgiveness and change is possible? Have you ever experienced anything like this in your own family or life? Why is Sam's gift of the house to the paralyzed girl significant? How is the mystery of conversion, reconciliation, and renewal present in the dramatic cycle of this film? Which scenes in the film impressed you the most? Why? Why is touch meaningful in the film? What is the significance of George and Sam jumping off the cliff into the ocean?

3. Only about 20 percent of Hollywood films have female storylines, but of those, very few even come close to dealing with the issues, problems, and values relating to the broad vision of human existence and experience that movies such as *Life As a House* portray. What accounts for the fact that movie studios tell more stories that plumb the depths of human experience from the (white) male perspective rather than from that of women? How does *Life As a House* reflect the universal human struggle for wholeness and love? List any films about women (or told from a woman's perspective) that explore similar issues of family, relationships, culture, values, and transformation the way that *Life As a House* does. How does a woman's perspective make

them different? Do these films appeal to you? Why or why not? Do you think it is important to think about the perspectives or points of view from which stories are told? Why or why not?

Prayer

Lord, as we celebrate your love through the image of the human heart of Jesus, help us to be truly loving and forgiving. Amen.

ALL SOULS DAY

Isaiah 25:6–9;
1 Thessalonians 4:13–18;
John 14:1–6

The Sixth Sense

U.S.A., 1999, 107 minutes
Cast: Bruce Willis, Haley Joel Osment, Toni Collette,
Olivia Williams, Donnie Wahlberg
Writer: M. Night Shyamalan
Director: M. Night Shyamalan

The Sixth Sense

Atonement and Purification

SYNOPSIS

Child psychiatrist Malcolm Crowe is celebrating the honor that the City of Philadelphia has bestowed on him for his work. That same night, a former client named Vincent Gray breaks into his house, accuses Malcolm of failing him, and shoots him. Some months later Malcolm is sitting in a park waiting for a young boy, Cole, with whom he wants to work.

The boy seems to have been violently treated but his injuries are a puzzle to his hard-working single mother. She takes him to a doctor but gets no answers. The boy encounters strange people, who are revealed to be dead. Gradually, he begins to talk to the psychiatrist and learns to trust him.

The psychiatrist goes to the hospital with Cole as well as to his school play. In the meantime, Malcom's wife seems to be having an affair with an artist and leaves when he arrives at an anniversary dinner in a restaurant.

Cole's fellow students treat him badly and they lock him in a room. Another ghost reveals herself to him and indicates a video that shows how her mother was poisoning her. Cole finally tells his mother and the psychiatrist the truth: that he sees dead people and it is up to him to suffer for them and find a way to free them so they can go to heaven.

415

Malcolm realizes that he himself is dead, a ghost, and that Cole has been a means of healing and helping him to make reparation for failing his client, Vincent. Now he can be free of his purgatory.

COMMENTARY

The Sixth Sense is an atmospheric thriller where the psychiatrist character, Bruce Willis, excels as an actor who works well with children.

The movie was written and directed by M. Night Shyamalan. He uses angles and editing rather than special effects to create the film's eerie mood. Haley Joel Osment as Cole draws the audience in with so much intensity and sensitivity that they feel his torment. The film's frightening element is the dead people who Cole realizes are in some kind of purgatorial torment after their untimely deaths.

The American and worldwide response to *The Sixth Sense* has made this one of the biggest box-office successes of recent years. The film received six Academy Award nominations.

DIALOGUE WITH THE GOSPEL

Focus: The Sixth Sense, *like the reading from Paul, helps us reflect on how life and death affect all of us and how, as today's Gospel attests, God wants all of us to have eternal life through Jesus who is the way, the truth, and the life.*

Catholic theology teaches that the tradition of purgatory can be better understood as a "condition" rather than a place. The state of purgatory means that those who die without atoning for their sins will experience a proportionate suffering so that they will be purified and thus able to enter into God's presence. *The Sixth Sense* shows two groups of the tormented dead: those who cannot rest until they acknowledge what they have done and atone for their actions, and the dead who were victimized and continue to suffer, still in need of salvation. The traditional understanding of those in purgatory concerns the first group; in God's wisdom, we hope that the suffering that victims endure on earth will allow them to enter immediately into God's presence.

The reading from Paul to the Thessalonians invites us to reflect on how the life and death of each of us has an effect on the other—exactly what *The Sixth Sense* (through imagination) and the communion of saints (through faith) illustrates. Paul also knew that some people have no hope and grieve that the dead will not rise. Nevertheless, he promises that the Lord will come and that his words will offer comfort to believers.

Malcolm Crowe seems to have failed his client, Vincent Gray, although the audience does not know how. Vincent kills Malcolm and then kills himself, and this act of violent desperation brings grief and loneliness to Malcolm's wife, Anna. The boy Cole, with his preternatural gift of being able to see and communicate with those who have died and are in a "state of suffering," is able to help and free them. Cole's gift has a saving effect on Malcolm. It enables him to atone for failing Vincent Gray and to experience a purgation that in turn is salvific for Cole and his mother.

In John 14, Jesus urges his disciples not to be troubled, to have faith that Jesus will not turn anyone away, no matter what they have done. God's will, made known through Jesus, who is the way, the truth, and the life, is that no one is to be lost who wants to be saved. No matter what "purgatorial experience" they must endure, they can be saved. They will all be raised up to God on the last day and find their place in the many mansions in heaven. John says that this is eternal life.

KEY SCENES AND THEMES

- The eerie atmosphere of the opening, the shadow of the intruder, the confrontation and Malcolm's confession of failure, his being shot; Malcolm sitting in the park waiting for Cole, their discussions, going home with him; Cole testing him, stepping forward or back if Malcolm's guess is correct or not; the growing trust.

- Cole's seeing the ghosts, the sense of past executions at the school; Cole's rudeness to the teacher, the boys picking on him; his loneliness at home and the tension with his mother, especially at the hospital and regarding his grandmother's brooch.

- Cole going with Malcolm to the funeral reception, seeing the girl, getting the video, her father's seeing the truth about her death; Malcolm's realization of what has happened, that he is himself dead, a ghost, and that Cole has helped free him; that he has atoned for his failings and is free to pass from his purgatorial experience.

FOR REFLECTION AND CONVERSATION

1. For non-Catholic Christians, "purgatory" is a difficult concept to understand, as is the Catholic belief in the communion of saints. Purgatory is "the condition of purification after death in which good souls who are imperfectly prepared for heaven are cleansed of the effects of their sins before they enter heaven" (*Basic Catechism*, p. 70). The Church teaches that the link between life on earth and the afterlife can be summed up in the understanding of the communion of saints, which is that communion of spiritual help among all the members of Christ's body, the Church, living and deceased. How is *The Sixth Sense* about life on earth, in heaven, and in purgatory? Although the film may not be accurate theologically (similar to *What Dreams May Come*), which teachings does it reflect well, if any? Is the film meant to teach theology or is it a meta-

phor, allegory, or myth, and if so, how does it function as such? What do you think the film is trying to
say? Would you use this film to explore the concept
of purgatory? If so, how?

2. Did you guess the conclusion of the film the first time
you saw it? How did you feel when watching the film
and then learning the truth about the characters?
What cinematic devices does Shyamalan use to create the supernatural atmosphere of the film and to
hold our attention (camera angles, colors, music, repeated visual patterns and motifs)? Look at all the
occurrences when the color red is used; what do you
think it means or symbolizes?

3. Besides the famous "I see dead people" quote from
Cole, he says in another place the traditional prayer
for the faithful departed, "De profundis clamo ad te,
domine" or "Out of the depths I cry to you, O Lord."
This prayer is from Psalm 130 and it is a cry for pardon, penitence and mercy. "Depths" is the translation
of the Hebrew word "sheol," a symbol or metaphor
for complete anguish and misery. How are Malcolm
and the other dead people in the "depths"? How is
Cole a Christ-figure, who takes upon himself the sins
and sufferings of others to free them from the depths
or "purgatory," and allow them to go on to heaven?

Prayer

*Lord, we all fail and need to both atone and be purged of our sins
and our failures. On this day we pray especially for those who have
died that they may have eternal rest with you. Amen.*

THANKSGIVING
Deuteronomy 8:7–18;
Colossians 3:12–17;
Mark 5:18–20

Home for the Holidays
U.S.A., 1995, 103 minutes
Cast: Holly Hunter, Anne Bancroft, Robert Downey Jr.,
Charles Durning, Steve Guttenberg, Dylan McDermott,
Cynthia Stevenson, Claire Danes, Geraldine Chaplin,
David Strathairn
Writer: W. D. Richter
Director: Jodie Foster

Home for the Holidays

Rediscover Thanksgiving and Blessing

SYNOPSIS

Single mom Claudia Larson prepares to go to Baltimore for the family's annual Thanksgiving holiday. She has just lost her job at a Chicago art museum but she kisses her boss just the same. She is shocked when her teenaged daughter Kitt announces that she plans to lose her virginity while her mother is gone.

Caught up in the family frenzy, Claudia resents being treated as a child by her mother, Adele. Her father, Henry, withdraws from problems while her mother interferes all the time.

Tommy, Claudia's gay brother, turns up unexpectedly with a friend, Leo Fish. The family assumes he has separated from his boyfriend, Jack, with whom he has gone through a commitment ceremony. The truth is, Leo is straight and had come to meet Claudia. Adele's older, unmarried sister, Aunt Gladys, has also come for Thanksgiving. Claudia tells Tommy about Kitt and about her other problems and asks for his support. Their conservative married sister, Joanne, arrives with her husband, Walter, and their children.

Over Thanksgiving, matters get out of hand. Gladys remembers Henry's kissing her when she was young. Joanne

420

attacks Tommy's lifestyle. Tommy tells the family everything that Claudia had told him. The dinner becomes chaotic, with people making harsh accusations and bickering.

Kitt telephones to say that her boyfriend is immature and the relationship is off. Claudia is reassured by her daughter and feels that ultimately the bonds between herself and her parents are stronger. She goes back to Chicago. Leo takes the same plane.

Home for the Holidays is another view of a loud and dysfunctional American family gathering for a disastrous Thanksgiving dinner. The reunion is seen through the eyes of Claudia, played by Holly Hunter. She is the contemporary single mother with a precocious teenage daughter played by Claire Danes. Claudia has lost her job and is overwhelmed by her chain-smoking, demanding mother, played by Anne Bancroft. In addition, Claudia is alienated from her stuffy sister, played by Cynthia Stevenson, but not from her gay brother, played by Robert Downey Jr. Charles Durning is the retired and retiring father of the family and Dylan McDermott of television's *The Practice* plays Leo, the romantic interest.

Jodie Foster directs this surprisingly raucous film, a change from her role as a serious actress in films such as *The Accused* and *Silence of the Lambs* or from lighter fare such as *Maverick* and *Anna and the King*. She made her directing debut with *Little Man Tate*.

The screenplay is based on the 1995 short story by Chris Radant. It is a mixture of the serious, the comic, and the farcical, a kind of sit-com that wants to make its audience think, especially in the context of the traditional, supposedly happy, celebration of Thanksgiving.

Focus: Claudia Larson in Home for the Holidays *is experiencing turmoil in her life. Her celebration of Thanksgiving at first aggravates the situation, and then offers some hope. The*

Scripture readings show a Thanksgiving pattern: God's bless-ing, the human struggle with selfishness, and God's renewed blessings.

The celebration of Thanksgiving is a memorial of God's graciousness in providing for early North American settlers struggling to establish themselves in the new and sometimes inhospitable land. This graciousness is echoed in each reading: God's provident care is recounted for the Hebrew people in the book of Deuteronomy as they entered into the promised land and settled there; Paul's Letter to the Colossians praises God, who offers an ideal for society, community, and family life that is characterized by integrity, goodness, and kindness as manifestations of God's own love; Jesus drives out an unclean spirit from a man at the Sea of Galilee and urges him to tell others how gracious God had been to him.

Thanksgiving is a time for acknowledging and appreciating God's blessings. But it seems like the time is never right. Despite attempts at reconciliation and peace, many families are disturbed by bitterness and hostilities. They go through the motions of celebrating the holiday while wishing they were far away. Thanksgiving, therefore, is not only for remembering blessings, but a time for acknowledging that things have gone wrong and trying to right them.

The Larson family in *Home for the Holidays* once again experiences what has gone wrong in their family. While Adele and Henry want their children to celebrate and be happy, to know the blessings they have received, the children are caught up in their own messy lives as well as in petty squabbles, deep rifts, and confusion among themselves and their parents. For them to grow in an understanding of the gifts they have received, it might be more appropriate to read, not just the conclusion of the passage about the man possessed by an unclean spirit, but the whole story about this terribly tormented, possessed man who sees no way out of his misery.

Thanksgiving is a time to know that there are "ways out." God blesses us with riches of all kinds and we do bless God. But we also get caught up in greed and possessions, and neglect God's commandments. God calls us back to repent and to renew God's covenant of love. By the end of *Home for the Holidays*, Claudia Larson has experienced something akin to the hope that this reconciliation brings.

KEY SCENES AND THEMES

- The Thanksgiving setting and the presuppositions about families coming home to celebrate blessings, to be with one another, and to share and appreciate family life; Claudia's disappointments, perspective, and hopes.

- The Thanksgiving family portrait: Adele and Henry and the long years of their marriage; Aunt Gladys going senile; Joanne and the conservative family, Tommy and his gay lifestyle, Claudia and her career, being a single mother; Kitt and her plans; the celebration as the occasion for clashes and for telling the truth; possibilities for reconciliation.

- Claudia's Thanksgiving; her life that seems to be a mess, her need to confide in family, her relationship with Kitt and her concern about her, getting everything out in the open, the fights, the resentments, feeling the support of her parents; her life and hopes until next Thanksgiving.

FOR REFLECTION AND CONVERSATION

1. Cycle B of *Lights, Camera…Faith! A Movie Lectionary* uses the multicultural, though no less conflicted, *What's Cooking?* for Thanksgiving reflection and dialogue. Cycle A uses *Pay It Forward*, which is more about the theme of thanksgiving than about the actual holiday itself. Which of these three films, if you have seen

them, do you prefer as a scriptural and cinematic context for your own observance of Thanksgiving? Can you think of other films that reflect your own family's experience more accurately? In your opinion, is there a Thanksgiving movie that better reflects, parallels or contrasts with the selected readings for today? If so, what is it and why (e.g., *Avalon*)?

2. Identify some elements or characteristics of Thanksgiving that make it special for you. In a spirit of discernment, think about your past experiences of Thanksgiving and how you will spend the day now. How can you be an agent of change in your family so that Thanksgiving can be a time for celebrating family values and encouraging reconciliation? One way is to ask all members present to write one thing they are grateful for on a small piece of paper and then read them at the blessing before the meal. Often, the children have the greatest insights into the family dynamics, love, peace, and shared blessings. As the Good Book says: "[You] are to be clothed in heartfelt compassion, in generosity and humility, gentleness and patience. Bear with one another; forgive each other if one of you has a complaint against the other. The Lord has forgiven you, now you must do the same. Over all these clothes, put on love.... Always be thankful." How can you make this reading from Deuteronomy a "project" for your Thanksgiving?

3. Is Thanksgiving only for "Americans"? How can citizens of wealthier nations share their bounty in justice with people of the world in a globalized economy? How can we as Christians resist and transform the

commercialization of our holidays to focus on the events and values they celebrate?

Prayer

Lord, today is a day of blessing and we thank you. Where your blessings have been forgotten, may it also be a day of healing and reconciliation. Amen.

Appendices

Contents By Movie Title

Contents By Movie Title

Contents By Movie Title

Contents By Sunday/Celebration

Sunday/Celebration	Movie Title	Gospel Text	Page #
Advent Sunday 1	*Deep Impact*	Lk 21:25–28, 34–36	1
Advent Sunday 2	*Beyond Rangoon*	Lk 3:1–6	6
Advent Sunday 3	*The Year of Living Dangerously*	Lk 3:10–18	12
Advent Sunday 4	*About Schmidt*	Lk 1:39–45	17
Christmas Midnight	*Braveheart*	Lk 2:1–14	25
Christmas Dawn	*Powder*	Lk 2:15–20	30
Christmas Day	*Catch Me If You Can*	Jn 1–17	36
Holy Family	*Little Man Tate*	Lk 2:41–52	43
Christmas Sunday 2	*The Elephant Man*	Jn 1:1–17	49
Epiphany	*The Fourth Wise Man*	Mt 2:1–12	57
Baptism of the Lord	*The Saint of Fort Washington*	Lk 3:15–16, 21–22	62
Ash Wednesday	*On the Waterfront*	Mt 6:1–6, 16–18	67
Lent Sunday 1	*Quiz Show*	Lk 4:1–13	75
Lent Sunday 2	*Close Encounters…Third Kind*	Lk 9:28–36	80
Lent Sunday 3	*Bringing Out the Dead*	Lk 13:1–9	85
Lent Sunday 4	*A River Runs Through It*	Lk 15:1–3, 11–32	90
Lent Sunday 5	*Thelma and Louise*	Jn 8:1–11	97
Palm Sunday	*Mad City*	Lk 19:28–40	102
Holy Thursday	*The Shipping News*	Jn 13:1–15	108
Good Friday	*Changing Lanes*	Jn 18:1—19:42	114
Easter Vigil	*Green Dragon*	Lk 24:1–12	120
Easter Sunday	*Fearless*	Jn 20:1–9	127
Easter Sunday 2	*Wit*	Jn 20:19–31	133
Easter Sunday 3	*Gods and Generals*	Jn 21:1–14	139
Easter Sunday 4	*Grapes of Wrath*	Jn 10:27–30	147
Easter Sunday 5	*Schindler's List*	Jn 13:31–33a, 34–35	153
Easter Sunday 6	*Star Wars…Episode IV*	Jn 14:23–29	159
Easter Sunday 7	*Chariots of Fire*	Jn 17:20–26	165
Pentecost Sunday	*Road to Perdition*	Jn 20:19–23	173

Contents By Sunday/Celebration

Contents By Sunday/Celebration

Sunday/Celebration	Movie Title	Gospel Text	Page #
Week 29	*The Winslow Boy*	Lk 18:1–8	348
Week 30	*A Few Good Men*	Lk 18:9–14	354
Week 31	*Regarding Henry*	Lk 19:1–10	361
Week 32	*Truly Madly Deeply*	Lk 20:27–38	367
Week 33	*Far East*	Lk 21:5–19	372
Christ the King	*Cool Hand Luke*	Lk 23:35–43	379
Holy Innocents	*Bless the Child*	Mt 2:13–18	385
Mary, Mother of God	*One True Thing*	Lk 2:16–21	391
St. Joseph (March 19)	*Frequency*	Lk 2:41–51a	397
Ascension	*Signs*	Lk 24:46–53	403
Sacred Heart of Jesus	*Life As a House*	Lk 15:3–7	409
All Souls	*The Sixth Sense*	Jn 14:1–6	415
Thanksgiving	*Home for the Holidays*	Mk 5:18–20	420

Contents By Gospel Text

Contents By Gospel Text

Gospel Text	Movie Title	Sunday/Celebration	Page #
Lk 6:17, 20–26	*Shine*	Week 6	212
Lk 6:27–38	*As Good As It Gets*	Week 7	219
Lk 6:39–45	*Amadeus*	Week 8	225
Lk 7:1–10	*The Green Mile*	Week 9	231
Lk 7:11–17	*The Deep End of the Ocean*	Week 10	236
Lk 7:36—8:3	*The Accused*	Week 11	241
Lk 9:11–17	*Eat Drink Man Woman*	Body &Blood of Christ	184
Lk 9:18–24	*Falling Down*	Week 12	247
Lk 9:28–36	*Close Encounters…Third Kind*	Lent Sunday 2	80
Lk 9:51–62	*The Sound of Music*	Week 13	255
Lk 10:1–12, 17–20	*Pale Rider*	Week 14	260
Lk 10:25–37	*Amistad*	Week 15	265
Lk 10:38–42	*Babette's Feast*	Week 16	270
Lk 11:1–13	*Groundhog Day*	Week 17	276
Lk 12:13–21	*Meet Joe Black*	Week 18	283
Lk 12:32–48	*Mrs. Brown*	Week 19	288
Lk 12:49–53	*The Straight Story*	Week 20	294
Lk 13:1–9	*Bringing Out the Dead*	Lent Sunday 3	85
Lk 13:22–30	*The Shawshank Redemption*	Week 21	301
Lk 14:1, 7–14	*Evita*	Week 22	307
Lk 14:25–33	*Gallipoli*	Week 23	313
Lk 15:1–3, 11–32	*A River Runs Through It*	Lent Sunday 4	90
Lk 15:1–32	*Restoration*	Week 24	319
Lk 15:3–7	*Life As a House*	Sacred Heart of Jesus	409
Lk 16:1–13	*Wall Street*	Week 25	325
Lk 16:19–31	*What Dreams May Come*	Week 26	330
Lk 17:5–10	*Leap of Faith*	Week 27	337
Lk 17:11–19	*Philadelphia*	Week 28	342
Lk 18:1–8	*The Winslow Boy*	Week 29	348

Contents By Gospel Text

Movie Ratings Chart*

Movie Title	MPAA (1)	BBFC (2)	OFLC (3)	USCC (4)
About Schmidt	R	15	M	A-III
Accused, The	R	18	M	O
Amadeus	PG	PG	PG	A-II
Amistad	R	15	M	A-III
As Good As It Gets	PG-13	15	M	A-IV
Babette's Feast	G	U	G	A-II
Beyond Rangoon	R	15	M	A-III
Bless the Child	R	15	MA	A-IV
Braveheart	R	15	MA	A-IV
Bringing Out the Dead	R	18	MA	A-III
Catch Me If You Can	PG-13	12A	M	A-III
Changing Lanes	R	15	M	A-III
Chariots of Fire	PG	U	PG	A-I
Close Encounters...Third Kind	PG	PG	PG	A-II
Contact	PG	PG	M	A-III
Cool Hand Luke	GP**	15	M	A-IV
Deep End of the Ocean, The	PG-13	12	M	A-III
Deep Impact	PG-13	12	M	A-III
Eat Drink Man Woman	N/A	15	PG	A-III
Elephant Man, The	PG	PG	M	A-III
Evita	PG	PG	PG	A-III
Falling Down	R	18	M	O
Far East	N/A	15	M	N/A

* Information regarding the rating codes may be found on each organization's Web site.

(1) MPAA: Motion Picture Association of America, United States; www.mpaa.org

(2) BBFC: British Board of Film Classification, United Kingdom; www.bbfc.co.uk

(3) OFLC: The Office for Film and Literature Classification, Australia; www.oflc.gov.au

(4) USCC: United States Catholic Conference, www.nccbuscc.org

**GP = General patronage, from MPAA rating before the current system

Movie Ratings Chart

Movie Title	MPAA (1)	BBFC (2)	OFLC (3)	USCC (4)
Fearless	R	15	M	A-II
Few Good Men, A	R	15	M	A-III
Fourth Wise Man, The	N/A	U	G	A-I
Frequency	PG-13	15	M	A-III
Gallipoli	PG	PG	PG	A-III
Gods and Generals	PG-13	N/A	N/A	A-II
Good Will Hunting	R	15	M	A-IV
Grapes of Wrath	N/A	PG	PG	A-II
Green Dragon	PG-13	N/A	PG	N/A
Green Mile, The	R	18	MA	A-III
Groundhog Day	PG	PG	PG	A-II
Home for the Holidays	PG-13	15	M	A-III
Leap of Faith	PG-13	PG	PG	A-III
Life As a House	R	15	MA	A-IV
Little Man Tate	PG	PG	PG	A-II
Mad City	PG-13	15	M	A-III
Meet Joe Black	PG-13	12	M	A-III
Mrs. Brown	PG	PG	PG	A-III
On the Waterfront	N/A	PG	PG	A-II
One True Thing	R	15	M	A-III
Outlaw Josey Wales, The	PG	18	M	O
Pale Rider	R	15	M	O
Philadelphia	PG-13	12	PG	A-IV
Powder	PG-13	12	M	A-III
Quiz Show	PG-13	15	M	A-II
Regarding Henry	PG-13	15	M	A-III
Remember the Titans	PG	PG	PG	A-II
Restoration	R	15	M	A-III
River Runs Through It, A	PG	PG	PG	PG

Movie Ratings Chart

Movie Title	MPAA (1)	BBFC (2)	OFLC (3)	USCC (4)
Road to Perdition	R	15	MA	A-III
Saint of Fort Washington, The	R	15	M	A-II
Schindler's List	R	15	M	A-III
Shawshank Redemption, The	R	15	MA	A-IV
Shine	PG-13	12	PG	A-III
Shipping News, The	R	15	M	A-III
Signs	PG-13	12A	M	A-II
Sixth Sense, The	PG-13	15	M	A-III
Sound of Music, The	G	U	G	A-I
Star Wars...Episode IV	PG	U	PG	A-II
Straight Story, The	G	U	G	A-I
Thelma and Louise	R	15	M	N/A
Truly Madly Deeply	PG	PG	PG	A-III
Wall Street	R	15	M	A-IV
What Dreams May Come	PG-13	15	M	A-III
When a Man Loves a Woman	R	15	M	A-III
Winslow Boy, The	G	U	G	A-I
Wit	PG-13	N/A	M	N/A
Year of Living Dangerously, The	PG	PG	M	A-III

Suggested Scenes for Viewing / Discussion

Movie Title	Suggested Movie Scenes (most are 2–5 minutes in length)
About Schmidt	Sister Nadine's letter
Accused, The	The final court scene and Sarah's vindication
Amadeus	(1) Mozart listening to Salieri's welcoming piece and then playing the variations; (2) Salieri declaring his jealousy to the priest
As Good As It Gets	Melvin, Carol, and Simon's trip to visit Simon's parents
Babette's Feast	(1) The captain's speech during the meal; (2) The dance of life after the meal; (3) The final conversation between Babette and the sisters
Beyond Rangoon	Aung Sang Suu Kyi's walk through the soldiers
Bless the Child	The final scenes, beginning with the satanic ritual
Braveheart	The death of William Wallace
Bringing Out the Dead	(1) The scene in which the dispatcher sends Frank back out; (2) the final "Pieta" scene
Catch Me If You Can	One of Frank's Christmas Eve calls to Agent Hanratty
Changing Lanes	Gavin entering the Church for confession
Chariots of Fire	(1) The opening; (2) The hidden glance; (3) The race in the quad
Close Encounters ...Third Kind	At the mountain with the space ship
Contact	(1) Ellie's interview about her faith in God; (2) Her journey into space
Cool Hand Luke	(1) The scene in church and Luke being shot; (2) The prisoners reminiscing about Luke
Deep End of the Ocean, The	(1) Sam meeting his birth family again; (2) Sam playing basketball with his brother
Deep Impact	The meteor crash and the tidal wave
Eat Drink Man Woman	The preparation for the first meal
Elephant Man, The	(1) John Merrick yelling, "I am a human being"; (2) John talking about being happy because he is loved

Suggested Scenes for Viewing / Discussion

Movie Title	*Suggested Movie Scenes* (most are 2–5 minutes in length)
Evita	Evita singing "Don't Cry for Me Argentina"
Far East	The social worker being tortured
Fearless	(1) The crash, Max walking out; (2) Max and Rosie in church; (3) Max on the roof
Few Good Men, A	(1) Colonel Jessup on the stand; (2) The final scene in which Daniel talks to Harold about honor
Fourth Wise Man, The	Jesus appearing to Artaban
Frequency	The father and son communicating on the radio
Gallipoli	Frank's final run and Archie's death
Gods and Generals	(1) General Lee's speech about not loving war; (2) The conversations between Jackson and his wife, or Chamberlain and his wife
Good Will Hunting	Dr. Maguire talking to Will about his wife
Grapes of Wrath	Tom Joad's final speech
Green Dragon	(1) Minh searching for his mother; (2) Tai and Jim showing the men what post-camp life will be like; (3) The marriage ceremony
Green Mile, The	John Coffey healing the warden's wife
Groundhog Day	Phil waking up on February 3, transformed
Home for the Holidays	The meal
Leap of Faith	(1) Jonah and the crucifix; (2) Jonah healing the boy
Life As a House	George and Sam finally communicating after the town's inspection of the bathroom situation
Little Man Tate	Fred bewildering DeDe
Mad City	The television interview with Sam
Meet Joe Black	(1) The final scene in the library; (2) Bill Parrish and Death/Joe walking away together at the party
Mrs. Brown	(1) John Brown waiting by the horses; (2) Visiting the family in Scotland

Suggested Scenes for Viewing / Discussion

Movie Title	*Suggested Movie Scenes* (most are 2–5 minutes in length)
On the Waterfront	(1) One of Fr. Barry's sermons; (2) Terry Malloy's final walk
One True Thing	The mother explaining to the daughter how she tries to bring happiness to others
Outlaw Josey Wales, The	Lone Watie talking to Josey about "losing his edge"
Pale Rider	(1) Megan going into the woods to bury the dog and praying Psalm 23; (2) The pale rider coming down from the mountains
Philadelphia	Andy and Joe sitting in the kitchen listening to Callas
Powder	(1) The science class; (2) The final scene: power in darkness
Quiz Show	The interviews in which Herb and Van Doren are asked to cheat
Regarding Henry	(1) Henry and Bradley sharing a beer; (2) Henry's daughter teaching him tie his shoes; (3) Henry making restitution to the family he cheated in court
Remember the Titans	Confrontation between the players concerning leadership
Restoration	Robert Merivel with the Quakers
River Runs Through It, A	The final fishing scene in which Paul catches the big fish
Road to Perdition	John Rooney's speech about none of them ever seeing heaven
Saint of Fort Washington, The	The scene when Jerry anoints Matthew as a saint
Schindler's list	(1) Schindler watching the destruction of the ghetto; (2) The final scene in the factory; (3) The end of the film in Jerusalem
Shawshank Redemption, The	(1) Red reading the note that Andy leaves about hope; (2) Red's speech in which he says to "...get busy living or get busy dying..."; (3) Red wanting to see the both the Pacific and his friend

Suggested Scenes for Viewing / Discussion

Movie Title	*Suggested Movie Scenes* (most are 2–5 minutes in length)
Shine	(1) David Helfgott playing the piano; (2) Visiting his father's grave
Shipping News, The	Quoyle in the boat, sinking and drifting away
Signs	Graham and Merrill's conversation about faith
Sixth Sense, The	(1) The final scene in the car; (2) The last scene with Malcolm
Star Wars…Episode IV	Obi-Wan Kenobi advising Luke about the Force
Straight Story, The	(1) Talking to the pregnant girl about family; (2) Talking about the war in the bar 3) Arriving at Lyle's house
Thelma and Louise	The final scene, as they are poised to drive off the cliff
Truly Madly Deeply	Nina's final farewell to the ghosts
Wall Street	(1) Gordon Gekko's speech to the stockholders; (2) Bud entrapping Gekko
What Dreams May Come	(1) Heaven and the paintings; (2) Hell and the sea of faces
When a Man Loves a Woman	Michael listening to Alice's speech at the A.A. meeting
Winslow Boy, The	(1) Sir Robert's interrogation of the boy; (2) Sir Robert's speech in Parliament
Wit	(1) Vivian, Susie, and the Popsicles; (2) Dr. Ashford reading from the book, *The Runaway Bunny*
Year of Living Dangerously, The	Billy's challenge to Guy about the situation in Asia

Recommended Reading on Movies and Religious Themes

Complied by Peter Malone, MSC, and Rose Pacatte, FSP

Baugh, Lloyd. *Imaging the Divine: Jesus and Christ-figures in Film.* Kansas City, Mo., Sheed & Ward: 1997.

A thesis-based study of the Jesus movies and some selected Christ-figure movies; defines what Christ-figure means, extensive and thorough, if somewhat controversial in interpretation.

Belknap, Bryan. *Group's Blockbuster Movie Illustrator.* Loveland, Colo.: Group Publishing, 2001.

Over 160 film clips are presented according to theme. Includes Scripture references, cue times to start and end the clips, and questions. Suitable for teenagers.

Blake, Richard A. *After Image: The Indelible Catholic Imagination of Six American Filmmakers.* Chicago: Loyola Press, 2000.

An exploration of imagination and its religious dimension in the movies of six Catholic-educated directors: Capra, Coppolla, De Palma, Ford, Hitchcock, and Scorsese.

Eilers, Franz-Joseph. *Church and Social Communication, Basic Documents.* Manila: Logos Publications Inc., 1993.

The texts of nine Vatican documents from 1936 to 1992, with the addresses for World Communications Day and quotations on communication from other official documents. Eilers provides introductions and some structural outlines of the documents.

Fields, Doug, and Eddie James.. *Videos That Teach.* Grand Rapids, Mich.: Zondervan, 1999.

"Teachable movie moments from seventy-five modern film classics" suitable for use with teenagers. Offers clip selection, themes, reflections, and Scripture references.

Fields, Doug, and Eddie James. *Videos That Teach 2.* Grand Rapids, Mich: Zondervan, 2002.

"Teachable movie moments from seventy-five more modern film classics to spark discussion," suitable for use with teenagers. Offers clip selection, themes, reflections and Scripture references.

Fraser, Peter. *Images of the Passion: The Sacramental Mode in Film.* Westport, Conn.: Praeger Publishers, 1998.

Selected movies are examined to illustrate how they implicitly dramatize aspects of the Gospel and the sufferings of Jesus.

Fraser, Peter and Vernon Edward Neal. *ReViewing the Movies: A Christian Response to Contemporary Film.* Wheaton, Ill.: Crossway Books, 2000.

An application of the theory in Fraser's *Images of the Passion* to contemporary popular cinema in a wide-ranging survey.

Jewett, Robert. *Saint Paul at the Movies.* Louisville: Westminster/John Knox, 1993.

A New Testament scholar writes an enlightening book about the Greco-Roman world of Paul. A movie enthusiast, Jewett has chosen ten popular movies to illustrate the virtues that Paul holds up to the Roman Empire.

Jewett, Robert. *Saint Paul Returns to the Movies.* Grand Rapids, Mich.:Ecrdmans, 1999.

A sequel that is as good as, perhaps better, than the original.

John Paul II, *Giovanni Paolo II e il Cinema, Tutti i discorsi.* Roma: Ente dello Spettacolo, Roma, 2000.

A collection of eight speeches by the Pope on cinema. Texts in Italian and in English with commentary articles on the Church and cinema.

Johnston, Robert K. *Reel Spirituality: Theology and Film in Dialogue.* Grand Rapids, Mich.: Baker Academic, 2000.

A theologian from Fuller Theological Seminary who loves cinema asks basic questions about the religious dimension of movies, opening up the spirituality implicit in so many mainstream movies. It has a wide range of film references.

Maher, Ian. *Reel Issues: Engaging Film and Faith.* Swindon, U.K. Open Book Bible Society, 1998.

Produced for the Open Book program of the British Bible Society, this booklet is designed for use with Christian groups.

Maher, Ian.*Reel Issue: Five More Films to Engage Film and Faith.* Swindon, U.K.: Open Book, Bible Society, 2000.

Produced for the Open Book program of the British Bible Society, this booklet is designed for use in Christian groups and continues the approach of its predecessor by considering five new films.

Mahony, Roger M. *Film Makers, Film Viewers, Their Challenges and Opportunities.* Boston: Pauline Books & Media, 1992.

The text of Cardinal Mahony's pastoral letter to the diocese of Los Angeles, his synthesis of a contemporary Catholic approach to cinema.

Malone, Peter, MSC, with Rose Pacatte, FSP. *Lights, Camera... Faith! A Movie Lectionary, Cycle A.* Boston: Pauline Books & Media, 2001.

Scripture readings for each Sunday of the common lectionary in dialogue with popular Hollywood films. Cycle B, 2002: Cycle C, 2003.

Malone, Peter. *Movie Christs and Antichrists.* New York: Crossroads, 1990; Sydney: Parish Ministry, 1988.

A study of movies and meanings, focusing on the Jesus movies (the Jesus figures) and the movies of characters, who resemble Jesus (Christ-figures); also chapters on movies and antichrist symbols.

Malone, Peter. *On Screen.* Manila: Daughters of St. Paul, 2001.

An introduction to the study of movies and meanings.

Malone, Peter. *Myth and Meaning: Australian Film Directors in Their Own Words.* Sydney, Australia: Currency Press, 2001.

Fifteen interviews with Australian film directors like Bruce Beresford, George Miller, Fred Schepisi, Scott Hicks, and Gillian Armstrong on the values and spirituality underlying their films.

Marsh, Clive and Gaye Ortiz, eds. *Explorations in Theology and Film.* Oxford: Blackwell, 1997.

A collection of theological essays exploring specific contemporary popular movies like *The Terminator, The Piano, Edward Scissorhands.*

May, John R. *Nourishing Faith Through Fiction, Reflections on the Apostles' Creed in Literature and Film.* Franklin, Wis.: Sheed & Ward, 2001.

An American pioneer in the studies of cinema examines stories that evoke the presence and images of the Trinity, the Creator, the Savior, and the Holy Spirit, the Life-giver. Classic movies and novels are considered in reference to many contemporary movies.

May, John R. *New Image of Religious Film.* Kansas City, Mo.: Sheed & Ward, 1997.

A collection of theological essays that examine theoretical aspects of religion, society and cinema.

McNulty, Edward. *Films and Faith: Forty Discussion Guides.* Topeka, Kans.: Viaticum Press, 1999.

As the title indicates, discussion material for forty films. They are designed for the nonexpert in cinema and provide detailed information about each film as well as some theological background. There are extensive questions for reflection.

McNulty, Edward. *Praying the Movies: Daily Meditations from Classic Films.* Louisville, Ky.: Geneva Press, 2001.

A collection of thirty-one devotions that connect movies and the spiritual life of moviegoers.

McNulty, Edward. *More Praying the Movies.* Louisville, Ky.: John Knox Press, 2003.

A second collection of thirty-one (one for each day of a month) devotionals built around a film scene, includes related passages from the Hebrew and Christian scriptures, a film synopsis and scene description, questions for reflection, a hymn suggestion, and a closing prayer.

Romanowski, William D. *Pop Culture Wars, Religion and the Role of Entertainment in American Life.* Downers Grove, Ill.: InterVarsity Press, 1996.

A wide-ranging study of entertainment, including cinema, noting the hostile U.S. religious tradition as well as the movements to find the religious values in media and entertainment.

Rosenstand, Nina. *The Moral of the Story: An Introduction to Ethics.* Mountainview, Calif.: Mayfield Publishing, 2000.

This popular textbook uses film stories in particular to explore ethics and ethical theories.

Sanders, Theresa. *Celluloid Saints: Images of Sanctity in Film.* Macon, Ga: Mercer University Press, 2002.

A search for "authentic accounts of saints and of the miracles, healings, ethical questions and challenges to holiness," a masterful analysis of the finest cinematic presentations of holiness" in the history of the movies.

Schreck, Nikolas. *The Satanic Screen: An Illustrated Guide to the Devil in Cinema.* London, U.K.: Creation Books, 2001

A book that documents the devil's twentieth-century celluloid history and locates three hundred or so films in the culture of the years in which they were made.

Scott, Bernard Brandon. *Hollywood Dreams and Biblical Stories.* Minneapolis: Fortress Press, 1994.

The author brings his scriptural background to modern, popular movies and highlights the links between the biblical stories and the new cinema stories to draw out their meanings and their myths.

Short, Robert. *The Gospel from Outer Space, The Religious Implications of E.T., Star Wars, Superman, Close Encounters of the Third Kind and 2001: A Space Odyssey.* San Francisco: Harper & Row, 1983.

The author of *The Gospel according to Peanuts* and *The Parables of Peanuts* offers the text of a multimedia presentation of Gospel parallels in popular science fiction and fantasy movies.

Solomon, Gary. *The Movie Prescription: Watch This Movie and Call Me in the Morning: 200 Movies to Help You Heal Life's Problems.* New York: Lebhar-Friedman Books, 1998.

Solomon, Gary. *Reel Therapy: How Movies Inspire You to Overcome Life's Problems.* New York: Lebhar-Friedman Books, 2001.

Dr. Gary Solomon has registered "Cinema Therapy" and "The Movie Doctor" as his trademarks and blends a popular approach to movies along with the academic. Though these two books are not specifically religious, he has selected a great number of films that can be used for "cinema therapy," that is, for healing and inspiration.

Stern, Richard C. and Clayton N. Jefford, and Guerric Debona. *Savior on the Silver Screen*. Mahwah, N.J.: Paulist Press, 1999.

The authors have run courses on the principal Jesus movies from Cecil B. De Mille to *Jesus of Montreal*. This is the expanded course with a thorough rationale for studying these movies.

Stone, Bryan P. *Faith and Film: Theological Themes at the Cinema*. St Louis: Chalice Press, 2000.

The framework for examining a range of generally well-known movies is the Apostle's Creed, enabling the author to highlight religious themes in movies in a context of faith and the exploration of faith.

Vaux, Sara Anson. *Finding Meaning at the Movies*. Nashville: Abingdon Press, 1999.

The author wants to encourage study groups in schools, universities, and parishes by taking a range of popular movies and showing how they can be fruitfully discussed.

Voytilla, Stuart. *Myth and the Movies: Discovering the Mythic Structure of 50 Unforgettable Films*. Los Angeles: Michael Wiese Productions, 1999.

The author draws on the culture of referring to and using myths, especially the hero's journey, to look at a number of popular screen classics.

Film Websites

Film and Spirituality

www.signis.net

The international Catholic association for communications includes current jury prizes for film festivals and reviews by Rev. Peter Malone, MSC, President of SIGNIS.

www.daughtersofstpaul.com/mediastudies

Media literacy in faith-communities includes some in-depth movie reviews and links, sponsored by the Daughters of St. Paul.

www.nationalfilmretreat.org

Information on the National Film Retreat, an annual interfaith gathering that screens and prays several films over a weekend (Friday evening to Sunday noon).

www.HollywoodJesus.com

This ecumenical Web site is dedicated to finding Christian spirituality in movies, with a searchable archive.

www.catholic.org.au

Four film reviews a month beginning in 2001 from the Australian Conference of Catholic Bishops.

www.chiafilm.com

This site is named for *chiaroscuro,* the interplay of light and shade in an image, and seeks to move beyond the culture wars and encourage a conversation between the cinema and Christian spirituality. Contains new reviews, retrospectives, and essays.

www.beliefnet.com

Comparative religion community includes movie reviews.

www.cityofangelsfilmfest.org

Interfaith film-festival site with reviews, resources, and events.

www.spiritualityhealth.com

Fred and Mary Brussat offer an e-course, "Going to the Movies as a Spiritual Practice," as well as current film and video reviews with a searchable database.

www.FilmClipsOnLine.com

Hollywood filmmaker Michael Rhodes and industry colleagues and educators offer clips from popular films to use in educational settings.

www.christianitytoday.com/ctmag/features/columns/filmforum.html

Christian film reviews that integrate and analyze commentaries from several sources, both from religious and from the mainstream press.

www.unomaha.edu/~wwwjrf/

Articles and reviews by the *Journal of Religion and Film,* University of Nebraska at Omaha.

www.christiancritic.com

The Christian critic's movie parables.

www.textweek.com

Sermon helps with a movie concordance for the Catholic and Anglican lectionaries.

www.visualparables.com

> *Visual Parables* is a monthly review of films, videos, and the arts with lectionary links.

www.udayton.edu/mary/

> This site features the videos on Mary and Marian subjects archived by the University of Dayton's Marian Library/International Marian Research Institute.

Cineandmedia@yahoogroups.com

> E-group for those interested in cinema, spirituality, and theology.

Film/Media Education

www.bravo.ca/scanningthemovies

> Canada's BRAVO! Channel presents a media-education perspective based on the television program "Scanning the Movies," hosted by Neil Anderson and Rev. John Pungente, SJ, with study guides.

www.filmeducation.org

> This U.K. film-education site is provided for secondary school teachers to encourage and promote the study, evaluation, and analysis of a wide range of media, including film, within the curriculum. Free online study guides and resources.

www.udayton.edu/~ipi

> *The Pastoral Communication and Ministry Institute (PCMI)* of the University of Dayton is an annual summer program to prepare leaders to proclaim the Gospel using all the means of pastoral communications available today. The program includes courses on film, theology, and spirituality.

Film and Families

www.daughtersofstpaul.com/myfriend

> Movie and video reviews by kids for kids.

www.americancatholic.org

> *St. Anthony Messenger*'s "Eye on Entertainment" section and the *Every Day Catholic* newsletter's "Media Watch," feature movie reviews and articles.

www.moviemom.com

"Helping families share great times, great movies, and great conversations."

www.screenit.com

Entertainment reviews for parents with a searchable archive.

Film Review Sites

www.usccb.org

The United States Catholic Conference site includes current film reviews, searchable archives, and "information for guidance."

www.imdb.org

The Internet Movie Databases is the largest movie archive on the web and includes industry information and a multitude of links to sources and reviews.

www.suntimes.com/index/ebert.html

The index on this website contains famed movie critic Roger Ebert's film reviews since 1985, along with a searchable database of these reviews.

www.movie-reviews.colossus.net

Film reviews since 1996 by James Bernardelli.

Film Ratings

Please note: while all of these sites list film ratings, only a few list their criteria for judging films.

www.mpaa.org

The Motion Picture Association of America (U.S.A.) film ratings.

www.ccr.gov.on.ca/ofrb/

Ontario Film Review Board.

www.media-awareness.ca/eng

Film-rating links for all other provinces of Canada.

www.bbffc.co.uk

The British Board of Film Classification.

www.oflc.gov.au

The Office for Film and Literature Classification, Australia.

Movie Licensing Information

For the United States and Canada:

If you wish to show a video/film in a group setting that is not included in the regularly structured curriculum of an educational institution, then you need to acquire a license.

The Motion Picture Licensing Corporation/Christian Video Licensing International can issue an umbrella license for many of the studios. Please visit them on the web, www.mplc.com, or call 888-771-2854.

Swank Motion Pictures can issue licenses for films from Miramax, Warner Bros. and HBO: 800-876-5577.

Twentieth Century Fox can be contacted directly: 310-286-1056.

For all films/studios that are not covered by the licenses these companies can provide, please contact the studio directly and ask for the licensing or legal department.

Movies in *Lights Camera...Faith! Cycle A*

A

Apostle, The

At Play in the Fields of the Lord

Awakenings

B

Bagdad Cafe

Beach, The

Ben Hur

Big Night

Bob Roberts

Born on the Fourth of July

Bridges of Madison County, The

C

Chorus Line, A

City of Joy

Civil Action, A

Cookie's Fortune

Crossing Guard, The

Crucible, The

Cry Freedom

Cry in the Dark, A

D

Dead Man Walking

Devil's Advocate, The

Doctor, The

E

E.T.: The Extra-Terrestrial

End of Days

Entertaining Angels

Erin Brockovich

F

Family Man, The

Fisher King, The

Forrest Gump

G–H–I

Girl, Interrupted

Horse Whisperer, The

Hurricane, The

Insider, The

It's a Wonderful Life

J–K–L

Jesus' Son

Killing Fields, The

Les Miserables

Lion King, The

Lorenzo's Oil

M

Man for All Seasons, A

Marvin's Room

Matewan

Men With Guns

Message in a Bottle

Miracle Maker, The

Miracle Worker, The

Mission to Mars

Music of the Heart

My Life

O–P

October Sky

Oscar and Lucinda

Paradise Road

Pay it Forward

Phenomenon

Places in the Heart

Pleasantville

Prince of Tides, The

R–S

Return to Me

Saving Private Ryan

Secrets and Lies

Shadowlands

Shoes of the Fisherman, The

Simon Birch

Sister Act

Snow Falling on Cedars

Superman: The Movie

T

Tender Mercies

Terminator 2: Judgment Day

Touch

True Confessions

U

Unforgiven

W

What's Eating Gilbert Grape

Where the Heart Is

Movies in *Lights Camera…Faith! Cycle B*

2001: A Space Odyssey

A

A.I.: Artificial Intelligence

Absence of Malice

Agnes of God

Alive

Angela's Ashes

At First Sight

B

Beautiful Mind, A

Bed of Roses

Billy Elliot

Black Robe

Bram Stoker's Dracula

Bronx Tale, A

Brother Sun, Sister Moon

Burning Season, The

C–D

Cast Away

Chocolat

Dances With Wolves

Daylight

Dead Poets Society

Disney's The Kid

E–F

Edward Scissorhands

End of the Affair, The

Exorcist, The

Finding Forrester

Firm, The

Flatliners

G–H

Godfather, The

Harry Potter and the Sorcerer's Stone

House of Mirth, The

J

Jesus of Montreal

Joy Luck Club, The

Judas

K–L

Keeping the Faith

Kundun

Last Valley, The

Legend of Bagger Vance, The

Life is Beautiful

Lilies of the Field

Little Women

Long Walk Home, The

Lord of the Rings, The: The Fellowship of the Ring

M

Magnificent Seven, The

Mass Appeal

Matrix, The

Mighty, The

Mission, The

Molokai: The Story of Fr. Damien

Moonstruck

Mr. Holland's Opus

Mumford

My Left Foot

O–P

Omega Man, The

Patch Adams

R

Rain Man

Remains of the Day, The

Romero

S

Savior

Second Best

Seventh Sign, The

Simple Plan, A

Simply Irresistible

Sommersby

Spitfire Grill, The

Stanley & Iris

Steel Magnolias

T–U

Test of Love, A

Third Miracle, The

Thirteen Days

Titanic

To Kill a Mockingbird

Truman Show, The

Unbreakable

W

What's Cooking?

Index

C

G

gaining life versus losing life *(Falling Down)*, 247–252

Gallipoli, 313–318

gangster movies *(Road to Perdition)*, 172–177

Garcia, Andy *(When a Man Loves a Woman)*, 190–195

Garibaldi, Giuseppe, 317

Garner, Jennifer *(Catch Me If You Can)*, 36–41

Garr, Teri *(Close Encounters of the Third Kind)*, 80–84

gecko, characteristics of, 328

George, Chief Dan *(The Outlaw Josey Wales)*, 206–211

Gettysburg, 140

ghosts
  Sixth Sense, The, 415–419
  Truly Madly Deeply, 367–371

Gibson, Mel
  Braveheart, 24–29
  Gallipoli, 313–318
  Signs, 403–408
  Year of Living Dangerously, The, 12–16

Gielgud, John
  Chariots of Fire, 165–170
  Elephant Man, The, 49–54
  Shine, 212–216

gifted children. *see also* intelligence
  Little Man Tate, 42–48
  Powder, 30–35

gifts
  Chariots of Fire, 165–170
  Fourth Wise Man, The, 56–61
  of the Holy Spirit, 177

Little Man Tate, 42–48
  and vocation, 204

Glenn, Scott *(The Shipping News)*, 108–113

globalization, effects of, 376

Glover, Danny *(The Saint of Fort Washington)*, 62–66

God. *see also* image of God
  manifestation of, 61
  mystery of, 178–183

Gods and Generals, 139–144

Goldberg, Whoopi *(The Deep End of the Ocean)*, 236–240

Goldblum, Jeff *(Powder)*, 30–35

Goldenberg, Michael *(Contact)*, 178–183

Goldman, Bo *(Meet Joe Black)*, 282–287

Gone to Texas (Carter), 208

Good Samaritan
  Amistad, 265–269
  Fearless, 126–132

Good Shepherd *(The Grapes of Wrath)*, 146–152

Good Thief-character *(Cool Hand Luke)*, 378–384

good versus evil
  Shine, 212–216
  Star Wars (Star Wars: Episode IV—A New Hope), 159–164

Good Will Hunting, 201–205

Goodall, Caroline *(Schindler's List)*, 153–158

Goodfellas, 86

Gooding, Cuba, Jr.
  Few Good Men, A, 354–358
  As Good As It Gets, 218–224
  What Dreams May Come, 330–335

Goodman, John *(Bringing Out the Dead)*, 85–89

Goodwin, Richard *(Remembering America: A Voice from the Sixties)*, 76

ABOUT THE AUTHORS

PETER MALONE, MSC, is a Sacred Heart Father from Australia currently living in England. In 1998, he was elected president of the International Organization for the Cinema (OCIC), an appointment which received immediate Vatican approval. He is currently president of The World Catholic Association for Communications (SIGNIS).

Peter is known worldwide for his pastoral approach to integrating film, faith and life. He has served as juror at film festivals throughout the world, and is currently a consultant to the Bishops' Committee for Film in the Philippines.

Father Malone is the author of *Myth and Meaning: Australian Film Directors in Their Own Words, On Screen, Movie Christs and Anti-Christs, The Film, Films and Values,* and a co-author of *Cinema, Religion and Values,* and is a regular columnist in *The Universe* Catholic newspaper in the U.K. He is also author of the first two volumes in the *Movie Lectionary Series: Lights, Camera...Faith! Cycle A* and *Lights, Camera...Faith! Cycle B.*

ROSE PACATTE, FSP, is a Daughter of St. Paul and the Director of the Pauline Center for Media Studies in Los Angeles, CA. She has an MA in Education in Media Studies from the University of London, and is a frequent speaker at conferences throughout the U.S. and abroad.

Sr. Rose is an active member in several Catholic and ecumenical communications and film organizations, including the U.S. affiliate of SIGNIS. She has been a jurist at the Venice Film Festival, and a panelist at the City of Angels Film Festival and Boston's Faith & Film Festival. She is one of the founding directors of the annual National Film Retreat and is the author of *A Guide to In-House Film Festivals in Ten Easy Steps* as well as co-author of *Lights, Camera...Faith! Cycle A* and *Lights, Camera...Faith! Cycle B.*

BOOKS & MEDIA

The Daughters of St. Paul operate book and media centers at the following addresses. Visit, call or write the one nearest you today, or find us on the World Wide Web, www.pauline.org

CALIFORNIA
3908 Sepulveda Blvd, Culver City, CA 90230   310-397-8676
5945 Balboa Avenue, San Diego, CA 92111   858-565-9181
46 Geary Street, San Francisco, CA 94108   415-781-5180

FLORIDA
145 S.W. 107th Avenue, Miami, FL 33174   305-559-6715

HAWAII
1143 Bishop Street, Honolulu, HI 96813   808-521-2731
Neighbor Islands call: 800-259-8463

ILLINOIS
172 North Michigan Avenue, Chicago, IL 60601   312-346-4228

LOUISIANA
4403 Veterans Memorial Blvd, Metairie, LA 70006   504-887-7631

MASSACHUSETTS
Rte. 1, 885 Providence Hwy, Dedham, MA 02026   781-326-5385

MISSOURI
9804 Watson Road, St. Louis, MO 63126   314-965-3512

NEW JERSEY
561 U.S. Route 1, Wick Plaza, Edison, NJ 08817   732-572-1200

NEW YORK
150 East 52nd Street, New York, NY 10022   212-754-1110
78 Fort Place, Staten Island, NY 10301   718-447-5071

PENNSYLVANIA
9171-A Roosevelt Blvd, Philadelphia, PA 19114   215-676-9494

SOUTH CAROLINA
243 King Street, Charleston, SC 29401   843-577-0175

TENNESSEE
4811 Poplar Avenue, Memphis, TN 38117   901-761-2987

TEXAS
114 Main Plaza, San Antonio, TX 78205   210-224-8101

VIRGINIA
1025 King Street, Alexandria, VA 22314   703-549-3806

CANADA
3022 Dufferin Street, Toronto, Ontario, Canada M6B 3T5   416-781-9131
1155 Yonge Street, Toronto, Ontario, Canada M4T 1W2   416-934-3440

¡También somos su fuente para libros, videos y música en español!